THE AUTOBIOGRAPHY OF
G. LOWES DICKINSON

Lowes Dickinson in middle age

The
Autobiography of
G. Lowes Dickinson

AND OTHER UNPUBLISHED WRITINGS

Edited by
DENNIS PROCTOR
with a Foreword by
NOEL ANNAN

DUCKWORTH

First published in 1973 by
Gerald Duckworth & Co Ltd
The Old Piano Factory, 43 Gloucester Crescent, London NW1

Recollections, The Wandering Jew, Poems, Body and Soul,
Introduction and Notes © 1973 Sir Dennis Proctor

Foreword © 1973 Gerald Duckworth & Co Ltd

All rights reserved. No part of this publication
may be reproduced, stored in a retrieval system,
or transmitted, in any form or by any means,
electronic, mechanical, photocopying, recording
or otherwise, without the prior permission of
the copyright owner

ISBN 0 7156 0647 6

Printed in Great Britain
by W & J Mackay Limited, Chatham

Contents

Preface	ix
Foreword	xi
Introduction	1

RECOLLECTIONS

1. Childhood, 1862–1872	35
2. Day School, 1873–1874	45
3. Boarding School, 1874–1881	49
4. Cambridge, 1881–1885	59
5. Postgraduate, 1885–1886	73
6. Early Verses	81
7. Roger Fry and Ferdinand Schiller	89
8. Ferdinand's Letters	97
9. Some Letters of 1896 to Ferdinand	115
10. Oscar Eckhard and Peter Savary	123
11. Young Don and Writer, 1887–1897	137
12. Mrs Webb	149
13. Greece and Writing, 1897–1901	161
14. American Tours and Writing, 1901–1910	167
15. Eastern Travel, 1912–1913	177
16. The War and After, 1914–1921	189

THE WANDERING JEW	201
POEMS	229
BODY AND SOUL	271

List of Illustrations

(between pages 34 and 35)

Frontispiece: Lowes Dickinson in middle age
1. Lowes Dickinson 1922
2. Lowes Dickinson 1884
3. Roger Fry as a young man
4. Ferdinand Schiller *c.* 1885
5. Original manuscript (page 12)
6. Original typescript (pages 161–2)
7. House party at Gersau 1888
8. Oscar Eckhard in his first year at Cambridge
9. Oscar Eckhard, Manchester Regiment 1915–18
10. E. M. Forster *c.* 1900
11. Peter Savary *c.* 1942

Preface

This book represents the discharge of a trust committed to me by the late E. M. Forster over seventeen years ago, when he asked me if I would be willing to take over from him the unpublished writings of G. Lowes Dickinson, the gift of which to him, with the copyright, had been confirmed in Dickinson's Will. I said that I would gladly do so, on the understanding, which he accepted, that I should not be able to attend to them until after I had retired from my then employment. Nothing was said on either side about eventual publication of the writings, but it was understood that there would devolve on me the expressed provision of Dickinson's Will that 'my friend E. Morgan Forster . . . is to be at liberty to publish them or withold them from publication as he may in his uncontrolled discretion think fit'.

The first acknowledgment, therefore, which I wish gratefully to declare is to the Vice-Provost of King's College, Cambridge, as E. M. Forster's Executor, for confirming my freedom to proceed to publication of the autobiography and the other writings which I have selected to go with it. I should like to associate with this acknowledgment an expression of my gratitude to Dr A. N. L. Munby, who has agreed to accept the papers themselves in due course for the College library, for his unstinted help in assembling various related documents and for lending me a number of photographs from the College collection.

A score or more of those who figure in the autobiography have gone with the flowers of the forest; but one, Peter Savary, is still alive, and to him I am deeply grateful for his warm encouragement to go ahead with publication of it, and for lending me two of the photographs which are reproduced in this book. Mrs Doris Eckhard, without in any way being a party to what is here revealed about her late husband's friendship with Lowes Dickinson over half a century ago, has responded most generously to my request for information on the subject, and to her too I am indebted for the loan of two photographs. Mrs Pamela Diamand has very kindly lent me the photograph of her father, Roger Fry, as a young man. To the kindness and ingenuity of Mr N. C. Buck, of St John's College, Cambridge, in unearthing an ancient group photograph in the College library, and to the skill of Mr Edward Leigh in converting it into an individual portrait, I

Preface

am indebted for the only photograph of Ferdinand Schiller which I had been able to discover until his nephew, Mr Alan Harris, produced one of a houseparty at Gersau which he had himself had made from a faded original in his possession, and which not only includes Ferdinand Schiller but shows Lowes Dickinson himself in company with two of his other great friends of that time.

Nick Furbank read an incomplete version of the autobiography at an early stage, and, but for his encouragement, I doubt whether I should have persevered on the road to publication. George Rylands and Tim Munby gave me some sound advice at the start, and Noel Annan has lent me a generous helping hand on the way. No traveller on that road could have had a kinder reception at his destination than I have had from Colin Haycraft as publisher. Oliver Stallybrass gave me invaluable help in establishing a text of the 'Recollections' when the book was going through the press, by checking it with the numerous quotations in E. M. Forster's biography.

DENNIS PROCTOR

Foreword

Lowes Dickinson died in 1932 three years before I went up to King's as an undergraduate. So I never knew him. But I already knew two of his books. At school I had learnt to parody and plagiarise *A Modern Symposium*, to this day the most perceptive vignette of English political ideas at the turn of the century, and *The Greek View of Life* was still part of the working library of liberation for that generation of schoolboys.

His spirit still floated in the air at King's. Few of the junior members of the College remembered him, but the younger Fellows kept his memory from fading. A Lowes Dickinson Society existed to discuss the topic nearest to his heart in his old age—how best war could be outlawed and peace preserved. There was no subscription and anyone could join: most Kingsmen who wanted to discuss politics seriously gravitated to it at some time. The President was Gerald Shove, an austere man of great purity: he was an economist who had been an intimate of the original Bloomsbury group. Another Fellow who often attended its meetings and who, like Shove, was at that time a dedicated pacifist, was Christopher Morris, my director of studies in history. Both had been close friends of Lowes Dickinson and remained true to his principles. They upheld his commitment to the League of Nations and, as I recollect, annoyed the Marxists by arguing that if war between nations was folly, civil war was no less barbaric, and both fascism and communism led to civil war.

I suppose I was too sceptical, or not ardent enough, to become committed to the particular version of internationalism associated with Lowes Dickinson, but when I had to choose between that or the dogmatic Marxism which was fashionable in the thirties, I never doubted which was the more humane or indeed which was nearer to the truth about politics. For despite the romantic mists which swirled across the surface of his utopia, they parted often enough to show how wiry were the propositions on which his humanism depended. Once you had submitted yourself to his argument, you were likely to question whether, if a revolution swept away the present social system, peace and justice would at once assume their reign. You were also likely to distrust those superior realists who preened themselves on interpreting politics solely in terms of power and denouncing morality in politics as a delusion. Lowes Dickinson's disciples suggested

Foreword

to you that a vision of political life which was not inspired by personal liberty and tolerance was meagre and dispiriting and would probably be destroyed by cynicism or violence.

When I returned to King's after the war as a young Fellow I found that the Lowes Dickinson Society had dissolved. Shove grimly remarked that the cold war was too blighting a climate to revive a club which was supposed to discuss peace. Lowes Dickinson's spirit became fainter. It did not quite vanish because the older Fellows still mentioned his name, his biographer and friend, E. M. Forster, had come to live at King's, and a fountain built and inscribed in his honour stood in one of the courts. But, despite the coaxing of plumbers, it symbolically refused to play. He had become an historical figure.

As such he holds a special place in the golden age of friendship between dons and undergraduates. In early Victorian times the word 'don' conjured up the image of a dry stick, at best a man who withdrew into the maze of his own scholarly pursuits and defied the young to find him, at worst a man who neglected his students and idled life away dining and wining in the tranquil backwater of his college. When Lowes Dickinson came up to King's in 1881 dons were beginning to change. There had always been closer relations between them and undergraduates at King's than at any other college: as they were all Etonians, the undergraduates already knew the younger Fellows. But in 1865 the Fellows had at last been able to implement their long-desired intention to throw fellowships and scholarships open to all comers. Lowes Dickinson and Nathaniel Wedd, neither of whom was an Etonian, were among the early beneficiaries and became the prototype of a new kind of King's don. Oscar Browning entertained undergraduates and became their friend, but they stood for the life of the mind and were an intellectual influence: philosophers as well as guides to the young.

That generation of dons did more than be the first to treat undergraduates as their equals. Ten years before Lowes Dickinson came up the College's annual income from endowments was £30,000 and a Fellow was paid £280 a year. By the time he had become a Fellow, the agricultural depression had impoverished all the colleges and, since their revenue came almost entirely from farm rents, some were brought near to ruin. It was all the more galling for King's: the scheme of reform which threw the College open to non-Etonians and was intended to make ample provision for poor students had been held in check for thirty years until the holders of vested interests had vanished into limbo. Now that the way was clear, it suddenly looked as if the funds would not be available to implement the scheme to found scholarships and exhibitions and research studentships and to erect buildings so that the number of undergraduates could be doubled. It

Foreword

would have been natural enough if the Fellows had put the scheme on one side. But Lowes Dickinson was one of the leaders who insisted that the scheme should go through, and the salaries of Fellows were cut again and again until they were no more than £80 a year: only then was the appropriation for scholarships diminished. These heroic days of self-sacrifice seem long ago. Dons no longer follow a calling: they belong to a profession. Yet without the idealism of Lowes Dickinson and his colleagues, would the English notion of a university have developed in this century as it has done?

He was not ashamed to have ideals, but he knew that ideals are illusory, and even dangerous, unless you relate them to each other and to language and to the scheme of things. In common with some of the finest minds in late Victorian Oxford and Cambridge Lowes Dickinson was preoccupied by ethics and eventually published a Socratic dialogue entitled *The Meaning of Good*. A year or so later he wryly watched his junior, Moore, sweep aside his offering and in the same devastating manner refute the metaphysics of his friend McTaggart which up to that time had captivated Cambridge. The new philosophical climate was too bracing and rigorous for him, and he turned more to the study of history and politics which were then still concerned with people.

But however starkly these three friends differed in their philosophic method, they held almost identical notions of value. For Moore the states of mind which were produced by the pursuit of truth and knowledge, or by the contemplation of beauty, were excellent: but yet more excellent was the state of mind which could be achieved by communion with the beloved. McTaggart dismissed as delusions the existence of God, material objects in space and the self-contradictions of time, but—though it went against the grain to do so—he admitted that *something* existed, and by the process of deduction concluded that the universe consisted of souls in ecstatic communion with each other. Lowes Dickinson too put the love of friends first. In his search for the meaning of good he argued that human beings in love come nearer than in any other of their experiences to what we might conceive as absolutely good: 'Whatever Reality may ultimately be, it is in the life of the affections, with all its confused tangle of loves and hates, attractions, repulsions, and, worst of all, indifferences, it is in this intricate commerce of souls that we may come nearest to apprehending what perhaps we shall never wholly apprehend, but the quest of which alone, as I believe, gives any significance to life . . .'[1] What could be more appropriate than that Dennis Proctor, the last of those to whom he offered his heart, should edit his autobiography?

[1] G. Lowes Dickinson, *The Meaning of Good* (Glasgow, 1901), pp. 177-93, 231.

Foreword

Just as he ended his book on ethics with an allegory, so in the most characteristic paper he ever read to the Apostles he imagined a meeting of the Society taking place in heaven. The celestial Apostles were emphatically not Peter, Andrew, James and John, but Goethe, Hegel, Turgenev and Victor Hugo. They are discussing, as the Society on earth often did, whom to elect to it and before them is the proposal: 'Shall we Elect God?' For a number of reasons they are disposed to think that it would be unwise, but before the question can be put, there is a knock at the door and God enters. He tells them that their doubts are mistaken: they cannot refuse to elect him. He is all they believe in, all they see, all they deny, all they affirm: he is the doubter and the doubt and the founder of their Society. They still remain unconvinced and, since his face is hidden by his cloak and hat, they ask him to reveal himself. As he does so they all recognise him and each calls him by his name—Goethe 'Das Schöne!', Turgenev 'La Vérité!', Hugo 'L'Idéal!', Hegel 'Das Absolut!' Whether or not you believe that men's notions of perfection can be reconciled, to discuss whether it is possible to do so with the intensity and devotion which Lowes Dickinson did, is in itself a sufficient justification for the existence of a university. It needs none other.

NOEL ANNAN

Introduction

Some fifteen years ago four people were coralled in the precincts of King's College, Cambridge, to hold a conversation to be recorded for radio about the well-known writer Goldsworthy Lowes Dickinson, a former Fellow of the College who had died a quarter of a century before. The four were: E. M. Forster, his old friend and biographer; Reginald Fuller, who had been his 'gyp' or personal servant; and two who had come to know him well as undergraduates in the last few years of his life—Patrick Wilkinson and myself. I shall not easily forget the dreary scene that was enacted.

The setting was a side court of the College which in those days, before recent efforts were made to redeem its former squalor, had long been consigned to outer barbary; except that in a set of rooms over an archway in the middle of one side there had once lodged in state the great Maynard Keynes; and it was in those very rooms that the gathering was to take place. They had, however, undergone a sea change since those palmy days. Gone were the life-size figures in the manner of Signorelli with which Duncan Grant and Vanessa Bell had decorated the walls for their Bloomsbury friend; gone were all the other appurtenances and comforts of former grandeur. The room into which we were now ushered appeared to be in the early stages of a removal. Some half-opened packing-cases stood in no particular order on the bare boards of the floor; the marks where pictures had been removed still showed on the grimy walls; and the only furniture was a deal table and some chairs, on which we four were invited by our radio *compère* to seat ourselves. Such, it transpired, was the daily habitation of the present tenant, a higher mathematician, who, being away that weekend, had kindly put his rooms at our disposal.

It was a bleak December afternoon, and through the uncurtained windows, which had to be kept open to admit a festoon of electric cables from a van in the court below, there entered a piercing winter wind. No form of heating appeared to be available, and no antecedent cheer had been provided to thaw us out. In freezing cold we took our seats: stone-cold in every sense we set about our task. Forster was in the throes of 'flu; but he nobly came for the first five minutes, swaddled in mufflers and great coats, to start us off. For the next hour and a half Wilkinson and I patted the ball, ever more aimlessly, backwards and forwards across the net, while Fuller

Introduction

sat tongue-tied on the side-lines. At last the umpire, to our relief, said it was enough; the cables were coiled up, the battery disconnected; and only then, when that which had never in fact come alive was now irretrievably dead, did Fuller pronounce the one memorable sentence uttered by anyone that cheerless afternoon. 'I remember,' he said, 'when Mr Gandhi was paying a visit to the College, and Mr Dickinson was to meet him at lunch. I asked him, when he came back, how he had got on with him. "Couldn't get a damned thing out of him" was his reply.'

Everything about that occasion and its close—the racy tone of Dickinson's reply to Fuller's question, its hint of exasperation over a missed opportunity, and our own failure to communicate it to a listening audience—seems somehow characteristic now of a man who, when he died forty years ago, would have needed no editor to introduce his autobiography to the reader. He was an established writer with a devoted and extensive readership, a successful broadcaster in the early days of radio, and a much-loved presence in a wide circle of friends of all ages. Now his memory has fallen into that trough which seems to lie in wait for everyone in the second generation after they are gone. Today the fountain which was erected in his memory in the court where he lodged in his first year in College is kept permanently switched off because the students complain of the noise.

It is not easy to find the right label to attach to Lowes Dickinson for a generation to whom the name means nothing. I described him in the article about him in the Dictionary of National Biography as 'humanist, historian and philosophical writer'; and this is perhaps as good a caption as any. He referred to himself, in one of his own papers, as 'a teacher and man of letters'; and the latter expression was the one he used for the description of Geoffrey Vivian, the character whom he cast in the role of himself, in the Dramatis Personae of *A Modern Symposium*,[1] the most popular, and I am inclined to think the best, of all his published works. He also, rather surprisingly, applied it to Shelley, as the reader of the following pages may notice, though it hardly conveys any hint of that perpetual wrestling with the world around them which was common to both of them. *The Times* once described him, on the strength of his early historical works on the Puritan Revolution and nineteenth-century politics in France and England,[2] as 'an anti-democratic publicist'; but that is not likely to appeal to a modern reader either; nor would it have pleased Dickinson himself in his later years. I shall simply mention some of his different manifestations and leave it at that.

[1] Brimley, Johnson & Ince, 1905, reissued by Allen & Unwin, 1930.
[2] *From King to King*, George Allen, 1891; *Revolution and Reaction in Modern France*, George Allen, 1892, revised edition, Allen & Unwin, 1927; *The Development of Parliament During the Nineteenth Century*, Longmans, Green, 1895.

Introduction

He was, first and foremost perhaps, a don who loved youth, and therefore a teacher from whom it was impossible not to learn, even if all one learnt was how to think things out for oneself. He was a born writer, as he himself remarked.[1] He was never not writing something, and what he wrote was pure, clear English prose. His style, like his matter, was a little *too* pure and clear for today's fume-charged atmosphere; but his turn will come again, and the pabulum he left is plentiful and various. He was—yes, one has to admit the horrid word—a publicist. Throughout his life he recognised an obligation to bring his brain to bear on the problems of the world in which he lived, and to send forth his message to anyone who cared to listen. 'I never wanted to write learned or scholarly works,' he said; 'I wanted to influence opinion and the course of events;' and, looking back when just on sixty, he wrote: 'Love, literature, natural beauty, are the things I really care about. Yet I have spent most of my life in writing and thinking and inquiring into political facts and tendencies; with no result I imagine!'

When the outbreak of war in 1914 dashed all his hopes for the future of humanity, he threw himself at once into practical activity to establish an international system, which alone, in his view, could prevent future wars. He was the moving spirit in founding the 'Bryce Group', which eventually became the principal nucleus of the League of Nations Union; and throughout the war he poured forth a stream of articles, pamphlets and books, which were undoubtedly influential in swinging public opinion in England, and perhaps still more in America, towards the idea of a League of Nations, and were responsible for some of the actual provisions of the Covenant.[2] After the war was over, he devoted five years of research into the documents of the pre-war diplomacy to produce his most authoritative work on the subject, *The International Anarchy, 1904–1914*,[3] with which he brought all these labours to a final consummation.

But the heart of Dickinson's writing, to my mind, was in the half-dozen books he wrote between 1901 and 1911 when he was in his forties,[4] after he had turned away from the themes of past political history and before the shock of 1914 drove him to take an active part in contemporary

---

[1] p. 159 below.
[2] E.g. *The War and the Way Out*, Chancery Lane Press, 1914; *After the War*, A. C. Fifield, 1915; *The European Anarchy*, Allen & Unwin, 1916; *Economic War after the War*, Union of Democratic Control, 1916; *The Choice Before Us*, Allen & Unwin, 1917.
[3] Allen & Unwin, 1926.
[4] *The Meaning of Good*, James Maclehose & Sons, 1901; *Letters from John Chinaman*, R. Brimley Johnson, 1901; *Religion: a Criticism and a Forecast*, Brimley Johnson & Ince, 1905; *A Modern Symposium*, Brimley Johnson & Ince, 1905; *Justice and Liberty*, J. M. Dent, 1908; *Religion and Immortality*, J. M. Dent, 1911.
Note: All these titles were transferred to Allen & Unwin in 1930.

Introduction

politics. These are the books I had in mind in the other two terms of my original caption, 'humanist and philosophical writer', and I still cannot think of any better category into which to fit them. Dickinson himself gave a very fair description of these books in the words he used to introduce the character of Geoffrey Vivian in *A Modern Symposium*:

> He concerned himself, directly or indirectly, with philosophic problems. But he never wrote philosophy; his methods were not those of logic; and his sympathies were with science and the arts. In the early age of Greece he might have been Empedocles or Heraclitus; he could never have been Spinoza or Kant. He sought to interpret life, but not merely in terms of the intellect. He needed to see and feel in order to think. And he expressed himself in a style too intellectual for lovers of poetry, too metaphorical for lovers of philosophy.

I cannot say that these books have had any great lasting influence: whatever effect they had at the time must have been quickly blotted out by the war of 1914. But they occupy, it seems to me, rather a special place in our social history. They were exactly contemporaneous with the first beginnings of the Bloomsbury group; yet their purport was something very different from the characteristic ethos of that essentially inward-looking élite. Though its members, with the exception of Dickinson's lifelong friend, Roger Fry, were born the best part of a generation later than he was, he saw deeper below the surface of modern society, and further into the future, than most of them did. His books of that period were the first intellectual stirrings in England of the twentieth century, whereas the thoughts and aspirations of Bloomsbury at that time were still rooted in the nineteenth. He understood the ferment that was going on beneath the sun-kissed Edwardian crust, and he welcomed it. There is no echo in him of that footling chirrup with which Lytton Strachey is said to have hailed the publication of G. E. Moore's *Principia Ethica*: 'The age of reason has arrived.'

Dickinson was deeply obsessed all his life by the sheer fact of poverty: he saw that it pressed like a deadweight on the great majority of the world's inhabitants; and in the two central books of this period—*A Modern Symposium* and *Justice and Liberty*—he was trying to think out how society could best be transformed, as he knew it must be, to remove it. He had approached the problem by a philosophic discussion of the ultimate end in view, in *The Meaning of Good*. All three of these books were cast in the form of dialogue or symposium modelled on Plato, and they are penetrated through and through, like all his writing, by his love of that philosopher; but Dickinson could never bring himself to deny, as Plato did, the reality of Evil, especially in its one great omnipresent manifestation—poverty. His discussion of the ultimate good led him, just as it had led Plato, to search

Introduction

for an absolute good existing independently of life on earth; and this produced the two beautifully written essays, *Religion: a Criticism and a Forecast* and *Religion and Immortality*, which must, I think, be unique in the literature of that subject in not attempting to probe the mystery of life beyond the grave (though Dickinson would dearly have liked to be able to do so), but in discussing, coolly and objectively, not whether such a life existed, but whether it was desirable that it should, and whether, in any case, it was desirable to believe that it did. His other production of that time, *Letters from John Chinaman*, an exquisitely urbane criticism of western industrialism, thinly disguised, in the manner of *Candide*, as coming from a visiting Chinaman, may still be read with pleasure; and it probably made more impact at the time than any of his other books of the period.

All of them are written in a beautifully modulated English prose, taking off at times into sustained passages of poetic, but still Attic, eloquence, which are more like Landor than any other parallel in English that I can think of. In these books, at any rate, Dickinson did not deserve the strictures of Virginia Woolf in *A Writer's Diary*, twice published to the world by Leonard Woolf, still less the criticisms which he himself threw in for good measure of 'a weakness, a looseness of fibre' and 'a thin vapour of gentle high-mindedness'.[1] Dickinson's conclusions, certainly, were usually agnostic; but the thought in these books is firm and clear, the reasoning tight, and the style pellucid.

I am reminded here, strangely enough—for no two people could well have been more different—of Jowett, who had also been in his forties—just about the same age as Dickinson was then—when he made his controversial contributions to *Essays and Reviews* in 1860. Yet Leslie Stephen, summing up, nearly forty years later, the life of 'a man of mark and intellectual authority at a time when vital questions were being eagerly agitated and the most various conclusions reached', felt obliged to conclude that, to the question 'Will the future historian of English thought be able to show that any of the important contributions to speculation bear the impress of Jowett's intellect?', 'one can hardly deny that the answer must be unequivocally in the negative'.[2]

If this was true of an Oxford prophet who cast a spell over his disciples which lasted all their lives, it is not surprising that the same should have been the fate of a Cambridge don, anxious, as Leslie Stephen also put it, 'rather to disavow than to assert any such personal influence as is independent of downright logical argument'. Dickinson, like Jowett, had worked his way through Hegel; and Plato, as I have said, was with him all

---

[1] *Beginning Again*, Hogarth Press, 1964, p. 190.
[2] *Studies of a Biographer*, Duckworth, edn. of 1931, vol II. pp. 130–1.

Introduction

his life; but Dickinson did not, any more than Jowett did, leave any philosophic system behind him; and he was, of his essence, a Cambridge man. His own words in an obituary article of 1930 on his old friend C. P. Sanger, and afterwards quoted by Maynard Keynes in a memorial of Frank Ramsey,[1] may fittingly be applied to himself:

It does not become a Cambridge man to claim too much for his university, nor am I much tempted to do so. But there is, I think, a certain type, rare, like all good things, which seems to be associated in some peculiar way with my alma mater. I am thinking of men like Leslie Stephen (the original of Meredith's Vernon Whitford), like Henry Sidgwick, like Maitland, like one who died but the other day with all his promise unfulfilled. It is a type unworldly without being saintly, unambitious without being inactive, warm-hearted without being sentimental. Through good report and ill such men work on, following the light of truth as they see it; able to be sceptical without being paralysed; content to know what is knowable and to reserve judgment on what is not. The world could never be driven by such men, for the springs of action lie deep in ignorance and madness. But it is they who are the beacon in the tempest, and they are more, not less, needed now than ever before. May their succession never fail!

Yet the chief impression left on one by his own autobiography is of something more positive than this—something which is not, I think, communicated by Forster's *Life*,[2] and which was certainly not divined by those who only knew him as a charming elder in the last few years of his life at Cambridge—that, before he reached that last quiet haven, he had been rent all his life by storms of passion. It was a capacity for strong passion and the pain it brings, rather than a sort of brooding melancholy, as one might gather from Forster's book, that animated his lifelong concern for the sufferings of humanity, and caused him to write, when he saw the world moving, soon after the end of the First World War, from one disaster to another:

The pain becomes almost unendurable, and I can only stave it off by plunging into some kind of work, which yet must bear upon it.

And it was the same capacity for passion strong and deep that continually plunged him into the abyss and lifted him to the heights during fifty years in which he was never not hopelessly in love with another person.

Dickinson tells the story of these unrequited passions in the four central chapters of his autobiography. He tells it with unflinching candour, and sometimes with such dryness as almost to forfeit the reader's sympathy; but

[1] *The Nation*, 22 February 1930, and *Essays in Biography*, Macmillan, 1933, pp. 302–3.
[2] *Goldsworthy Lowes Dickinson*, Edward Arnold, 1934.

Introduction

there is no mistaking the agonies he went through. His account of the first two love affairs, both of them with men of about his own age, was written in retrospect in his sixtieth year after they were over, though it incorporates letters and poems written while they were in progress; but the third affair (with a much younger man) had not yet ended when he was writing; and the fourth began before he had laid down his pen. It is a moving record of suffering and devotion, whatever one's views of sexual morality may be. Dickinson does not spare himself; and he allows one to understand, as he himself clearly understood, the embarrassments of the others, none of whom shared his homosexual temperament. Since I myself was the fifth and last in the series (after the close of the period covered by the autobiography), I feel I can testify on behalf of us all that we loved Goldie (as I propose now to call him) dearly, and treasured his friendship as a precious possession; and each of us did his best in his own way to assuage his physical desires. His relationship with each of the other four ripened, after the passion had subsided, into a lasting friendship. In my case there was no time, alas, for that. It has left me instead with this opportunity to present his autobiography to a modern reader.

Goldie kept the typescript of these four chapters separately, and did not include them in the text, entitled 'Recollections', of which he had a professional typescript made. They do, however, contain indications, as the reader may notice, that he expected them some day to be published with the rest of the book; and he affixed instructions at the head of each of them as to where it was to be fitted in. E. M. Forster, who had been his friend for over thirty years when Goldie died in 1932, inherited these chapters, together with the rest of the autobiography and all his other unpublished writings, under his will; and Forster has left notes of the dates on which he read them within the first three weeks after Goldie's death. He devoted himself at once to writing his friend's biography—with such effect that the book was published in less than two years' time[1]—and he worked with the transcript of the 'Recollections' at his elbow, following it closely in matter, in arrangement, and often in actual wording. But, the climate of opinion about homosexuality forty years ago being very different from what it is now, and all the other persons concerned being still alive, he banished all reference to these particular chapters from his book.

One can well imagine how he must have chafed under the necessity of describing his friend's life without mentioning the rarest thing about it, the almost continuous experience over a lifetime of passionate love for another human being, merely because the other human being was always someone of the same sex. It was indeed a serious omission in the portrait as well as a gaping hole in the narrative. For Goldie's loves for other

[1] *Goldsworthy Lowes Dickinson*, Edward Arnold, 1934.

Introduction

persons—particularly the second in the series, his love for Ferdinand Schiller, which was the richest and most formative—were the source that fed all his transcendental yearnings for the truth about the universe; his long familiarity with personal anguish was what constantly renewed his determination to bend his mind to the problems of suffering humanity; and it was the way in which he learnt to live with this and command it that made him a stronger, more positive person than one would gather from Forster's biography.

But Forster also omitted, besides these chapters on Goldie's love affairs, a great deal that *was* included in the version which he had at his elbow, beginning with the significant sentence placed early in the book by Goldie,

It is my object, in these reminiscences, to tell what is usually not told,

and continuing to suppress all that flowed from it. Goldie has given, as the reader will see, a quite exact account of his sexual make-up and his gradual discovery of his sexual propensities from early childhood onwards. His very first sexual sensation—before puberty, he says—was connected with boots, which he liked to be elegant well-polished ones; and this fetish remained with him all his life. He was already masturbating, to the accompaniment of boot fantasies, before he went to his first boarding school at the age of twelve. He must, I think, by then have had some proclivity, almost unbeknown to himself, for casting himself in the woman's role, for he relates how he was warned by his first schoolmaster that he must 'resist and resent being treated like a girl', and how he enjoyed his success when he acted the part of Mrs Bouncer in *Cox and Box* and 'was got up to look pretty'.

He went through Charterhouse, however, in a house which he describes as 'what would be called a "hothouse of vice" ', without experiencing any sort of sexual attraction, or even one of those romantic attachments which are almost normal in English boarding schools, for another boy. He was masturbating—but still the fantasies, he says, were connected solely with boots—until his father extracted a promise from him to stop—a promise which he faithfully kept, with remarkable strength of character, for eight years, until he was forced to give way under stress of frustrated passion when he had by then discovered that his sexual desires were exclusively fixed on other men. He had gone through the whole of his undergraduate career at Cambridge before he made the discovery. He was 24 when it happened—quite suddenly, one evening with Roger Fry, his first love. And from there the story continues, as I have said, through his successive love affairs, with Roger Fry, Ferdinand Schiller, Oscar Eckhard and Peter Savary, and later, in his last years, with myself—never, as far as one can

Introduction

make out, manifested in orgasms produced by any form of copulation, but only by kisses and warm embraces accompanied by fantasies about boots, and these intertwined with musings and longings for the Infinite.

I find a certain dryness in Goldie's account of all this in his autobiography, most of which was written in 1921, his sixtieth year, when he was looking back, after the ravages of the war, on his past life. Even the story of his passionate loves for Roger Fry, Ferdinand Schiller and Oscar Eckhard, which were the most important in his whole life, is told coolly, and not altogether persuasively. I am going to redress the balance, therefore, by drawing on another, far more impassioned, document which he had written eleven years earlier when the stress and strain were at their height. It is a manuscript of forty large pages written in his own hand, which he never typed or had copied. The writing is a mere agonised scrawl, extremely difficult to decipher; but I am satisfied that I have puzzled it out in the end. There is no sign that Forster had read this particular document (which, indeed, is no easy task), although there is an explicit authority on the cover, addressed personally to him and Roger Fry, to do so: it bears no note such as he left on other papers when he had read them. It is headed 'A chapter in my autobiography—Privatissimum'. It was begun at Diessen in Bavaria, and it is dated 'September 7 1910, in the 49th year of my age'.

Goldie's note on the cover was mainly intended, I think, as a warning to his two friends to make sure that his sisters did not see the document. He left similar warnings to that effect on other chapters which he clearly meant, as I have said, to be included with the rest of the autobiography. There is a clear indication that he thought that this document too might one day have a wider circulation, for he writes on the first page that he is going to make the attempt to set down an account of his own homosexual experience,

partly to fix for myself what the years are already beginning to blur and obscure, partly in the hope that what I am writing, if it should ever see the light, may bring some help and encouragement to others who have the same temperament; or may contribute to enlighten and humanise public opinion on a point as to which, especially in England, it is singularly irrational and cruel.

The cause has now been gained, and, to that extent, the justification for publishing what Lowes Dickinson wrote on behalf of it in 1910 has evaporated; but much of what he wrote is so impressive, both for its own sake and for the further light which it throws on himself, that I feel entitled to attach this piece of his own embroidery to the somewhat too seamless garment he made later.

Introduction

He begins with a recapitulation of his earliest sexual experiences, going into more detail than he does in the autobiography about his various devices in childhood for satisfying his shoe-fetichism, but adding little that is significant, except for one thing. He does here identify his shoe-fetichism as 'part of a general "femininity" in my physical feeling towards men'. 'My dream', he says, 'is always to be dominated, not to dominate. I have, so far, a woman's soul; and the only thing for which I should like to be a woman is that I might experience the dominating and aggressive love of a man.' This recalls his letter to Ferdinand Schiller, written (but not sent) not long before, in which he said:

It's a curious thing to have a woman's soul shut up in a man's body, but that seems to be my case.[1]

Only, he adds here the important corrective:

This physical impulse, however, has never given the key to my relations to men, because, on the spiritual side, I have a much more imperious need to preserve my independence and self-respect, and have, in fact, had at least as much to give as I have received.

There was certainly nothing feminine about Goldie's *mind*, and I should not myself have said that his soul was feminine either. I do not recognise anything in my own intimacy with him that seems in any way akin to those which I have had with women.

There follows a passage—a more extended treatment of the subject than the corresponding passage in the autobiography[2]—justifying the practice of masturbation as

the proper and healthy course to adopt by anyone having the homogenic temperament who cannot otherwise satisfy his sex, and who has sufficient self-control and preoccupation with higher interests to prevent him from taking too seriously, or indulging to excess, a mere animal need.

For his own part, he sadly explains:

Probably, if I had ever loved a man who returned my love in the same kind, some kind of sexual intercourse would have resulted, and been natural, healthy and good. But my fortune has been otherwise. There has been no alternative but masturbation or abstention. And I have, rightly, as I think, practised the former.

[1] p. 111 below.
[2] p. 91 below.

Introduction

This leads on to general discussion of homosexuality, which, again, is a much fuller treatment of the subject than is to be found in the autobiography. He introduces it by some remarks about himself which are likely to strike a chord in others:

In my emotional life I have had such experience as I would hesitate to exchange for the normal satisfaction of love and marriage. I am like a man born crippled; will and character may make more of such a life, through the very stimulus of the defect, than many normal men make of theirs. Whatever I feel about my life, it is not shame or humiliation, rather the contrary. It presents itself to me sometimes as tragic, but never base.

He goes on, more generally:

The homosexual temperament must, I think, be regarded as a misfortune, though it is possible, with that temperament, to have a better, more passionate and more noble life than most men of normal temperament achieve.

He adds the interesting comment that, since 'a homosexual man is often attracted only to those who are normal', so that 'on the physical side . . . the passion is constantly unsatisfied',

it is as though the earlier phases of love between a man and a woman should be indefinitely prolonged, with all their ferments, turmoil and bitter-sweet distress. This means, of course, the perpetuation of romance, and in fact, I suppose, homosexual men have a more romantic and passionate life than others; but also, a more tragic one, and in some cases, perhaps in most, an unhealthy, unbalanced, perhaps ultimately insane one. That this can be successfully avoided my own experience shows. But the strain is often very great; and one requires, perhaps, an unusual measure of self-control, and an intense preoccupation with intellectual or practical pursuits.

Now comes a fine political diatribe, fifty years before its time, it seems, on the state of the law and the prevailing prejudice against marriage between two men; who, he says,

ought to be able to meet and love and publicly and permanently evince their relation;

and he points out the hindrance thereby erected to the fruitful contribution which such men are often capable of making to the good estate of society:

Introduction

Whether this prejudice will ever be overcome by experience or knowledge or reason I do not know. It is the last stronghold in society of sheer irrationality. And England is the keep and centre of it.

He ends this section of the paper with a moving declaration of his own testament:

No words of mine can tell what I have found of happiness and despair, of greatness mixed up with baseness, of nobility crossed with mere evil, in my emotional life. All insight I have had into life and the world has been rooted in my friendships. They have struck deep into my intellectual and spiritual life; they have made me what I am. And if anyone values anything that I have done, they should value also the passions that alone have made it possible.

Interspersed between the excerpts which I have been quoting from this 'most private' paper (which yet seems to have been conceived, as it largely continued, almost as a manifesto) are passages telling the story of Goldie's passions. Those describing his love affairs with Roger Fry and Ferdinand Schiller (both by then over) do not differ significantly from the account of them which he gave eleven years later in his autobiography; but a third passion, for Oscar Eckhard, had just befallen him when he was writing, and his description of this is so much more moving than the greatly condensed account he gave later,[1] that I feel constrained to reproduce a large part of it here. Goldie himself, after all, when he was recording his next love affair, with Peter Savary, included in his autobiography some long passages which he had written earlier while the affair was still in progress;[2] and since I feel that he failed to do justice to himself in the few pages which he devoted to this one, or to give its due weight to a love affair which lasted for twelve years and occupied, in its way, as important a place in his life as his previous passion of about the same duration for Ferdinand Schiller, and since there are no 'revelations' in these passages of anything that is not plainly recorded in the autobiography too, I am going to quote from them at some length.

The first (which preceded the long discussion of homosexuality from which I have just quoted some extracts) is as follows:

As I write, I am involved in a relation which I find more difficult to handle, and more problematical in its outcome, than any I have yet experienced. Three years ago there came up to my college an undergraduate whom I will call O., with whom I quickly formed a close intimacy. We rode together regularly, talked together, went to concerts and theatres; and in his second year he began to do

[1] pp. 123–5 below.
[2] pp. 128–33 below.

Introduction

work with me. The first two years of his residence at Cambridge were among the happiest I have known. It was like a new youth. I hardly knew why I was so happy; my feeling at that time was one of pure delight in watching the development of a very charming and beautiful personality, in giving all I could, and receiving in return more than he or I knew. There was then no element of passion, nor did I think it likely any would arise; for I had never loved anyone so many years younger than myself.

I was, however, mistaken. My feeling followed the course usual with me in such cases. I began to find an irresistible attraction in his face, his mouth, his eyes, and his voice, all his ways and manners. I thought a day wasted in which I did not see him. Finally, the desire to come into physical contact with him grew more than I could resist. I do not, of course, mean any sort of sexual relation; I could never alarm or insult a young man entrusted to my care with such suggestions, nor do they occur to me. But I wanted to touch him, and once or twice I allowed myself to do so. I do not think that he then understood the nature of my feeling. But he is independent, and he developed rapidly. He began, I think, without ceasing to have a regard for me, to find me a little importunate. Some talk we had made it clear to me that he wished to see less of me. I acquiesced, and only then discovered that it had become almost impossible for me to live without him.

I was in a kind of fever during the week he didn't come to see me. It was the end of term, and he was leaving Cambridge. Under the influence of a feeling I could not control, and which at the time I judged to be right, I wrote him a long letter explaining my temperament and the character of my love for him at length. I then went abroad. I heard from him at Taormina, a brief letter, but kind and affectionate, in which he assured me he valued my friendship, and, in his own way (not mine, of course), returned it. This letter made me very happy. I accepted it as a kind and attractive account of his feelings, and on my return to Cambridge endeavoured to renew relations on the old terms. Gradually I found that things were not as before. He was embarrassed and bored or impatient in my presence; he made no attempt to see me; and showed no pleasure in my visits to him. This I did not fully make clear to myself until the end of the term. I found then also that he himself was in love with a woman.

He went abroad, to this place (Diessen), with his family, and the lady; and the result has been (so far) that she does not return his love and will not marry him. Meantime, I was suffering more than I thought I could ever suffer again from such a cause. I reproached myself with writing to him; I reproached him for heartlessness. Day and night I could not get the thought of him from my mind. At the end of August I came out to join the family at Munich, to go to Wagner's 'Ring'. I had intended to go on to France, for a trip with R., after the opera was over. But all I really wanted was to come here with him and his family. The day I should have left Munich something took hold of me, carried me to the telegraph office, and sent a wire abandoning the tour. I then came here, to Diessen. I do not know whether I did right, nor how it will issue.

O. accepts, and I think really values, my sympathy in his trouble. I see little of him, but he is friendly and kind; and I half hope our relation may resume a

Introduction

happy and harmonious course. Much, I feel, will depend on myself. I must have more self-control than I have ever had before, more, perhaps, than I am capable of. For I love him with an extraordinary intensity. If I can make out of this relation, too, something permanent and beautiful, it will be one of the chief gains of my life. I do not know whether it will be possible. But upon the possibility, or the reverse, must turn a great part of my happiness in the future.

Next comes the following short note, dated '25 September 1910, Cambridge':

On 18 September 1910, received at Baden Baden, sent from his room to mine, Oscar's intolerable note breaking off all relations. Nothing had passed between us to account for, or justify, this since our affectionate, and, as I thought, frank, conversation at Diessen. I left at once, in two hours.

Is this sordid, ugly, unnecessary stroke the end? Is he, after all, worthless?

The story is resumed nine months later, on 11 June 1911, still on the numbered pages of the same paper:

From Diessen I went with O. and his mother to Baden Baden. We were to spend a fortnight there. I went feeling happy and secure, and looking forward to seeing a great deal of O. in the most pleasant conditions. The third morning (I think) after our arrival, I found this letter in the box outside my room. There had been no warning of any kind. I have never received such a blow. I walked up and down the room, I remember, saying 'This is death'. Then I decided to leave by the next train. I saw O., as I had to settle one or two things; but nothing was said, except with regard to his mother's attitude. The journey to England was the most horrible experience I have ever had. I suppose I was really mad. I wrote a line to the mother, from Cologne, because I felt I must get expression somehow. This was a slight relief. I knew she would not be unsympathetic. I managed, with infinite difficulty, to prevent myself from writing to him what I might have regretted saying all my life.

I cannot dwell on my state of mind in the weeks that followed. I was utterly obsessed by this misery. It seemed to me cruel, unaccountable, almost incredible. Morning after morning I woke saying it must surely be a nightmare. I experienced then the full horror of unrequited and slighted love. There is, I suppose, no pain worse. I, certainly, have known nothing like it. R. and another friend (H.O.M.) were my chief comforts. Ultimately, H.O.M. acted as intermediary between O. and me; O. wrote me a letter which I received on 7 November. I replied, saying that I should leave it to him whether or no he could renew relationship with me, and made no advances from my side. I kept to this, always with a great deal of suffering, but feeling that the bitterness was over, and that there was at least a possibility of a future.

During last term, and this, he became more friendly and less embarrassed, rode with me frequently, and came to my rooms. On Wednesday May 31, he

Introduction

came to supper with me. We had an intimate conversation, and finally I asked him whether he felt he could now continue a permanent relation with me. He said he was sure he could, and that he now really liked me—he used some stronger phrase. There was no concealment on his part, and no illusion on mine, as to the nature of his feeling, or of mine. We recognised that I loved him, body and soul, and that his feeling for me had no 'love' in it at all. I kissed and embraced him then for the first time, and he acquiesced without apparent reluctance. Some days later (it was last Tuesday June 6) we had another intimate talk. I then put it to him whether he disliked physical contact, kissing etc.. He was perfectly candid; said he would think it over; but kissed affectionately at parting, and said he would always do that on saying good night. That kiss and embrace lingers with me as a moment of supreme happiness.

But since then I have not seen him; and I have been suffering acutely. I want him every minute. And I cannot get rid of the idea that he is undergoing the same reaction as at Baden Baden—that another dreadful Doom is hanging over me. This dread became almost a certainty when I received on Friday a few words, in answer to a note of mine asking him to ride, in which he declined briefly, signed his name, scratched this out, and substituted initials. This reproduced in me the whole dreadful horror of last winter. I seemed to lose my balance, almost my senses. I wrote him a passionate letter, begging him to be candid with me, and not to go back on me again. He wrote a reply, very brief, saying it was a 'fuss about nothing'! Perhaps it was. But I have not heard from him, or seen him, since. I wrote asking him to supper tonight, and he sends no reply.

My state of mind is contemptible to myself. I am physically upset. And though I do not give way, and do my work, and see people as usual, I am suffering torments. I know that if I saw him for a few minutes, and he was still friendly, all this would disappear. And I do not think my love would assume this intolerable form, if I could be sure of his faithfulness. I know that I have no claims on him. I make none, in my heart. I want his happiness and his well-being, and I know he must find it independently of me. In the future, I know, when the strain is past, I shall get nothing but good from this. But only if he told me the truth when he said he now cared for me. Did he?

I write on purpose this frank record of my present state. But I find it curiously disagreeable to write, and feel that it somehow does me injustice. It is impossible to render either the intensity or the conflict of my feeling; nor its intermixture with the texture of my ordinary life. The strain is almost unbearable. But I would far rather have it, than not love. If he knew, would he torture me so? But the torture is in the situation, and he is not to blame, nor I.

A fortnight later, on 24 June, he records the dénouement as follows:

I leave the above as I wrote it; it describes my feelings; but it *was* all a 'fuss about nothing'. On that day, 11 June, O. broke off his engagement to H.G. I went to see him, and try to comfort him, in the evening, and he was friendly and affectionate. Still, I was disturbed and unsettled. But he supped with me and passed

Introduction

the evening on June 14. It was the night of the College concert, to which we had both intended to go. But neither of us went. We sat till 11, in the dark, by the firelight, in my red room. I sat at his feet, and we embraced often, and talked over everything. Then, and later—on a ride, my last with him here, alas! June 16—he told me, for the first time, the truth about his feelings. My letter of March 1910, in which I told him I loved him, had made him furiously angry. His instinct and desire was to break off all relations; and he was only prevented from doing so by his mother, to whom he had told everything, and to whom he showed my letter! The letter he wrote me in reply (received at Taormina), which I took as a full acceptance by him of the situation, was intended to convey exactly the opposite—he now admits that it could not have done so, to me. Hence his irritation when I renewed relations with him in the following term, and all that led up to the break in the September of that year. But now, he says, he does really like me. He can allow me to kiss him, i.e. without pleasure on his part, but, so far, without sensible annoyance! This is a point I must watch carefully. It seems as though we have, at last, got on to a basis of truth, and that, with care and unselfishness and self-control on my part, and frankness on his, we may retain and develop a relation very beautiful to me, and perhaps helpful and pleasant to him. More depends on me than on him. And so, for the time, I leave it. I feel very sad and flat that he is gone. But behind all that a sense of happiness and hope.

The next entry is a brief one, written over a year later, on 19 August 1912:

Re-reading the above, I think it as well to bring it up to date. There was to be more trouble. Though O. permitted me to kiss him, i.e., as I sincerely thought, without distaste, he had afterwards violent reactions. There was a dreadful week-end at his home, followed by a kind of reconciliation and explanation. Between July 1911 and November 1911 I did not see him. We met then, and once after. In the spring of 1912 I stayed ten days at his home. There was no physical intimacy, and all went well. At present he is very friendly, and I have had great happiness from him. In a month I go to the East. I hope to see him before, and to carry happiness about him in my heart.
I don't blame him. Nor myself. Though I suppose most people would blame me. But then they speak from outside.

Here the numbered pages of the original paper come to an end; but Goldie jotted down a series of notes, which he kept in the same envelope, recording the progress of his love affair with Oscar over the next ten years, including the war years when Oscar was on the Western Front; and these convey such a different impression of their meetings during that period from the dismal account in the autobiography,[1] written after the

---

[1] pp. 124-5 below.

Introduction

affair had ended, that I am going to quote from them too, to redress the balance in a different sense.

The first is a note on two pages with the letter-heading of The Royal Hotel, Winchester, dated 26 June 1915. It is a happy description of an idyllic week-end in the country with Oscar just before he went to the front —the meeting recorded in a single bare sentence of the autobiography. At the end of it Goldie writes:

I record this, to remind me that this meeting, if it is to be the last, as I fear it may and must be, was perfect and beautiful, and O. very tender and generous. So from all the stress and strain an eternal moment has been saved. If I could have died then!

I write this next morning, the rain pouring outside, and death in my heart.

The mood of the next entry, describing another week-end, also at Winchester, when Oscar was home on leave from France in November 1915, is still more serene; and what is even more striking is the goodness it reveals of a man who had just returned from the trenches towards his homosexual lover:

All his character has come out—his courage and cheerfulness and endurance. Also, he has no sentiment or romance, and was clever. I admired him very much. He was better to me than he has ever been. He came to my room both nights and talked. The first night I lay on the floor by the fire, and held his naked feet. The second night he came into bed with me. I felt almost no sexual passion; only deep happiness and love. I think he was happy too. He goes back to France tomorrow. It seems to me that all the troubled story has run clear and beautiful. If it ends now, at least it ends beautiful. Quamquam oh sic! The love and the pain are almost unendurable.

There are other entries on a similar note recording further meetings, until Oscar returned at the end of the war, unscathed except for a slight wound from which he had recovered. The last entry, dated 22 November 1922, records the final end of the affair in much the same terms as the account of it in the autobiography, written not long afterwards;[1] but the last words here are more moving:

So this, which has been so much to me, runs into the sand. . . . The end can't now be far off. I have only to wait for it, and live as decently as I can, till it comes.

So Good-bye, my dear, whom I love still, and shall never see again, except in some brief accidental meeting and parting.

[1] p. 125 below.

Introduction

At about the same time as he was writing his autobiography and these later papers of the 'Privatissimum' collection, Goldie was writing another work on the theme of homosexuality which was almost equally autobiographical. It is a dialogue between 'Vivian' and 'Audubon', the names which he had given to the characters cast in the roles of himself and Ferdinand Schiller respectively in *A Modern Symposium*; in which the former reveals to the latter, for the first time in a long friendship, that his feelings for him have always been those of passionate love, as it might be of a man for a woman; and then, after breaking it to him, gently but firmly, that his son has the same temperament, tries to convince the father, a business man retired after a life in India, with a wealth of illustration and argument drawn from physiology, Plato and various historical examples, and from his own life, that he need not be plunged into utter despair at the news. The dialogue rehearses, with curious exactitude, many of the details of Goldie's own life, and his relations with Ferdinand Schiller, which are related in the autobiography. It had a certain currency among his friends, but it was never published; and I do not think it would have much appeal for a modern reader. Goldie attached to the typescript a scrap of paper, dated February 1931, reading as follows:

This was written some time after the war and read to the Society [of Apostles]. It took about two hours. The general verdict, if I remember right, was 'what a fuss about nothing'.

If I have seemed to dwell too much on Goldie's homosexuality, it is because it was an essential element in his make-up and a constant ingredient of the whole of his adult life, which had to be, or anyway was, suppressed in Forster's biography. I want now to turn to another ingredient, intimately connected with the former and almost equally pervasive throughout his life—his poetry. Goldie poured out poetry when he was a young man, and continued to write it at intervals for most of his life. It was the form of expression which came most naturally to him, and he evidently versified with great facility. He records in his autobiography how, on sitting down to write *Revolution and Reaction in Modern France* when he was nearly 30:

I had not written any prose to speak of, and had to learn how to do it.[1]

A great mass of poetry, from his early twenties onwards, is preserved among his papers. He himself has quoted some examples in the chapter of his autobiography which he devoted to his early verses;[2] and I have

[1] p. 143 below.
[2] Chapter VI below.

Introduction

thought it right to reprint, at the end of this book, the privately printed *Poems*, 1896,[1] since there are frequent references to them in the autobiography, and he himself said that they contained all, or nearly all, of his verse that had any merit.[2] The series of 'Shakespearian' sonnets which formed the largest section of that volume are the outpourings of his love for Ferdinand Schiller; and of these he wrote:

They are only what is called a 'cri du coeur' and no proof that I could have been a poet. But they are raised, I think, to poetry by the passion they express[3]—

a sentiment entertained by every writer of love poems, and generally endorsed (as it was in this case) by the recipient, but hardly a sound principle of literary criticism.

Some seven or eight years earlier, when he was 23 and had resolved on a misconceived attempt to turn himself into a doctor, Goldie had written, in a letter to his father seeking his approval of this new departure:

I don't find in myself on the whole a creative gift: i.e. I shan't be an artist of any kind.[4]

This was too sweeping, as the event was to show, for the artist's hand is manifest in everything he wrote. All his books are written, and felt, with an artist's sensibility; and almost all of them, except one or two of his early books which were conceived almost as historical text-books, contain sustained flights of poetic prose. But of his gifts as a poet in the formal sense his early judgment was, I think, a true one; and he himself seems to have come to the same conclusion when he commented in the last few years of his life:

If I *had* been a poet, I should, I suppose, have *had* to be one. . . . Anyone who reads this memoir will quickly perceive that I had no overmastering impulse at all, but a wide range of sensitiveness.[5]

Yet even this does not quite hit the mark, I feel. It was not the impulse, it was the charge itself, that was lacking. Verse flowed from Goldie's pen with the greatest of ease, and poetic diction was a currency he constantly handled and lovingly disposed. The trouble is that the coins he used were rubbed, and the rate of exchange was always the gold standard. He could

[1] pp. 229 ff. below.
[2] p. 84 below.
[3] p. 107 below.
[4] p. 76 below.
[5] p. 158 below.

Introduction

not find a rhythm or intonation of his own, or strike a new image; and his themes were unsparingly lofty. His account of the way in which Shelley gripped him as a young man, 'not as a poet, but as a visionary about life—his landscapes, always shimmering with moonlit streams, his loneliness, his passionate and ideal love'[1]—might almost be a description of his own poetry. Forster knew very well that Goldie's poetry did not reach the heights, and he was honest enough to say so, though he mixed some faint praise with his condemnation; and I share the same disability to which he confessed, that none of Goldie's three prophets, Shelley, Plato and Goethe, has meant much to me. The poetry of a friend is nearly always moving, and so I found Goldie's privately printed *Poems* when I first read them as a young man over forty years ago; but now that the arteries have hardened, I fear I cannot be as kind about them as Forster was.

There is, however, one other, much later poem, written about 1928–9, when Goldie was 66 or 67, which is such an extraordinary summation of his whole sex life that I have thought it right to print this too.[2] It is a dialogue in smoothly-flowing rhymed couplets entitled 'Body and Soul', in which those two contestants rehearse all the episodes of his sexual history in terms of the conflicts which have taken place between them. The reader of the autobiography will recognise at once all the twists and turns referred to. I find it remarkable that Goldie should have had the interest, the remembrance, and the facility, to compose such a compendium of this aspect of his own past life, when he was about the same age as I am now.

Of his other unpublished writings, the only ones mentioned by Goldie in his autobiography are three plays: one on Mirabeau, which he wrote during his stay in Paris with Roger Fry when he was 26 or 27;[3] *Business*, which he wrote on his return from his second American tour in 1910;[4] and one on Lassalle, which has been lost.[5] The play on Mirabeau (written partly in blank verse, partly in prose) is interesting to me as being the only instance I know in the whole of Goldie's work in which he portrayed love between a man and a woman. It is also the only instance of his taking as his hero a dynamic, thoroughly worldly character. The scenes between Mirabeau and Madame de Nehra when he escapes from the intrigues and agitations of revolutionary Paris to spend a night with her in the country, and later dies in her arms, are conceived on the same plane of mature relations between a man of action and his mistress as those of Shakespeare's *Antony and Cleopatra*. I think Goldie must, without knowing it, have fallen under

[1] p. 61 below.
[2] pp. 271 ff. below.
[3] p. 140 below.
[4] p. 172 below.
[5] p. 172 below.

Introduction

the spell of the Parisian atmosphere, despite his disclaimer that 'the principal interest of Paris, women, was no interest to me'.[1] I need hardly add that Forster found this play, according to the note which he wrote on the cover, 'of no value'. While this seems to me too severe a judgment, I would not dispute the view (which was evidently that of Goldie himself) that the play does not merit publication. The same applies to the other surviving play mentioned by him in the autobiography, *Business*, which is a tragedy of human lives wrecked by the juggernaut of big business. It was written when the impressions of his American tour were fresh in his mind, and it was an essay in the kind of thing which Galsworthy was doing better, at about the same time, in *Justice* and *Strife*.

Several other literary compositions (mostly unfinished) have been preserved; but, with one exception, none of them, in my opinion, deserves publication, though there is another complete play, *War and Peace*, which might make a highly entertaining stage production as a period piece with appropriate musical accompaniment. It is a satirical extravaganza, in somewhat the same manner as the plays which C. K. Munro wrote later on similar themes, in which Reason and Violence dispute in neatly turned verse for the votes of the Great Powers, Capital and Labour, Church and State, etc., much as the Just and the Unjust Logic dispute in *The Clouds* of Aristophanes. According to Forster, it was written before the outbreak of war in 1914.[2] It was extraordinarily prophetic, for it contains quite specific forecasts of the extraction of nuclear energy from uranium, and the atomic bomb.

The exception, which is the first of the previously unpublished pieces printed at the end of this book, is *The Wandering Jew*,[3] and this is the most remarkable of them all. It is quite unlike anything else Goldie wrote; and not the least surprising thing about it is that neither he himself in his autobiography nor Forster in his *Life* ever mentioned it. It is a fantasy narrated in the first person by Lloyd George's private secretary during the Versailles Conference. He describes how he had got into conversation with a stranger in the Luxembourg Gardens, who turns out later to be the legendary Wandering Jew, and how Lloyd George, when he tells him about his talks with him, says he would like to meet this fascinating stranger himself. A meeting over lunch is duly arranged, and this is followed by a similar meeting between the Wandering Jew and Clemenceau—the young private secretary who records the conversations being present at both of them. Before the two meetings, the Wandering Jew had told him the mournful story of his own journey through all the tribulations inflicted on men by

[1] p. 150 below.
[2] *Goldsworthy Lowes Dickinson*, 1934, p. 178.
[3] pp. 201 ff. below.

Introduction

the conquerors and rulers of the last 2,000 years. He explains that he is serving his sentence on earth until his master, Jesus, comes again, in expiation of a taunting word which he had spoken to him on the way up to Golgotha; and he says that he has never since forgotten how he, and he alone, had looked into his eyes.

It is only a fragment: it was never finished, and the parts are not properly joined together; but there is more force and passion in it than Goldie ever allowed to appear in any of his published works. It must have been written sometime in 1921–2 (for it contains an anachronistic reference to Lord Reading as Viceroy, and Edwin Montagu as Secretary of State for India), i.e. soon after Goldie had settled down, in a mood of bitter disillusionment, to studying the documents of the pre-war diplomacy which had led up to the outbreak of war in 1914, in preparation for writing *The International Anarchy*.[1] This must have been an outlet from that painful task in which he gave vent to his own feelings, just as he had found relief the year before in another fantasy on the vileness of war (though the treatment had been very different), *The Magic Flute*,[2] published in 1920. It is a pity, to my mind, that he preferred to publish the rather limp poesy of the latter instead of finishing, and publishing, this much stronger work.

Its inspiration, clearly, was *The Economic Consequences of the Peace*, which Maynard Keynes had written and published in 1919 after he had resigned from the British delegation at the Versailles Conference in protest against the policy of the Allied Powers towards the defeated Germans. For the vehement denunciation of a Carthaginian Peace which Goldie has put into the mouth of the Wandering Jew, and the vivid characterisations of Lloyd George and Clemenceau in the two interviews, must derive directly from that book—though, curiously enough, he never mentions it, or for that matter (with one trifling exception) Keynes himself, in his autobiography. Nor did he anywhere in his published works, except for one glancing reference in a short paragraph near the end of *The International Anarchy*, condemn as explicitly as he does here the penal clauses of the peace treaties.

There is another detail which interests me in both of these fantasies into which Goldie escaped at that time through the strangely different gateways opened for him by Mozart and Maynard Keynes. He makes both Tamino in *The Magic Flute*, and the Wandering Jew in this one, catch their message of compassion from a look in the eyes of Jesus; and there is no mistaking the passionate sincerity which he has breathed into the Wandering Jew's speeches of yearning for his master's return. This is something quite exceptional in Goldie's work. His own saint was Socrates: it was to Greece, not Palestine, that he would have looked for the dawn of the

[1] Allen & Unwin, 1926.
[2] Allen & Unwin, 1920.

Introduction

world's great age; and I do not recall any other such salutes of his to the Galilean.

The Wandering Jew is thus, in several ways, *sui generis* in Goldie's work, and it is a pity, as I have said, that he never finished it. He bent himself instead to the sterner labour of *The International Anarchy*. He felt the need to bring the full rigour of historical scholarship to bear on the thesis which he had never ceased to advocate in books and pamphlets during the war itself:[1] that 'war guilt' could not be fastened on any one country; that the sheer *vis inertiae* of Great Power politics had led inevitably to war; and that the same thing would inevitably continue to happen unless or until some effective international authority were established.

It took him five years to complete the work. With the publication of the book in 1926 he could write *nunc dimittis*, as he himself expressed it,[2] on his long wrestling with the problems of world affairs. He had nobly fulfilled the obligation he had always recognised to apply his own gifts of mind and spirit in a way which would do some service to his fellow men. With this behind him, he took up again the autobiography which he had written six years before, and put some finishing touches to it in 1927 as though he were ringing down a curtain. He never continued it any further, except for some purely updating footnotes inserted in the last year of his life.

So the end of the autobiography coincides with the time when I myself first came to know him, and it will fall to me to try to fill in the missing final section. Before I do so, however, this is perhaps the place to say a few words about my editing of the book. I have left the wording exactly as Goldie wrote it except for such minimal rectifications as were needed to correct obvious mistakes. There are very few places where I have been left in any doubt that I have correctly puzzled out his wayward typescript, with all its engagingly random manuscript corrections. I have, however, corrected his spelling mistakes, some of them habitual (*schwärmerisch*, for instance, a favourite word, is regularly written 'schärmerisch'), and also the punctuation, which is equally unprincipled. (Lest anyone should think that I have been too liberal with commas, I must add that Goldie himself was greatly addicted to them. Indeed, he often inserted them in places where I myself would not.) Apart from these modifications, the autobiography is here printed as Goldie wrote it, revised it, and evidently intended it one day to be published. And now I will try to take up the story of his last few years myself.

Although he had not been a conscientious objector in the war,[3] and although, since he agreed that, after the invasion of Belgium, England

[1] See p. 3 above, n. 2.
[2] p. 151 below.
[3] p. 190 below.

Introduction

could not have kept out of it,[1] he had never advocated a negotiated peace before Germany was beaten, the fact remains that all the work which Goldie had done during the four years of war had been work for peace, not 'war work'. At the time when most of his colleagues over military age were engaged in some form of Government service in support of the war effort, he was identifying himself more and more strongly with the cause of world peace, and working harder and more publicly on behalf of it than he had ever worked for a political cause before. It is not surprising, therefore, that he suffered all the obloquy that was heaped on 'pacifists', and felt a terrible isolation even from some of his old friends. And when the young men who had fought in the war began coming up again to Cambridge, and he found that they too shared the one idea that obsessed the old, that the way to make a 'land fit for heroes to live in' was to hold on to the gains of victory and go 'Back to Pre-war'—that Pre-war which to him now seemed to have been a hideous, inevitable prelude to catastrophe—his loneliness became bitter indeed. He shut himself up, concentrating on his research work for *The International Anarchy*, and stayed quite out of touch with any of the life that was going on around him, for five years.

But then, with *The International Anarchy* behind him, he began to come out of his shell; and just about the same time there began to arrive in the College a new generation of undergraduates comparatively untouched by the war, for whom Cambridge opened new horizons of beauty, truth and love, just as it had for Goldie himself on his own arrival nearly fifty years before. We did not share his romantic *Schwärmerei*, still less his idealism—or, at least, we did not think we did. We regarded ourselves as very modern young men, realists and sceptics, though not, I think, cynics. Yet, in a way, we were much closer to what he himself had been as a young man than we thought we were—certainly closer than any generation of undergraduates has been since. For we were living, though we did not know it, in a little bridge-period, and the bridge was shortly to collapse.

The great slump had not yet broken, and mass unemployment had not yet spread across the land. The British Empire was still intact; our social conscience slept peacefully in the enjoyment of more favourable terms of trade than the inhabitants of these islands have ever known since. The bogey of the balance of payments had not yet appeared. Marx had crossed the Channel, but had not yet arrived on the Cam, where Robertson and Keynes were proclaiming all the economics that mattered, and philosophy could safely be left to Russell and Moore. The Cavendish, everyone knew, led the world in physics, and Rutherford was about to split the atom. Mussolini, it is true, was making trouble abroad, but he was only a Mediterranean *farceur*. Hitler, if we had heard of him at all, seemed a mere cloud

[1] p. 194 below.

Introduction

of the Niebelungen not yet the size of a mailed fist. The grim polarity of communism and fascism that haunted our successors had not yet forced its challenge to enrol under some 'student' banner on our attention. We were still 'undergraduates'; and, for those of us who were not too impecunious, they were halcyon days.

So we drank gratefully of the springs of poetry and art and a little 'charming divine philosophy'; and Goldie too seemed to find his way back to them with us. If it was a false dawn for us, it was a St Martin's summer for him. He began to trust himself again to new relations with other people, after the long period in which he had been too much hurt to venture far outside himself. He seemed to have found a new zest for the enjoyment of life. Whereas, in the dark days ten years before, he had written:

That sense of being an alien. . . . I have never lost it. Indeed, in my old age I feel it as I never felt it before. Men become to me simply unintelligible;[1]

and, recalling his postgraduate years,

I had no notion how to get into touch with ordinary people;[2]

he could write now, in an entry in his diary of May 1931:

I will record also that in these days I get on very well with every kind of man I meet.

He got to know more and more undergraduates, for whom he was a gay, charming and utterly unpompous companion. He became such a sought-after person in the social life of the College that by the end of his life his engagements were getting quite unmanageable.

And so he went back to writing on the old themes, which were not greatly different from the ones that interested us. I should have mentioned before now *The Greek View of Life*,[3] in which he had celebrated his love of Greece when he was still a comparatively young man. No civilisation, as Spengler remarked, has been so passionately adored by its successors as that of ancient Greece; and though, no doubt, every generation has to make its own re-interpretation of it, few have done this better than Goldie did in that book, which seemed to me, when I was young, to distil the whole message of the ancient Greeks, just as it has continued to be an inspiration and revelation for many thousands of readers ever since. Yet

[1] pp. 53–4 below.
[2] p. 73 below.
[3] Methuen, 1896.

Introduction

still finer, in my opinion, is his short treatment of the same theme—the very last thing he ever wrote—in *The Contribution of Ancient Greece to Modern Life*, an inaugural lecture given at a Cambridge summer school only a few weeks before he died, and published just after his death.[1] By then, his early love of ancient Greece had been suffused with all the hard experience of his later years, and the harvest he reaped had become still richer.

It was to Plato that Goldie had always felt most closely drawn, and it was to him that he now returned, casting him this time as speaker in a dialogue with a modern young man, in *After Two Thousand Years*,[2] the last of his own 'Platonic' dialogues. In the covering letter with which he sent me a copy of the book, he wrote;

I don't think you'll care about it, and it is not likely that any young man will, I fear, and my generation don't matter—

a remark which shows how well he knew me, for I cannot even now deny the truth of it. He referred to this book again as follows in another letter to me, about a year before he died:

I doubt if I shall want to write another book, at any rate not one expressing my view on things in general. Somehow that dialogue has in a queer way set me free, into the void, or whatever it is.

A passage from it was chosen as a last salute from his friends, to be read by me at his funeral.

In between those two letters Goldie had found a still wider public in a series of broadcast talks on Plato, which were afterwards published in an expanded version as *Plato and his Dialogues*.[3] He had already made his début as a broadcaster in 1929, when he was invited by the British Broadcasting Corporation to give the first and last talks in a series called 'Points of View';[4] and his happy touch in acting as a catalyst of the younger generation in that series moved the B.B.C. to call on him twice again to perform a similar role, once in a broadcast discussion with John Maud, called 'Then and Now', in 1931, and a third time, later in the same year, when he gave the last of a series of broadcast talks under the title 'What I would do with the World'.

Three other broadcast talks of his, one in 1930 and two in the last

---

[1] Allen & Unwin, 1932.
[2] Allen & Unwin, 1930.
[3] Allen & Unwin, 1931.
[4] Reprinted, with an Introduction by Lowes Dickinson, as *Points of View: a Series of Broadcast Addresses*, Allen & Unwin, 1930.

Introduction

months of his life in 1932, were devoted to the subject which came more and more to occupy the chief place in all his thoughts during these last few years—Goethe. He had read *Faust* as a young man and written in admiring terms about it to Ashbee in 1885;[1] but, after that, there is only an occasional passing reference in the autobiography, until Goethe's arrival in his life in a far more important way is briefly signalled on the very last page, where Goldie says that he has just been working on a translation of *Faust* (which has never been published) with Melian Stawell. He also collaborated with her (though this is not mentioned in the autobiography, and, according to Forster,[2] Goldie's share in the book was slight) in *Goethe and Faust: An Interpretation*,[3] which was published in the following year. But he continued to jot down his reflexions on life and letters in a thick sheaf of papers which have been preserved, and these are full of passages expressing his admiration for Goethe, which became, indeed, the dominant theme towards the end. He frequently mentioned him, too, in his letters to me during the same period. It is a matter of regret to me, now that I have just reread those letters, that I may have left it too late to follow his example and soak myself in Goethe.

For Goldie has some very interesting things to say about him, and they are so closely intertwined with his thoughts about his own life, that, both for their own sake and for that reason, some of them are worth quoting here. They revolve round the antithesis between thought and action, which, as he himself had said,[4] kept him all his life in a kind of tension, and which he thought Goethe had solved better than anyone else—though even he not completely; for 'even Goethe', he wrote, 'whom I regard as almost the type of the great man . . . was defective on the side of action'. But Goethe, he thought, had got much closer to the perfect life than he had. 'A perpetual action,' he wrote another time, 'always growing wider and wiser in scope, is the best life, and a refusal to despair. This is what makes Goethe great.' The besetting defect in his own character, he wrote, had been 'the lack of energy, expressing itself in pessimism'; and he copied down Goethe's aphorism:

Die Hoffnung ist eigentlich eine gute That.

Reviewing his own life, when he felt, as he constantly did in these last few years, that he was nearing his end, he contrasted it with that of Goethe, his ideal of what a man should be.

[1] p. 74 below.
[2] op. cit. p. 202.
[3] Bell, 1928.
[4] p. 145 below.

Introduction

Except for action [he wrote in 1927] life seems to have no meaning. For contemplation is but an etiolated life. Goethe, who felt the problem, was saved from the consequences by his irresistible drive to literature and art. He attempted also, for ten years, the life of action. But he could not stick it in the end. But my own vein of artistic creation was thin and intermitted.

And again, reading Goethe's *Wanderjahre*, which he described as 'queer stuff, often dull, but fundamentally very interesting', he wrote:

At the time he wrote that—he was, I think, getting on for 80—it is clear that action of a practical kind was the key to everything in his view. Art was secondary to that, and existed mainly to inspire to cheerful action. I believe that is the right view, though I have altogether failed to accommodate my own life to it.

Goldie himself was only 66 when *he* wrote that; but he was casting forward all the time to his end, and, even though his life had not been at all like Goethe's, his aim was to make his end, and his closing years, as much like his as he could.

That drive of the unsatisfied soul [he wrote in 1927] . . . Goethe kept it most wholesomely, and to the bitter end; as I would wish to do;

and, reading the *Wahlverwandschaften* about a year later:

Now, in my old age, I seem to be fit to begin living right, just as I am about to die. All of which I write without bitterness or even regret—for what would be the good? What is left I hope to live cheerfully, and without remorse. But Goethe! 'Es ist in den Wahlverwandschaften überall keine Zeile welche Ich nicht selber erlebt hätte.' And so throughout.

Yet Goldie himself was experiencing, as he felt the end drawing near, a sense of liberation from all the circumscriptions of his own past life. 'The point of life', he wrote in 1930, 'is to arrive at death courageous, and with your vision enlarging and your sympathies extended;' and, later in the same year:

This morning I was thinking it is time I turned my thoughts more to the possibilities of the other side and less to the troubles of this. Of course we don't and shan't know anything about that. But it seems natural that one's speculation should become freer . . . We should venture to expand, if we have done what we could here, and are near the end, and I am inclined to think that the kind of escape outlined at the end of my forthcoming dialogue [*After Two Thousand Years*] may be some kind of anticipation of truth.

Introduction

His letters to me—cheerful, gay, tender letters—were sprinkled with similar thoughts. In 1930 he wrote:

The thing I desire is to die with courage and hope. But I well know that that all depends on the brute facts, which no one can control. Meantime I feel curiously happy so far as personal life is concerned, but very much the contrary so far as those public things go which I have (rather vainly) devoted too much time and worry to.

As he passed into what were to be the last twelve months of his life, the sense that the end was near seemed to press on him more and more strongly —although, when actually awaiting the summons to go into hospital for the prostate operation from which he died, he was utterly matter-of-fact about it. His very last words to me, just before the operation, were:

I cannot doubt, with my mind, that a quick and painless extinction would be best for me; but I do not anticipate that. People are always clinging to the bridle rein, as that excellent and sympathetic poet, Mr Rudyard Kipling, remarks, and May [his sister] would be about finished, I fear, if I peter out.

But, a month before, he had felt the approaching end almost with a kind of exaltation. He had written to me:

Pain is the bother—physical more than mental, since the latter may have its uses and I'm damned if I see how the former has. Everything begins to dazzle before me now; yet I seem to be physically well and mentally clear. Only I hardly know where I am and what I'm doing! Still less *why*!

'Everything begins to dazzle before me now.' It is extraordinary that he should have used those words; for this was exactly the impression he made on his hearers when he was talking to a gathering of the Apostles in London in the very same week in which he wrote that letter. He had been asked to speak to the text of 'Youth'; but, on the pretext that old age was second childhood, he talked about old age and death instead. Ostensibly, he was summing up the condition at which he had arrived; but as he talked on, more and more abstractedly with a rapt smile on his face, he seemed almost to go into a trance while he was speaking. It was as though he were penetrating, at that very moment, further than ever before into the mystery he had wanted all his life to unlock. He seemed to assume without any question that it was the last time he would be there; and somehow he made us feel the same thing, although, at that time, there was no known reason why he should not live for any number of years more. It was as though he was already bidding us farewell from the other side.

Introduction

However, I do not want to end on such a solemn note, for being with Goldie in those last few years was generally not at all like that; nor was he himself usually so introspective with others. At the luncheon parties which he used to give in his rooms on Sundays it was *his* gentle, despairing gaiety, making play all the time with his fancied incompetence as host, that made the party go; and in the friendly, light-toned conversations it was always the opinions and experiences of the others, especially if they were young, that were given priority—almost, one was made to feel, superior validity—over his own. For he always did more than justice to the importance of other people's emotions and convictions: it was one of his most endearing qualities. His utter modesty about himself came out in a touching remark he once made to me: 'Really I know very little what other people are like.' I sometimes felt that this was true, but it didn't matter: it only enhanced the kind of protective tenderness which I think we all felt for him.

I saw him often in London too, and we went to many concerts and plays together. But visits to him in his rooms in King's, and the care he always took for my comfort when I stayed there, are the ones I cherish most among the memories of our times together. I used to have the attic bedroom with an *oeil de boeuf* window in the pediment of the Fellows Building which belonged to his set of rooms on the top floor: a little spiral staircase led up to it from them. Up that staircase Goldie would climb on a Monday morning, sometimes more than once, to make sure that I did not oversleep and miss my train back to London and the office; a hot bath, timed to the minute on his antiquated geyser for my descent, would be ready for me when I came down; and Fuller and he between them would somehow have contrived to have a hot breakfast for me before I left, no matter how early the hour.

The great principle of his own domestic arrangements was to ward off cold—for one of the first things one got to know about Goldie was that he always felt cold. A Danish stove in his sitting-room was kept alight day and night throughout the year; during the day he was never without his celebrated Mandarin's cap, which he wore everywhere when indoors; at night he went to bed in a pullover and a thick woollen helmet, looking like a polar explorer; an electric mattress completed the precautions. The other great enemy was the weather. His conversation and his letters were peppered with remarks about it. 'Nice winter day, ain't it?' in a midsummer letter, or 'May indeed! My God! But it is idle to complain and you never knew me do it, did you?'; and so on. The weather, in fact, was the readiest vehicle for the kind of exasperated defeatism in the face of all inanimate things and objects which was a charming feature of his mental and social equipment.

Best of all my memories are the bicycle rides we used to do, especially

Introduction

in the May term. Our favourite ride was the one to Overcote on the River Ouse which Goldie has described on p. 117 below. The start, through the narrow Cambridge streets, was a bit hair-raising, even in those comparatively tranquil days; for he was a dogged bicyclist who rode fixedly ahead at an even pace, undaunted by the densest traffic. But, once we were out of the town, pedalling across the wide fens thick with buttercups and may under a Cambridgeshire sky, it was pure enchantment for both of us. At Overcote, where Goldie lifted up a tremulous shout to summon the innkeeper on the opposite bank to come and ferry us across, our clothes looked as though it had been snowing by the time he arrived, from the down that drifted gently all the time from the willows along the river bank. We used to make our way along the other bank of the river to Holywell, where we had supper on the terrace of a little inn looking across the water, and usually, so it seems to me in retrospect, towards a rising full moon. Then we would be ferried back again across the river and rode back along the straight Huntingdon road in the moonlight, getting back into College not much before midnight—though the very first time, when I was still resident in College, it was through the eye of a blinding, crashing tempest, and we got soaked to the skin. I remember that I took some brandy up to Goldie's rooms afterwards, thinking he might need it; and it was then that I first became acquainted with the domestic arrangements which I have described. However, he said that his usual cup of Ovaltine was all he needed. The next morning he sent me a note with a light-hearted reference to our having come unscathed through what he called 'a nice little performance by the Almighty'.

There is a radiance for me in all these memories, just as there was a radiance about Goldie himself at the time; and I like to think that I helped a little to keep it there. Though I was having my own love affairs with girls (into which Goldie entered with sympathy and understanding) and had no homosexual tendency, I loved him too; and since it has always come naturally to me to give expression to my affection for anyone I am fond of, I did so quite spontaneously with him. This, so he sometimes told me in very moving terms, gave him a happiness he had not known before —simply because he found in me a reciprocity which others had not been able to supply. There was never any 'trouble' for him in our relationship. For me it was pure gain to have the intimacy of such a man.

His autobiography is, of course, the life-story of a homosexual man, and I may have over-emphasised that aspect of it in this Introduction. But I hope it will not be taken as just one more manifestation of that particular strain in the Bloomsbury pedigree. For Goldie's way of life, and especially his way of love, were very different from those which were in fashion in that circle. Roger Fry, of course, was his dear friend all his life, and Goldie

Introduction

was on visiting terms with most of his friends; but few of their names will be found in the pages of the autobiography. Goldie thought his own thoughts, found his own friends, and led his own life. *Pleon hemisu pantos* (as he wrote it, for his typewriter had no Greek)—'the half is more than the whole'—was his favourite catchword, which I suppose means something like: 'Better to travel hopefully than to arrive'. He had not arrived when I knew him, and he never did; but he was still travelling hopefully. This we all knew, and this is what we loved in him. It was a commonplace among us to hope that one might 'grow old like Goldie'. Reminded of him, as I have been now after a long, long lapse, it may still just be possible for me, late though I have left it, to try to do so.

Recollections

1. Lowes Dickinson 1922

2. Lowes Dickinson 1884

3. Roger Fry as a young man

4. Ferdinand Schiller *c.* 1885

5. Original manuscript (page 12)

6. Original typescript (pages 161-2)

7. House party at Gersau 1888

Back row: G.L.D.   Roger Fry   Ferdinand Schiller   McTaggart

Middle row: Mrs Schiller (mother)   Mrs Steintal   Canning Schiller   Lisbeth Schiller (later Lady Harris)   Max Schiller   Max's wife Ellie née Stainer   Miss Rod (a governess)

Front row: W. W. ('Pup') Asquith   (later) Sir Charles Harris

8. Oscar Eckhard in his first year at Cambridge

9. Oscar Eckhard, Manchester Regiment 1915–18

10. E. M. Forster c. 1900

11. Peter Savary c. 1942

CHAPTER ONE

Childhood, 1862–1872

The earliest thing I remember—or rather remember to have remembered, for that is how it now presents itself to me—is looking out of a pointed window, opening like a door and filled with small diamond panes of glass, at the people coming home from church through the little gate of our garden. I may have been two years old and my nurse was holding me. This was in our cottage at Hanwell, then a little country village, now part of the suburbs of London. One or two other memories seem to float vaguely at this threshold of consciousness. Once, for example, stars looked large, with points all round them, as they used to be painted on the roof of the old St James Hall in London. For, I remember one night later, looking up and feeling surprised and disappointed to see nothing but pale tiny points of light. That seems to be all I can recover of these earliest days. After that, memory proper begins, treacherous, complicated, stratum piled on stratum, reflexion and comparison vitiating experience.

The Hanwell cottage still exists and I suppose is still called, as it used to be, The Spring Cottage. When we first went there my father thought it was Spring Cottage without a 'The', and associated it with the season. Then he found it was named after the big house, called The Spring, because it has a spring in its grounds which supplies an artificial lake. So the definite article was added to our note paper and a new association took the place of the old. About this cottage centre all my early recollections. I was born in London, but when I was a year old or so my mother and the children—at that time there were two older than myself—moved out into the country, and my father made every day the journey to his studio in London. He was a portrait painter, and his pictures perhaps will survive, hanging in Cambridge halls or private houses, long after I and my books have been forgotten. My mother had long chestnut hair reaching almost to her feet when it was let down. I still remember her at the time when I cuddled up to her in bed and when she took her bath in my almost infant presence. About her and about my nurse centred, of course, all my childish life. She brought up five of us, and taught as well as clothed and fed us; and in this she was seconded by our nurse Emma who served us all when we were children, then married a grocer's assistant, and still lives in Hanwell, and still from time to time sees us.

Her I remember in unconnected pictures, remaining, I suppose, in my mind not because they were characteristic but because they were striking. I see her fainting one day when she was bringing us our water in the morning, and our dismayed flight for aid to our mother's bedroom. I see her shaking my youngest sister, who seems to me to have been always crying, and who was, I suspect, at that time exasperating past endurance to a tired nurse. She bit me once, when I was a small boy, and I can still see the mark. I see also her head, banging against a cupboard under castigation, and it cannot have been very good for her. Then I see Emma sitting at tea in our nursery, with her young grocer, smacking her lips and talking mysteriously of Mrs R. and Mrs B. I used to think that I too would smack my lips when I was grown up.

Later, came our walks, which I associate with itching chilblains and hoops, but also with cemeteries. There were two large ones, close to Hanwell, as well as the churchyard, and Emma had a liking for taking us to them, watching the outdoor service from a distance, examining the tombstones, and reading the inscriptions. The funerals came down from London by road, and approached the cemetery at a slow walk, with much display of pocket handkerchiefs. But on the return journey they would stop at the public house, and then set off again at a cheerful trot. Later still, when I went to school every day in London, Emma used to receive me at the gate with gaiety and affection. She must have been a kind woman, sentimental and warm hearted. While she was being courted by the grocer he used to take her and us for drives in his cart. How exciting it was! How high up we were, and how far and fast we went!

The little house and garden are still very vivid in my mind. When first we went there, there were two sitting rooms only, both very small, and, above, two bedrooms, with a little kitchen and scullery projecting behind. In front ran a verandah covered with white roses. Above this, wistaria hung over the wall and peeped in at my parents' bedroom, where I still see my mother plucking a piece to put in her hair for dinner. All round was a garden, two lawns, flower beds gay. I still see the geraniums, verbenas, calceolarias, roses; a bush or two of laurel, a shrubbery; a fernery; an old fir, smothered in ivy, a chestnut by the road, where one could sit in the branches and see what passed by; a sycamore dropping seed on the fernery; a swing, and beside it a tar-covered shed through whose boards one could peep at the next door garden, where were the boys of a small preparatory school, and where we used to hear the long screams of pigs being killed. Then, chief of all, there was a cherry tree covered in spring with a cloud of double blossom, under which my mother would sit and work her sewing machine, while we read to her.[1] In front of the house, beyond the strip of garden, was a thorn hedge, and beyond that a meadow with a line of elms bordering the footpath. In this meadow were a cow and a heifer, very alarming when one had to pass them, because the heifer was skittish and would sometimes come galumphing after one, when one fled, with beating heart, to the stile. Across this meadow my father used to walk from the station, and call to us who were sitting at our nursery tea. We ran down and met him in the field.

This nursery was part of an addition made to the cottage by my father. It contained, below, what then seemed a large dining-room, and, above, day and night nursery. The windows in this new part were sashed and opened wide, so that one climbed in and out from the garden. A little greenhouse connected the new dining room and the drawing room of the old house. It had a door into each room, and also one opening on the garden, in which were panes of coloured glass. It fascinated me to look through them and see through the purple a world of snow, through the red and orange one of glowing heat. The building and furnishing of the dining room I still remember, the black clock on its mantel piece, the book cases with their red silk behind diamonds of gilt wire, the Hepplewhite chairs, the large library table full of drawers which now stands in the room in which I am writing at Cambridge, the 'high' chairs—how high they seemed—on which one climbed to eat one's meals; the Collard piano, in a boxwood case, sweeter, I think, in tone than pianos have since become; the Sheraton sideboard, still in our house at home. That was the new dining room. In the little drawing room of the old cottage were green velvet chairs, a walnut table of curious curling shape, and on the mantelpiece candlesticks hung with lustres and a vase supported by two little cherubs. The windows here reached to the floor, and opened on the garden under the verandah. Next to that room came the hall with the front door and then the other little room of the old cottage, which we called the study and where sometimes we sat in the evenings. It was dark and had two book cases, full of dark books, on either side of the fireplace. One of these books, I remember, was called *Curiosities of London*. It contained, among other things, an account of how a small boy was blinded by tying across his eyes two shells, in each of which was a live beetle. Whether this was true or not I cannot tell, but it made an impression on me, since it comes back to my memory even now. We used to shudder past the open door and dark gulf of this room on our way upstairs to bed.

[1] Curious how persistent are these childish memories. I never see the double cherry in our College garden without this scene recurring to me.

The garden hangs in my past like a vision of light. Flower beds are brighter than they have ever been since; shrubberies more mysterious; spaces larger, storms and rain more exciting. How I recall at this moment the oncoming of a storm, the black sky, the still air, and us in the twilight garden running and screaming with delight. And then the lightning, hour after hour, the sky opening and closing like an amazing flower, as I lay and watched it from my bed, till at last some elder pulled down the green venetian blinds, and there was nothing to be seen but the flicker of light at their edges. Then the kitchen garden, the gooseberries and currants and plums and pears, the lettuces and chives which we cut for salad; the playing at trains in the swing. At that time the Great Western still had broad gauge trains and huge engines with one great driving wheel. I got to know them all by name and used to impersonate them. To travel by one of the great expresses was a dream of joy beyond one's hopes. Even to drive in the new cab with its purple velvet plush was out of the question. But one got in and sat there while it waited on the rare occasions when my father engaged it.

The society of the village was self-contained, and of course, since it was English, split into social sets. There were the people you knew and the people you only knew about, and the tradespeople, who were outside the pale, and the poor who sat in what were called free-seats in church and were visited and helped, if they were good. My father, though not rich, was creditable enough, as an artist, to belong to the first circles of the village. These comprised, first, the Sir Alexander Spearman, who lived at The Spring. He was a civil servant of high rank. His wife was paralysed. She went about in a wheeled chair with her tongue projecting, a rather terrifying figure to us, though very kind. But our principal friend was the daughter, Miss Spearman, about whom there was a story that she had been engaged to be married but deserted on the marriage day before the ceremony, and had had nevertheless to dance at the ball in the evening. I don't know whether this was true. But she never married. And, as I remember her, was a kind of vision of light floating drapery, gaiety, sweetmeats, everything children love. She would run down the lane after dinner when we were in bed and bring us cakes. And every year she gave a children's party with Punch and Judy or a ventriloquist. The Spring was a charming house, still existing.[1] It had a large garden with the lake of which I have spoken, and swans swimming on it. And it communicated with a little cottage next door, with one story above ground and one below, where later Miss Spearman lived after her parents' death.

[1] When last I saw it, a year or so ago, it had been converted into a nursing home (1931).

Childhood, 1862–1872

Next to this cottage came the rectory, and beyond, the church. The rector was Derwent Coleridge, a son of the poet. He was very learned, too much so for his congregation, and of course I was always afraid of him. There lived with him, beside his wife and his daughter Christabel—named I suppose after the poem—a niece, Miss Edith, who knew Greek and taught my mother enough for her to begin to teach my brother and myself. But the most interesting feature about the rectory was the succession of young Americans who came to stay there to be initiated into English ways. They were an important element in our society, and a constant source of interest to our girls and young women, and especially to my elder sister. They took active part in our entertainments, theatricals and dances. I remember sitting on the knees of one and asking him in all innocence why his face was covered in spots; and I hate to think of it. I remember also how the rector once remarked to his wife, in a crowded drawing room: 'Mary my dear we must keep a small Poe in the drawing room'.

The rectory garden had a lawn running down to the stream of the Brent, and there the school treats were held, of which I still catch the curious smell. Just opposite the church was a thatched cottage, where Admiral Dennis lived with his wife. They were fond of children and very good to us. And, beyond, the Otters' house reached by a drive through a white gate. All these houses still exist, survivals in the flood of villas and streets. On the other side of our house, and towards the village, lay The Park, which was inhabited by a Mr Sharpe who had been an officer in the Navy. He had lost money, and the big house was in great part shut up. But he kept a carpenter on the premises making furniture, and we were sometimes allowed to go through the big closed rooms. He was a severe-looking man, with grey hair and whiskers. Having nothing much to do, he used to quarrel with the rector about the church services, for he was 'low' and they were made not indeed 'high' but less low, so that the choir put on surplices and the rector preached in white instead of black, and turned to the east when we said the Creed. This was too much for Mr Sharpe, who turned full round to the west, in his conspicuous pew, and engaged in acrimonious correspondence with the rector, whose side my father took. I still remember a long letter he wrote, in which he said he could not understand how the squire could strain at the gnat of turning to the east when the Creed was said, while swallowing the camel of coming to the Communion Table with such unchristian feelings towards the rector.

These theological differences were intensified by politics, for my father in those days was a Liberal and Gladstonian and Mr Sharpe a Tory and Disraelian, and fierce would be the battles after church. Mrs Sharpe had been very pretty, and was deaf and eccentric. I recollect her remarking once that my sister was a pretty child and adding 'but pretty children always grow up ugly'. There was a Miss Sharpe, who used to ride, and my mother sometimes rode with her, on a kind of cart-horse. I was allowed to sit on this horse when it went home to the Park, a rather fearful pleasure, for I was a very timid little boy. Miss Sharpe also played the organ, and had a small one in the house. And her brother used to try to teach me harmony. We went to The Park not through the big gate and drive, but through a side entrance, in what was called Cuckoo Lane. It was alarming in the dark. There was a hornets' nest, one year, which one had to pass. Also a pond full of tadpoles. Opposite our cottage was another biggish house, where the Buchans lived; and close by a cottage inhabited by an old lady and her daughter, called Edwardes. Miss Edwardes was deformed and very ugly. She used to say that she was not beautiful, but fascinating. She also sang and especially 'shook' in singing. She explained that for a long time she could not shake. Then she heard Grisi sing 'The Nightingale' and 'I shook and shook and have shaken ever since'. These two old ladies kept a number of small dogs, who used to sit up at table with them on chairs. Still farther up the lane towards the village were the Miss Haffendens, who had a garden containing a mulberry tree, from which we used to get leaves for our silkworms. I remember softly stroking the sealskin jacket of Miss Haffenden after church on Sunday, and also how shocked these ladies were because the men worked at the new railway station on Sundays. 'Believe me, Mr Dickinson, God's blessing will never rest upon it.'

These were the principal 'society' of the village. But as they were elderly and childless we played with the children of less eminent families. These seem, in my remembrance, to have been mostly girls. The boys, the Otters for example, were older than myself, and I had not much to do with them. And it is worth noticing in view of later events that in these very early years I seem to myself to have liked girls better than boys. I had indeed from the beginning a strongly feminine element in me, never cared for boys' games, but was affectionate to little girls, and even at times to older women, in a sentimental rather than sexual way.

In this place and society I passed my earliest years. Curious things come back to me like scents from the past. Lying in bed in the dusk, listening to the Moonlight Sonata played below; lying in bed in the morning reading a child's version of the *Arabian Nights*, sitting by the fire in the evening while my father read to us the novels of Scott; playing at Fairies with my father, which meant stealing up and tickling his bald head, while he pretended to be asleep; playing at oranges and lemons; dancing quadrilles; singing, in a little piping voice, a song about a little fish, that was foolishly caught by a little hook in defiance of its mother's warning; singing hymns on Sunday evening; sitting, or kneeling, through interminable church services; saying my catechism to my mother and my text every morning;

Childhood, 1862–1872

being naughty and saying I was sorry; being sent to bed, and crying for hours; being spanked (once only); rolling down the hill in the field by the church, walking to Greenford or to Osterley; a wood of bluebells beyond the canal; cowslip-balls. And then lessons, my sister and myself carrying our books and writing copies on a kind of desk we called the slab; pothooks and strokes, arithmetic, dictation, the Child's Guide of singularly uninteresting information; Little Arthur's history; Pleasant Pages which were very unpleasant; and, in all this, nothing that I can recollect that interested me at all, though also nothing that I much minded doing. My mother, with infinite patience, conducted us through this routine, as well as running the house, providing her little dinner parties, learning her Greek, and adoring my father who also loved her, yet, as I think, not as she loved him.

Then, every year, a month or so by the sea, sands and donkey rides, sea-anemones, bathing, blackberries and cream on Sundays, long drives or walks, Seaton, Croyde, Felixstowe, what not. A happy life, as I look back on it, and the happier because it was followed by such misery. For the time came when I was sent to school.

It will be convenient here to say something of my family. My father was a man of remarkable charm. Few men can have had so many friends. His father came up to London, from farming stock in Northumberland, near Bardon Mill, where the graves and monuments of his relations, Dickinsons and Lowes, may still be seen. My only married sister many years later went back to live there, having married a Lowes, and inhabited the house of Allens Green, which I suppose she will shortly leave, for her husband died last year. My father's father set up a print shop and photographing business in Bond Street, where the name is still to be seen. My father took early to drawing, and worked with his brothers in and for the shop. But when he was thirty, a friend gave him money to go to Italy. We have printed for private circulation the letters he wrote thence, very interesting and charming, as I think, and as most people who read them think. It was in 1850, or thereabouts, and the old Italy, very much more amusing for the traveller than the modern nationalistic State. On his return, he married my mother and settled down in the studio at 1, Langham Place, where also painted Millais and others. Later, he built there the house known as 1, All Souls Place, the red corner house one sees as one walks north from Oxford Circus, looking over the church. The windows thence seen belonged later to my room.

As I have said, a year or two after his marriage we moved to the cottage at Hanwell and my father went every day to his work in town. To us children he was charming, playing to us and reading to us in the evenings,

Scott and Shakespeare and the Ancient Mariner, and Christabel, always good literature, for which I think I then imbibed my taste. We, my sister May and I, sat on a kind of stool before the fire, which was a wood-fire, on dogs. My mother sat next my father, and sometimes I sat on her knee. My father always read the notes to Scott, holding up the story, to our great impatience, and my sister always looked on to see what was going to happen. This relation to both parents was very charming while we were children. But for me it was broken by school. My mother died in my first year at the University, so that I never formed with her the tie that so often exists between a mother and a grown-up son. My father lived to be a very old man. But in later life, though I was fond of him and he of me, we never had an intimate relation. Different opinions and different ages made and preserved a gulf.

I had a brother, Arthur, three years older than myself. He is now Sir Arthur, married, with two daughters, and well-to-do. As he was three years older than me, and went to school before I did, I was never intimate with him. He was very different in temperament and interests, and we have still few things in common, though I like and respect him and suppose him to have some regard for me. My elder sister, May, was the one with whom I was most thrown in my boyhood. We did our lessons together, sat up together for my father's readings and generally were very intimate. For a good many years we slept together, when we were both small, and every night my sister used to begin a romantic story about a young girl of singular beauty aged 17. But the stories were never finished.

The end of this period of sleeping together came in a curious way. I suppose I was about 9 years old, or younger perhaps. Observing our cat to be very big, I hazarded the guess that kittens were coming inside her. I didn't really believe anything so preposterous, because one knew that babies came under gooseberry bushes, and supposed that kittens did too. But to my surprise my grandmother seemed to take this remark seriously. She became rather sly, and I was told that henceforth I must not sleep with my sister. A curious example of how not to do it!

This sister May was, I believe, rather precocious and clever. She acted and sang and danced and certainly, to my remembrance, flirted. But girls in those days were not sent to Universities. Her education was rather accidental, though not altogether neglected, and she had neither the advantages, nor the contrary, of good training. The two younger sisters were called the 'Little ones'. May and myself felt ourselves to be separated from them by a great gulf of years, and were mainly anxious that they should not presume to intrude upon our sphere. However, we were all very friendly together, and, unless the sentiment of the past deceives me, the childhood of us all was on the whole very happy.

Childhood, 1862–1872

In the midst of these early recollections, there stand out certain experiences of sex. And as they were important for my later life, I shall speak of them. For it is my object, in these reminiscences, to tell what is usually not told. I am, I think, almost entirely free from false shame, and the absurd kind of moral judgments current on these subjects. On the other hand, I have no theories, and am rather sceptical about those at present in fashion. I think, therefore, that I ought to be able to speak without prejudice. My experience of sex seems to go back earlier than the age of puberty, or else that age came very early with me. I remember, when I was a very small boy, playing with my penis, and extracting something white, which I showed to my mother, who consulted my father. I think that I used to get erections, but without sexual feeling. Once my mother came into the room when I was doing this, and told me never to do it again, but as no reason was given this had no effect.

My earliest remembrance of sexual feeling was connected with boots. This form of fetishism, which has accompanied me all my life, and is still active, came to me long before sex was connected in any other way with persons. Possibly, under the method of psychoanalysis, my memory might be brought back to some origin for it, but I have no curiosity to try that method. What I actually remember is lying on the floor in our little drawing room, and my father patting me with his feet. It was, as it still is, from this earliest time, boots rather than feet, and polished boots that moved my feelings. And still I have the most curious taste in this matter, and am attracted by some kinds of boots and shoes and repelled by others. Like all forms of fetishism this seems to me very odd and unaccountable. It fills, in my boyhood, such sex life as I had. I used, later, to get my brother to tread upon me, or my sisters. I don't know whether he, at that time, had any sex feeling about it, but imagine he may have had. At night, when I had gone to bed, I used to steal out to my father's dressing room, and excite myself over his boots. Yet I believe this was before puberty, in the sense that there was no emission of semen. I never told anyone of course. How early, and predestined, is secrecy in these matters!

Neither at this time, nor during all my school life, nor even in the first years of my university life, were these sex feelings connected in any way with love. And in these early days they were not connected specially with either the female or the male sex, for I was at first indifferent between them. Later, the interest became exclusively attached to males. I have, of course, read since of what the Germans call Schuh-fetischismus. But I have never read anything which throws any light upon it. On the other hand, when I have seen e.g. a turkey cock treading the hens, I have supposed that it may go back very far into animal life. It appears also that these fetishisms often accompany the ordinary sex impulse, though becoming as it were fused with it. This morning, for instance, in a poem of Goethe's, I find him comparing himself to a dog lying at his mistress' feet, and the line occurs

Sie streicht ihm mit dem Füsschen übern Rücken,
Er denkt in Paradies zu sein.
(cited Ludvig I, p. 203)

I will add here that I never had any real instruction in sex life, at most only vague and alarming hints, until I was in my sixteenth year, and wrote to my father, as will be told later. And even then what he gave was hardly instruction. I have noticed since a curious reluctance on the part of parents to discuss the matter with their children. I wonder why. But I suppose I should feel the same difficulty. Whether an early discussion and explanation would have altered my own apparently precocious and predestined reaction, I cannot say.

CHAPTER TWO

Day School, 1873–1874

When I was ten or eleven years old I was sent to day school at the Misses Woodman, 13 Somerset Street, Portman Square. I am not likely to forget the address because we all, or almost all, got a prize-book every term, and on this book was stamped the monogram of the Misses Woodman, and, printed round it in an oval shape, the address, with the addition 'morning class for the sons of gentlemen'. Nothing could be more characteristic of English society, as it was and still is. 'Gentlemen' meant *not* tradesmen, or, rather, not any tradesmen except the very rich. For I remember that the son of Brassey, the contractor, was there, called then Tab, and afterwards Lord Brassey. There also were two of the sons of Tom Hughes, called Pip and Plump. They were little chubby boys, in sailor suits. I came into touch with both of them again in later life. Pip became an enthusiast for Wagner and Herbert Spencer and Emerson. He died only a year or two ago at Beccles in Suffolk, where for many years he had lived part of the year in rooms, spending the rest abroad. He was on the verge, and sometimes over the verge, of insanity. His brother, Plump,[1] was shipped off early to America, roughed it there, as a cowboy and the like, married, has a family, is a follower of Henry George, and one of the most amusing, realistic, racy people I know. Tom Hughes was one of my father's many friends and we knew more or less the whole family. But I will not digress upon them in this place.

At this school I was what is called 'grounded', and, no doubt, well grounded in the sense that I learned a great many things by heart. The Latin grammar, for instance, in the *Public School Grammar*, in Latin. I didn't understand the Latin, nor would it ever have occurred to me that the rules really applied to a language. 'Common are to either sex Artifex and opifex.' But one never came across these words in books, so one didn't have to think of the rule. It was just a kind of charm! 'Syllaba longa brevi subjecta vocatur iambus'. No doubt. But then we never read any iambics!

[1] Last year his daughter came to England; a pretty, racy, adventurous American girl. (1931)

The Autobiography of G. Lowes Dickinson

It was the same with everything. Geography was taught by blank maps drawn on a black board, with round blobs for the towns of which we were then taught the names, and afterwards examined as to whether we remembered them. We did then; but I have never remembered them since. All the teaching was done by ladies. Only later on was a man introduced, as an experiment. He was called 'the graduate', but he wasn't a success, I don't remember why. At any rate, one term saw the end of him; and at the prize-giving Miss Woodman remarked, with caustic wit, that should he turn up again it would be as an 'uninvited guest'.

There were two Miss Woodmans, Miss Woodman proper, who was stern and ironical, and Miss Maria, with a cast in her eye, who was violent and ugly. When we said our irregular verbs to Miss Woodman, she would repeat 'Yes! Fatiscor, fatiscor, I am weary. I am weary of you boys'. Meantime, from the room above, out of the floor of which a circular hole opened into the room below, would come the smack smack of Miss Maria boxing someone's ears. Miss Woodman would pause with a sigh and then resume operations. 'Fatiscor, I am weary.' About these two great goddesses the lesser mistresses revolved deferentially. One scene I never forget. Our geography lesson was interrupted by the arrival of Miss Woodman, dramatic and solemn. She asked us one by one whether we had been guilty of bullying on the way home through the streets. We all said 'No'. But when this 'No' proceeded from the lips of a red-haired boy whose name, I still remember, was Watson (is he alive I wonder? What happened to him?) Miss Woodman turned paler than usual, stepped back, and exclaimed in a terrific voice, 'William Watson, you have told a lie'. How we shuddered! Whether poor Watson had told a lie I don't know. But the assistant mistress said to us afterwards 'I thought Miss Woodman would have fainted'.

One term, when my parents were away in America, I boarded at the school. There were about half a dozen of us, and we were well fed and well treated. We used to take walks in Hyde Park, where I recollect the excitement of a steam roller, not like the modern ones, but all enclosed in a vermilion case. I became a favourite, I think, with both the Miss Woodmans and still more with an assistant mistress, being then a rather attractive cosseting kind of boy. We used to have dinner in a large underground room, lighted with gas, where dined also the boys who stayed for afternoon work. We were expected to provide the Miss Woodmans with what they wanted without their having to ask for it, and terrible it was when we heard a voice 'I have to *ask* for the salt'. I learned to say 'thank you' instead of 'please', and became conscious of a much improved style. A curious thing is memory. For now there comes back to me a picture of Miss Maria, in the water closet, trying in vain to flush it, and screaming 'some one has been using too much paper'. Many years later Miss Woodman married and

Day School, 1873–1874

Miss Maria separated from her. I suppose by now they are both dead. Well, they did 'ground' me according to their lights, and I feel nothing but friendliness for them.

It was only that one term that I boarded at the school. Otherwise, I went up and returned every day by train, walking to Somerset Street from Paddington station and back. I had a season ticket, which once I lost and my father insisted on my going up without a ticket and explaining the fact to the collector. How I trembled! How I tried to hide from his lynx eyes! How he found me out, and pitilessly exposed me before the carriage full of people! He was a rather famous detective, and passengers would sometimes make up an imaginary man of rugs, put it under the seat, and point it out to the collector, who then dashed into the carriage to extract it.

My life at this day school was thus really only a continuance of my home life and pleasant enough. The great break came when I was sent for the first time to boarding school. I was then, I think, twelve years old.

CHAPTER THREE

Boarding School, 1874–1881

Boarding school! What a flood of black memories! They start in a large empty room, smelling of soap and water, myself left there, my mother gone away, the other boys not yet arrived, but imminent at any moment, a disquieting thought, almost worse than solitude. This was at a house called Beomonds, in Chertsey. The school had just been started by Ernest Coleridge, the son of our rector at Hanwell. I remember him then as a fattish man, with a pompous manner. He was made for anything rather than a schoolmaster, and later found his proper work as an editor of Byron. Presently boys began to arrive. There were not many of them, but they were very mixed. There was one, perhaps two, of my own age. The rest were older, some of them failures from the public schools. Two I remember in particular, Grenville Kingsley, the son of Charles, a young man with a moustache who had been at Harrow; and a long lanky youth, almost imbecile, I think, whose family had dumped him at the school to get rid of him, who seldom or never, I think, went home, whom everyone, even the smallest of us, tormented, and who naturally from time to time went mad with impotent rage. Horrible to think of, even now! I was shy, timid, inexperienced. Everything alarmed and worried me.

The first Sunday morning my top-hat came in for severe comments, not undeserved, for it had belonged to my brother. Sitting round the table in the evening, supposed to be preparing unintelligible 'work', I was disturbed and perplexed by the talk of older boys. 'Bitches.' What was a bitch? Did I know? 'It's a female dog, isn't it?' said Kingsley, and I said yes, and thought perhaps it was. But then, why talk about it? Then someone put something cold down my back. Then prayers in the hall, all the servants trooping in, and Mr Coleridge in great form. Prayers, I think, always ended with 'For so he giveth his beloved sleep'. That sounded soothing. But then one went up to a bedroom with three other boys, one older, and inclined to bully, and there were many pains before sleep was given to one who I fear was not 'His Beloved.' My habit had been to wash at night, and only give myself a cold slop over in the morning. Schoolboy etiquette pronounced this to be dirty. They washed in the morning, and not at all at night.

A few days of discomfort, shyness, homesickness, reduced me to despair. I concocted (of all things!) a postcard, saying I was very unhappy and wanted to come home. It was, of course, seized and read, and Miss Coleridge (the Miss Christabel of Hanwell) sent for me to the drawing-room. She took me on her knees, cosseted me, talked to me, as they say, like a mother, and ended with 'and now we will destroy this unlucky postcard'. It went into the fire and with it my last hope and my last effort. I settled down to irremediable gloom. The letters we were allowed to write home every week were read by the master. There was nothing more to be done. Time stretched before one, infinite, endless, without a gleam of light to vary its bleak monotony. People talk of the troubles of later life. I have known none like the troubles of school. One suffers more later, but one has at least experience to correct it and character to fight it. At school a timid boy like me has no aid and no hope.[1]

What were these troubles? Nothing that seems anything to normal boys or unimaginative grown ups. Timidity, which itself is a curse, and I never got over it at school. Bullying, moral rather than physical. Cold—I seem to myself to have been always cold. There was nothing worse, I think, but it was quite enough. Or what was perhaps worse was obscure and dim, and in that I got no help. Mr Coleridge, before I left Hanwell to go to his school, had sent for me to the rectory. He wished to talk to me about sex; and no doubt he was right. But he did not know how to do it. Vaguely he said that I must resist and resent being treated like a girl. I listened and acquiesced in the weary way one did when grown-ups talked irrelevant and unintelligible things. It all meant nothing to me. And could Mr Coleridge know that my sex was excited by nothing but boots? I would rather have died than give away that curious secret. Later, at school, he sent for me to his study. I had been guilty of an offence. I had had a hot bath in the same tub with another boy. Nothing had happened, nor would it have been conceivable to me that anything should happen. For I knew nothing whatever about sex, and had no rudiments of sex feeling towards the boy in question, nor he to me. Mr Coleridge questioned me, and I answered wretchedly, not knowing what it was all about. Then he said—I still remember the words—'I don't know whether you are more fool than knave' and dismissed me. And all the time there was formed in me a 'complex' of which he knew nothing. I was masturbating at the time, stimulated by my usual theme, and perhaps to excess. Certainly I was not well. I had begun to endure life instead of enjoying it.

[1] 'Suffering,' says Wordsworth, 'is dark, obscure, and has the nature of infinity.'

Boarding School, 1874–1881

Everything was made worse, and every door of escape closed, by an unwise act of my parents, acting on an unripe character. We were forbidden, of course, to do various things, such as buying sweets at the tuck-shop. In my first term I learnt to ignore these rules like other boys. But on my referring to this fact, my mother was distressed, spoke to me seriously, handed me on to my father, who did the same, and I returned to school with the feeling that it was wrong to break rules. This put me out of touch with schoolboy ethics, without giving me any conviction or power to stand up against them. The effect was far greater than might seem probable. It formed a kind of complex which haunted me all through my school life. Perhaps it is at the root of my impatience now of most current rules of conduct. But now I have reason and character to justify myself to myself. Then it was a mere fetich, which had got hold of me to my undoing. *Why*, though, did it get hold of me, when most boys would have let it pass indifferently? That, I suppose, goes deep into my character. At any rate, a confusion of conscientiousness, timidity, hypocrisy, seized upon and held me for many years. I emerged from it ultimately a rebel, and at bottom have been so all my life. But by what strange and devious routes the approach was made!

These in retrospect seem to me the dominant facts of my school life at Chertsey. Of the rest, I recall as usual a series of dim flashes, arbitrarily selected by memory. For instance, a verse translation I made of one of the odes of Horace:

> Why love the pine and poplar white
> With mingling boughs sweet shade to spread?
> Why does the murmuring brook delight
> To hurry down its zigzag bed?

Reciting, from far out in the hall, to the schoolmaster in the schoolroom, Tennyson's 'Dora', and being applauded by Miss Coleridge, as she passed by, to the annoyance of Mr Boyd, who refused to give me the praise I supposed myself to deserve, and perhaps did. The bedroom, and myself and a smaller boy acting as target to a bigger one who threw slippers at us as we ran from bed to bed. Bed was 'home' and I remember putting my arms round the other boy and having a momentary thrill of something warm, comfortable and alluring, but that was all, and it had no future, and for me no association with sex. I see, too, Mr Boyd and another small boy playing with his watch chain, while he looked on with an odd and rather fatuous air of affection.

This Mr Boyd was the assistant master and the only element of order in the school. For we were afraid of him. When he went to town, as he often did, to concerts and theatres, pandemonium was let loose. He had an odd effect on me. I was so shy of him that I could hardly speak without stuttering. Yet also I was fascinated by him. He became a clergyman later, and long served a London church, and I used to hear of him, though I think I never saw him. He played the piano, especially, as I remember, Gounod's 'Funeral March of a Marionette', which I also used to try to play. And once he returned from town to tell us he had 'seen the sea'. The sea was Salvini in *Othello*, and, seeing him later, I endorse the verdict. With Mr Boyd we went to bathe in the Thames, from the bank, without bathing costumes, in the early morning. He tried to teach us to swim, and so far succeeded with me that I learned to swim a few strokes under water, but couldn't keep my head out. That I had to learn later. It was very cold, and I was of course very frightened, as I always was of everything. There was football, which, however, I seem seldom to have played. There was what was called a 'fight' between myself and another small boy, egged on by the bigger ones; a miserable demonstration, as I recall it. Then hours spent in the shrubbery in a vain attempt to learn to throw a cricket ball, a feat I could never accomplish in all my life. The lawn in the dusk evening, and myself, miserable panderer that I was, stealing out to kick the bottom of that poor lanky youth amid the applause of Mr Boyd and the elder boys.

What remembrances! In it all, only one thing stands out as belonging somehow to a more real me. That was theatricals. Under Miss Coleridge's supervision we acted *Cox and Box*. I was Mrs Bouncer. When the evening of the performance came I was first miserably afraid, then suddenly confident, happy and successful. My performance was much approved. I was got up to look pretty. And on descending, cleaned up and a boy again, to be introduced to the guests, I remember the crushing remark 'What! Was it that little whippersnapper!' How tactful grown-ups are!

That was Chertsey. Then, from my 14th to my 19th year, came Charterhouse, then recently moved down from London to Godalming. I was there the other day, an elderly stranger, and had still the remembrance of prison and the joy of one released. Charterhouse was the same thing as Chertsey, only longer and worse. I was in a house kept by a Mr Weekes. He never knew or cared, I think, anything about any of us, nor did his wife. He came in and read prayers, and made occasional inroads, in silent slippers, to the dormitories. Otherwise, the house was left to the monitors, who had powers to punish by boxing the ears (called 'swingeing') and beating with sticks (called 'cocking up', from the attitude assumed by the victim).

The house in my time was what would be called a 'hothouse of vice'. The odd thing is that, though in a sort of way I knew this, I wasn't interested in it and didn't attend to it. As I write, there comes back to me a picture, in the room where we changed for exercise, of a bigger boy

Boarding School, 1874–1881

masturbating against a smaller, amid a crowd of admirers. I passed on, feeling awkward but otherwise indifferent. For still my only sexual experience was masturbating under the stimulus of the idea of boots. I suppose I was not alone in this idiosyncrasy, for I remember once lying awake listening to the conversation of two other boys, and one of them saying (obviously I remember it because it excited me) 'I should stamp upon him with my dirty boots'. *I* always wanted to be stamped upon, that is the odd thing, or rather not odd, I suppose. What is one to do about these things? I remember Gilbert Chesterton once in conversation recommending flogging. It is the remedy that naturally appeals to a Britisher, but surely a very crude one. What happened to me was equally crude, but for the time being effective. It will be narrated presently.

To Charterhouse I carried not only my sexual complex but my timidity, my wretchedness, and my curious form of 'conscience'. On this latter point I remember a curious episode. The headmaster in chapel had preached us a sermon in which the importance of keeping rules was stressed. We were supposed not to talk in the dormitories, which were long rooms divided into cubicles. Of course everyone talked, and of course there was no reason why they shouldn't. But I became convinced, after the sermon, that it was wrong. That night accordingly, after efforts, fears, agonies, which even now dimly come back to me, I announced that I should not talk because it was against rules, and my people had told me not to break the rules. After this heroic announcement, I put my fingers tight into my ears and hid my head under the bedclothes. Some time afterwards I withdrew it, shuddering. The conversation had passed on and away from my concerns. Only later I heard one boy say to another 'Funny thing him saying that.' 'Yes', said the other, philosophically. Next morning I expected every kind of persecution, but nothing of that kind happened. On the contrary, a boy came up to me to make my acquaintance on the strength of the event. His name was Munro, and he is now Rector of Lincoln College, Oxford. He became my principal school friend, with, later, one other boy named Bowlby, now head master of one of our public schools.

'So,' some may say, 'virtue is rewarded.' But was there any virtue in it? It looks to me like a piece of foolish superstition. Still I admit it required courage. But then what an odd courage, how mixed up with fear, how inconsistent! For afterwards I did not keep my resolution. Yet I suppose that, by the effort and the shock, it had much effect (for good or evil or both) on my character. I have, I should say, never been what I should call courageous; but I have a kind of obstinate toughness which has stood me, on occasion, in lieu of courage. At any rate, it will be understood that this little episode at Charterhouse confirmed my antagonism to the ordinary view of things. That sense of being an alien was constant with me all through my school life, and I have never lost it. Indeed, in my old age I feel it as I never felt it before. Men become to me simply unintelligible.

Well, so much for that moment in my school life. For the rest, I crept about, cold, unhappy, alien; went through my work creditably enough, but with no kind of interest that I can remember; had my two friends, for neither of whom, however, had I any kind of sex feeling; did not know sex except in the form of my fetichism; played no games, except a very poor one at Fives; took walks, but always with a sense of banishment from the country through which I passed; struggled for bread and tea at a hatchway; endured the usual small bullying, physically, and the continual bullying morally, and so reached my 16th year. Then came another event of importance. We were being prepared for confirmation. Anything more absurd it is difficult to conceive. The head master used to lecture us in chapel, on the history of the prayer book, so far as I can remember. And we were given little books of self-examination. Unfortunately these had been drawn up for domestic servants (how characteristic of English society!) and had nothing in them relevant to our circumstances. I, with my unreal but conscientious religiosity, used to plough through the book, looking for something I had done and could be sorry for, and make good resolutions for the future. But it was very difficult when the whole book consisted of questions whether one had been properly obedient and submissive to one's master or mistress.

But one thing did happen in this pre-confirmation period. The headmaster made obscure and alarming references to sexual vice. This made me very frightened. I made one of my heroic efforts and wrote to my father explaining that I had been guilty of 'unclean actions' (I think that was the way the headmaster had put it) and asking advice. My father wrote back a very kind but very alarming letter, in which he dwelt on the frightful consequences of this act. One grew up, he said, 'ashamed in the presence of women and unable to hold up one's head among men'. I remember the phrase, because it made a tremendous impression. Was it wise? I doubt it. But it had, for the time being, its effect. From that moment I stopped masturbation. I learned even to wake myself in the night to stop it during sleep. And I remained what is called 'chaste' for the next eight years or so. Yes, but suppose some comprehending sympathetic, unsuperstitious person had talked to me. Suppose—I don't know. Perhaps it would have made no difference. But at least much confusion and superstition might have been cleared away from my mind. For the odd thing is—or is it anything except odd?—that even in this matter my attitude was the old superstitious one. It was *wrong* to do what I had done, like a taboo. Oh, how I hate taboos!

However, this taboo 'worked', in the negative sense. I daresay it was

Boarding School, 1874–1881

better for me, though I cannot remember any improvement in my school circumstances or outlook during the three remaining years I stayed there. I went mechanically on, from form to form, reached the sixth, became a monitor, kept some kind of miserable order in the house, but never got at home in the place, never felt happy, never, what is worse, felt genuine or myself. Was it anyone's fault? Probably not. I was what I was, they were what they were. It was the nearest thing to a 'state of nature' middle class modern life can show. Such unhappiness, such dumb despair, such a sense of alienation, I have never known since. I curse the time as I look back upon it. It seems to me all evil and no good. Cut off from home life, unknown to them and they to me, without a root to hold me that really sprang from myself, yet tormented by external ties of mere superstition, with not one of those passionate friendships or loves which redeem school for many boys, despised, and, as I think, rightly, yet by people who themselves were despicable, with no intellectual interest and no moral conviction, alone as I have never been alone since, physically unfit, mentally undeveloped—was ever a sadder, drearier, more hopeless entry upon life? And no one knew. And so, of course, no one cared.

It should, however, be added that there were some consolations, even at Charterhouse, as there had been at Chertsey. For instance, there was acting. I did not act myself. By that time I was too obscure, too shy, too unenterprising. But to watch the acting was a great delight. Companies of old Carthusians used to come down. And once there came with them one of the Miss Volkes (I think that was the name) at that time a rather famous family of actors. This one had a wonderful laugh, a kind of ripple strangely infectious. She also sang 'My Johnny was a shoemaker'. Was it a first awakening of the normal impulse to women that caused this performance to haunt me? If so, it was both the first and the last. Anyhow, I went mooning about, saw her with excitement next day in the racket court, and wrote out the whole play as nearly as I could remember it with a view to performing it at home; a superfluous exertion as of course it was printed. Miss Volkes, I seem to remember, was also a little intoxicated, or so rumour had it, which must have disturbed the equanimity of the doctor's household. This acting was one thing that delighted me.

Then there was the school orchestra, in which I used to play the violin, very badly but with some satisfaction to myself. At the end of every summer term there was a school concert. We wore dress clothes and Mrs Haig Brown gave us button-holes of syringa. The scent of this became associated for me with the approaching holidays and still produces a curious effect of excitement and release. I read also innumerable novels, nearly everything by Wilkie Collins, Bulwer Lytton, Harrison Ainsworth, Charles Reade. I seem to have been always reading, when I was not suffering, and got some compensation in that fictitious world for the futile boredom and distress of the 'real' one. I had pleasure too in the society of my two friends, disturbed, however, by the fact that we were marked figures known, as I remember, ironically as the 'Three Graces'. There were school debates too which excited me somewhat as acting did. I believe I took part, and with the same feeling of release and relief I had felt at Chertsey when I acted Mrs Bouncer.

In my work I remember no kind of interest except once when Mr Page, the sixth-form master, read us out a passage from Frere's translation of the *Birds* of Aristophanes. We were reading this play in Greek, and it presented itself to me as the usual dreary meaningless stuff which one got in the Classics. Then suddenly:

> At length in the dreary chaotical closet
> Of Erebus old, was a privy deposit,
> By Night the primaeval in secrecy laid
> A mystical egg that in silence and shade
> Was brooded and hatched; till Time came about
> And Love the delightful in glory flew out,
> In rapture and light, exulting and bright,
> Sparkling and florid with stars in his forehead,
> His forehead and hair, and a flutter and flare
> As he rose in the air triumphantly furnished,
> To range his dominions, on glittering pinions
> All golden and azure and blooming and burnished.

Was *that*, then, what we had been reading? For a moment a door sprang ajar, as once before at Chertsey, when Mr Coleridge read us Milton. It closed again. But the experience remains with me. I can read Greek now and know how the original transcends the translation. And that original now haunts my memory, as it was delivered in Cambridge by Clive Carey. But through what vain and wasted years I had to pass to that kingdom! And how few they were that ever entered it, of all those that began the laborious road.

Charterhouse I daresay when I was there was more sunk in barbarism than other public schools, and I myself was more incompetent for the life than most boys. I will not try to apportion the blame. Perhaps, as usual, there was no particular blame. But there is no doubt about the misery, the futility, the worse than waste of precious years. I make no generalisation. I record as faithfully as I can my own experience. But I believe that many boys would have something similar to say, if they revealed the secrets of the prison house. But they are more likely to forget, or to idealise, which

Boarding School, 1874–1881

is worse, and to say to their hapless sons entering on the same path: 'Remember, my boy, these will be the happiest years of your life.' No! Life is terrible, but not quite so terrible as that!

Holidays of course were a relief. I enjoyed myself at home. We used to act plays, which I liked, though I had, I think, no talent. My sister had, as she had in so many ways, none of them to bear any remarkable fruit, not through her fault, but because of her circumstances. We went up to town to concerts, and while I was still a boy I knew the *Elijah* and the *Messiah* almost by heart. We went to plays occasionally, and how they moved me, even the worst of them! I remember (but that was when I was a smaller boy) bursting into tears in the stalls, when the hero plunged into the water and saved the heroine, who had just been run down in a small boat by a realistic steamer dashing on to the stage. She had no sooner reached the shore in the hero's arms, than she discovered her long-lost father, and the climax of emotion was too much for my tender nerves. *Caste* too in those days I remember with the Bancrofts in it. *The Lyons Mail*, best of melodramas, with Irving, other Irving performances, *The Merchant of Venice*, Benedict in *Much Ado about Nothing*.

One thing also is worth recording, Wagner's first visit to England in 1870 or thereabouts. We went up to the Albert Hall and heard long extracts from the operas. I don't think really that I made, at that time, very much of them, though my sister did. But I remember well the appearance of Wagner, and how at the end he was crowned with laurel, amidst indescribable enthusiasm, and publicly kissed Richter, who did most of the conducting. It was some years later before his music really began to take hold of me.

I will add that it was while I was at Charterhouse that we moved from Hanwell to the house behind All Souls Church in Langham Place, to which I have already referred. It was also during these years that my mother contracted the illness from which she died. It was asthma, and she was ill for many years, and nursed chiefly by my sister May. My childhood relationship to her had ended when I went to school, and I had not time, before she died, to form a closer one, if I ever could have formed it. Perhaps I could not, for she would have been distressed at the line my thinking took at Cambridge. No mother I suppose ever devoted herself more wholly to her children. And if, in the most important things, she never got in touch with me, that was not her fault. The cleft between young and old is almost impassable, do what either party may. But it is, I think, less marked now than it was in my youth, and was less so in my family than in many others.

CHAPTER FOUR

Cambridge, 1881–1885

My school life lasted seven years, and what years! In the October of 1881 I went up to Cambridge, having secured a small exhibition at King's College. It was something of an accident that I went up at all, for in the examination I was only 'proxime accessit' and my parents decided that they could not afford to send me up. What would have happened, in that case, is conjectural, but I was to work for a clerkship in the Civil Service. Perhaps, in that case, I should never have developed at all. But, as it happened, one of the successful candidates did not take up his exhibition, and I was given £40, which determined the matter the other way. I seem to myself to have been curiously indifferent to what was to happen to me, and I don't know that I went to Cambridge with any particular expectations.

My brother had preceded me there, as he had at Charterhouse. I remember my arrival at the rooms I first had, in Bennet Street, and going over at once to lunch with him in his rooms, which were in College, looking over King's Parade. Some of his friends were with him, and everything still breathed the wearisome air of the public school. I wasn't at home with that kind of man and I hardly knew there were other kinds. One of his friends was Rowlatt, now a judge, another Chitty, afterwards also a judge, in India. My brother is knighted for war service, and a rich man. They were all, in fact, normal public school Britishers. I was anything but that. But at Cambridge one could escape, as one could not at school. To have one's own rooms and privacy, was a boon indescribably precious, after the forced and unsympathetic publicity of school. And then gradually to discover people who were really akin to one. That, however, took time.

I was very shy and timid and began at first in a purely conventional way to be 'tubbed' on the river, and all the rest of it. My friends at first were not particularly interesting to me. Nor was my work. I took classics merely because I was advised to, and began to read in the stupid pseudo-industrious way I had contracted at school, attending lectures religiously, from which I derived nothing, working at my authors with notes and counting my hours, and often, I think, half asleep. But I was throwing out tentacles. In that first year I tried all sorts of things which did not belong to me—bell-ringing, a class of poor boys at Barnwell, the Church of England Temperance Society, in connexion with which I recollect visiting an athlete who had been drunk the night before and inviting him to join. He had a headache and was rather repentant, but he declined the syren's voice. I joined the University orchestra, which was then conducted by Stanford, afterwards Professor Stanford in London (now dead), an old man and I daresay cantankerous and reactionary, but then inspiring, young and fresh. All those months I was endeavouring to discover myself and throwing off, though I did not know it, the uncongenial misgrowths of school.

Then, towards the end of my first year, an event happened which marks for me the transition from an alien life to my real one. One day, returning from a bicycle ride, I found a telegram telling me my mother was dead. As I have said, she had long been ill, but I was expecting no change. The effect of this telegram, perhaps, I do not justly recall. But, as it seems to me now, it was a curious blend of conventional and real feeling. The incredible had happened; for is not death always incredible? and I had not come across it before. There was something about that that stunned. Then there was the effort as it were to feel more than one did or could; a curious sense of the melodrama of the position. And grief? yes, I think so; and yet that not prominent and exclusive, as I supposed it would be. I rushed across to my tutor, showed him the telegram, and burst into tears. He was very kind, came back with me to my rooms and helped to send me off to town.

I see myself now ringing the bell, the door opening, my sister coming downstairs in tears, my own tears, the whole distressing scene. I remember mother, lying on the bed, looking calm and beautiful. I remember my father's grief. Yet, after the funeral, I remember also sitting at one of our drawing room windows with my sisters in a state of almost hysterical laughter, and one of my aunts remarking coldly that we had better not laugh so much as people might think it heartless. Then I remember lying on the sofa, trying desperately to realize the 'never again', the indubitable and yet inconceivable fact. I returned to Cambridge to finish my term, oscillated between the grave demeanour I felt to be appropriate, and the natural forgetfulness and cheerfulness produced by the company of my friends. I had to stay up late to keep my term, and there comes back to me a long solitary expedition to the Fens. With this event, the death of my mother, I connect my definite passage into a new phase of my life.

One of my then friends, now Principal Graham of Dalton Hall, Manchester, said to me later that in my first year I was a very insignificant undergraduate, and I am sure he was right. I was like a boy recovering from a

Cambridge, 1881–1885

long illness. But from now on my mind was in a ferment, a kind of ferment, however, which would hardly, I think, be intelligible to a contemporary undergraduate. It was as though, at last, the door that had once or twice swung ajar, now opened and let me out. What I saw was a dim and moonlit scene, infinite, exciting, perilous, full of adventure. It presented itself to me as the problem of existence, at once felt and thought about—if indeed what one did then can be called thinking. It was exciting, to a degree that no modern young man of intelligence could comprehend, to discover that Christianity was not, as it were, an inextensible box, very small, in which the whole world was packed, but that an immense world extended quite outside of it. That world I began to try to grasp in ways that seem now ridiculous but that had nevertheless an intensity, a passion and a romance that it is only given to youth to experience. It was exciting, then, to conceive that perhaps Jesus was not God but only an exceptional Being. It still seemed shocking at first that anyone should conceive him as only man. Then interest in him (such poor ignorant interest as it had ever been!) began to fade.

Shelley suddenly gripped me; I don't think as a poet, but as a visionary about life. His landscapes, always shimmering with moonlit streams, his loneliness, his passionate and ideal love were what seized me—Alastor and Adonais and the more ethereal and musical lyrics of Prometheus. I read Hogg's life of him (still in my deliberate judgment one of the most fascinating biographies in existence) as though it were a new gospel. Shelley at Oxford especially appealed to me. And then his political ideas! I thought with rapture and reverence of the youth of 19 dropping his leaflets among the crowd from a balcony in Dublin. I leapt with indignation and contempt at Godwin's solemn cry 'Shelley, you are preparing a scene of blood'. No one who has not felt Shelley once like that can know, I think, what Shelley is. I still recover those first feelings when I turn to him. And I still resent (rightly, as I believe) the elderly view of him as a man of genius gone astray, ignorant of life, wild and utopian. He had, in fact, a clear logical mind, a courage of conviction almost unique, and a burning passion for truth which is only not appreciated because it is of all passions the rarest. If there were indeed that world beyond, of which the Platonic Socrates used to dream, there is no one I would sooner meet; of all men of letters he is, I think, the most lovable, humane and genuine.

It was in the ferment of my first passion for him, and for poetry at all, that I made my own first poems. Certainly they had no value, but nothing I have written since has filled me with such excitement, such a sense of being inspired, that is, of something speaking through me which was not myself. I sent one of them to the 'Carthusian', then edited by my friend Bowlby. It was called, if I remember right, Ormuzd and Ahriman. I have forgotten it now, but I remember the emotion with which it was composed. Later, I got the prize medal for an English poem supposed to be about Savonarola. It had, I expect, no merit. But once more how it possessed me! In my first rooms at King's, on the ground floor of Chetwynd Court, looking on the King's Parade, I remember still my rapt contemplation of photographs of Shelley and of Schubert, whose music had seized me as had the other's poetry, but whose countenance was certainly less poetic; and the reading of Mrs Oliphant's *Life of Savonarola*, the only thing, so far as I remember, which I did read bearing on the subject. It mattered little because my poem was hardly about the subject; a way prize poems have, and no doubt a good way. I had to read mine, of course, as is still done, in dress clothes in the Senate House, to an audience of which a principal part was my admiring relatives.

It was by the route of Shelley that I first approached politics. Then came Henry George with his *Progress and Poverty*. I have not read the book since those days. It is, I daresay, vitiated by economic errors. But it had the curious effect every book has which is written by a convinced man who has a quite simple view of the causes of social disorder. I have known many followers of Henry George and never one that did not regard him as a prophet, and his solution as finally right. He came to Cambridge while I was an undergraduate accompanied by an odd sort of son, who said to us 'My father is a crank'. No doubt he was, and what would the world be without the cranks! He addressed a large public meeting in the Guildhall. One of the arrangers and doorkeepers of the meeting was Mr J. R. Tanner, afterwards tutor of St John's, a Conservative (or would he say a Liberal?), an ardent supporter of the Great War and—well, well, this is what life does to nearly all of us!

While the mists were thus drawing up before religion, poetry, politics, like curtains of gauze on the stage, I was gradually finding, for the first time, real friends. With my temperament friendship always meant for me more than for normal men. But I hardly knew it in my earlier years at Cambridge, and no touch of sex entered at this time into my relations. We feasted on ideas, on speculations, on poetry, music, or what not? The best of our life was long talks in our own rooms, or, in summer, pacing the grounds of King's, still, as I think, one of the loveliest spots in the world, and open still all night to talk, as well as to more noisy enterprises. The dedication to my unpublished volume of poems[1] recaptures the feeling of those hours better than anything I can say now, when I pace the same ground half a ghost and more haunted by memories than realities. But always the same beauty, as perhaps may be the case even centuries from now.

[1] *Poems*, 'Privately Printed at the Chiswick Press,' 1896.

Cambridge, 1881–1885

As to my friends of this earlier date, I have lost touch with some, in some sense, perhaps, with all; for it was others of later date who made more mark upon me. Of the earlier period those I principally remember are Grant, now Professor of History at Leeds, with whom I associate, at this moment, a moonlit evening spent in the grounds of Trinity, after we had climbed a locked gate to get in; and a trip on bicycles past Peterborough and Crowland into Lincolnshire. Professor Graham, of Dalton Hall, older than the rest of us, full of enthusiasm for Tennyson's *In Memoriam* and believing so ardently in progress that he would not have it doubted that art too must have steadily progressed, like everything else. Laurie, now head of a large technical college in Edinburgh, then the most speculative and bold of that little sect, a chemist, a Henry Georgite, a perpetual talker, with whom I remember an undergraduate tour in the Highlands. I met him again after many years quite recently, and found him much the same as before, only with all his opinions changed, critical of the 'working man' and enthusiastic about the entrepreneur. Others of that set have gone almost out of my mind, and some of them out of the world. But still their forms appear in the golden mist of dawn and almost I catch their voices through the talk of younger generations, heard under the same chapel walls, under the same chestnut grove, over the same great lawns, under the same stars reflected in the same sluggish yet lovely stream, that will hear perhaps for centuries yet the same voices at the same budding time of youth; unless perhaps, who knows?, they fall silent even before the eternal silence closes upon me.

My tutor at that time was Welldon, now, I think, Dean of Durham. His burly figure I can still see uneasily balanced on a bicycle along the Ely road. He had a curious effect on me, not unlike that once exercised by Mr Boyd at Chertsey. Why, I cannot tell. There was certainly nothing of sex in it. But I was at once shy and hero-worshipping. I doubt whether he deserved the hero-worship. At any rate he and I have moved too far apart since then for any mutual comprehension. He took trouble over us, wrote to us at the end of the year, and lectured, I daresay well, on Aristotle's politics. But I was unripe for that although I attended.

The don who really influenced me, perhaps I might say inspired me, was the once famous, or notorious, Oscar Browning, who still lives (1923) in Rome, at the age of 84. He was surely a remarkable man whose life ought to be written[1] in some form that would express him better than his own colourless reminiscences. In default of that, I will set down some things I remember of him. He came down to my brother's room, which was on the same staircase as his, when I was a freshman of only a few days. He came

---

[1] Has been by Wortham (1931).

rollicking in, already stout, already middle-aged, but with an air of equality with youth which I could not then comprehend. He carried me up to his rooms, took stock of me, no doubt, and left me alone for a year or so. Then I spoke at a debate when he was present. It was about ghosts. He was interested in my speech, came up to me afterwards and said 'I didn't know you were such a clever fellow'. This was characteristic, for his principal gift was the power of making men believe in themselves. I have seen a letter to him from Lord Curzon, saying that at Eton he had had just that effect upon himself. After that, I remember playing duets with him, on his grand piano, how his bulky form crushed me into a small corner of the seat and the tempo was judiciously manipulated to suit his not too agile fingers. We played, I remember, the slow movement of Beethoven's 7th Sonata, and it became very slow indeed when we reached the demi-semi-quavers. Then we sat by the fire and talked about 'vice' at school.

What Browning's attitude really was to this subject I hardly know. He had, beyond a doubt, the homosexual temperament, and that explains his influence at Eton and at Cambridge. But to what manifestations he would have allowed it to extend I do not know. He always had some boy or young man as a secretary and for many boys and youths he did much to start them in life. His interest was in the young aristocrat, on the one hand, and the obscure struggler on the other. His rooms at that time, and for many years, were the centre of all that was most sociable, genial and stimulating in Cambridge. Every Sunday evening he was 'at home'; and I heard at that time really good music there, for Gompertz used to play the violin and Row (was that the name?), a fellow of Trinity, the piano, and I have listened spellbound to the Kreutzer Sonata and other great works. Later, he got together some curious kind of harmoniums supposed to represent the different instruments of an orchestra. Undergraduates called them O-Beophones and I cannot pretend that I ever heard anything from them except cacophony.

He (O.B.) was secretary of innumerable clubs, including the swimming club, where his corpulent person was constantly to be found in the state of primitive nudity which, in those early and happy days, was characteristic of Cambridge bathing. For even in the meadows open to view, where the members of the town bathed, they ran in crowds, quite naked, over the green grass. O.B. conducted at that time the Political Society, which he had founded and of which I, though then studying classics, not history, became a member. A paper was read, during which the President reclined in his arm chair, a red pocket handkerchief, of enormous size, covering his face. Then we all spoke in turn according to an order dictated by lots drawn out of a bag. I have passed many dull evenings there, but some that were interesting. And interesting or dull, O.B. produced his usual effect. We felt that we were men, and history a serious subject. Mr Browning's ambition was to produce statesmen. The only one I remember as emerging from his hearthrug is Mr Austen Chamberlain, perhaps not the most intelligent of men, but always, so far as I know, kind, friendly, and honourable.

Later, when I became a teacher at King's, Mr Browning was my senior colleague. I cannot honestly say that I found it easy to work with him, for I often disagreed with him, and never was there a man more incapable of seeing another man's point of view. Still, we remained always friends, and I hope and think still are so. I found him once in his inner room, where he slept behind a screen, in the act of getting up. On one side of him was a secretary writing letters to dictation, on the other another secretary playing the violin. O.B. was seated in deshabille, between the two, and he began to speak on a subject always congenial to him, himself. Once, he said, he had his horoscope taken. He was born in the ascendancy of two planets, Capricorn and Saturn, the one elating, the other depressing. But, however much crushed by Saturn, he always knew that Capricorn would toss him up again to the sky.

He made once one of the wittiest and most pregnant remarks ever made about Cambridge. 'There are three things,' he said, 'that no Cambridge man can endure. One is, that a man should know anything outside his own subject. The second is, that his name should be known outside the University. The third, that he should be able to express himself lucidly, either in speech or writing.' That was the older Cambridge, when Thompson of Trinity was still paralysing the activities of his younger fellows. It is perhaps less true now. Mr Keynes for instance is still a resident at King's, and his book has gone over the world. But something of this 'lucifuge' spirit still maintains itself; and I do not know that, in moderation, it is regrettable.

Such, as I remember him, was O.B., Falstaffian, shameless, affectionate, egoistic, generous, snobbish, democratic, witty, lazy, dull, worldly, academic, but, and above all, with the Socratic gift of maieusis. How many young men did he stir to life who afterwards turned against him! They were wrong, though not without excuse. The man was more than his foibles; and I greet him here as many others might greet him, as one of those who discovered me to myself.

I took my degree in the summer of 1884, and then I went abroad. In the earlier part of this trip C. R. Ashbee was my companion. He may, or may not, be remembered for his creation of a 'Guild of Handicraft', first in East London, later transferred to Chipping Campden, in Gloucestershire, where I have often stayed with him, first in a fourteenth century house in the village, afterwards at the 'Norman chapel' outside, which he had rebuilt into a living-house. I will not digress upon that experiment, which was a very interesting one. It was finally broken up, like so many good things, by the Great War, and Ashbee blown upon because his mother was German. In 1884 he had just finished his first year at Cambridge. He was a long youth, enthusiastic, opinionated, 'Schwärmerisch', of whom, mainly, I remember, at that time, that he started a society for discussion, which was to spread throughout the world, and which, in fact, collapsed after his first term; and that he made a hole in one of the 'eights' by leaping awkwardly into it.

In regard to our tour of 1884, there floats before me a memory of the little carts drawn by big dogs at Rotterdam, of the unfavourable impression made on the inhabitants by my wearing a puggery; of Dordrecht, its air of a great solitary village, its huge church and pictures by Ary Schäffer, whom I pretended to admire and who was no doubt one of the worst of painters. From Dordrecht we went south and I found my way ultimately to the Odenwald, where my friend Ord was staying with the family of his German fiancée. The place was an old castle twenty miles or so from Reichenberg (I think that was the name). I had to drive in a coach, during the dusk and night, stopping at all the villages and feeling so desperately romantic that I filled, in pencil, pages of a notebook with my observations and reflexions. The castle was a lovely place, set in the woods.

The inhabitant was a parson who had somehow become a heretic from the Lutheran church. He held service on Sundays in the Castle chapel, a bleak whitewashed room in which I seem to recall a strong smell of the neighbouring privy. He also kept a school of boys of different nationalities, one or two English among them. At meals we had a kind of service before and after, prayers and a Lutheran hymn. 'Mögen Sie die deutsche Kost?' was a remark frequently made to my incipient German ear. 'Ja' I said, and indeed I think the deutsche Kost was good. As to the boys, they were a bit unruly; and the pastor, bursting one night into their dormitory, was reported (by the English of course) as delivering himself thus: 'What do you here in the night? This must not be so. No'! For my own part I sat out in the woods studying German, with Heine and a dictionary, reading *The Light of Asia*, dreaming in a mystic way, taking long walks and writing poems. It was all very enjoyable.

I left the place after a week or two and went to Heidelberg, returning, however, later to my friend's wedding. On that occasion I lost my luggage and had to appear in a tail coat of Ord's, which was built for a man about twice my size. Of the wedding I recollect long hours spent at table, health after health being drunk, and after each health everybody processing round the table to clink glasses with everybody else. Then there were games, peep-shows, fireworks, the whole going on from early morning to late at night. Ord brought his wife back to England, and they have lived ever since at Clifton, produced a family of children, of whom one has just been made a Fellow of King's College, and spent the evening the other day in these rooms. And so let that little bubble of the past float down the stream of time.

At Heidelberg I lodged with an old woman called Pfelstrich, in a little cottage somewhere on the way to the castle. Here too, oddly enough, I recollect the strong smell of the privy entering my bedroom window, and also how I was driven from bedroom to sitting room and back again by mosquitoes. These, however, in those days seemed negligible evils. My Heidelberg life was spent in the company of Plato and especially of Plato's myths. I ate little and mostly vegetables, sat in the woods or walked, was very solitary, and very happy. For was I not expecting that one day there would open before me the secret of the Universe? Meantime, there was Plato and Shakespeare, the castle with its 'gesprengter Thurm' by moonlight, and its great view over the plain, where I watched the storms coming up. Also at Mannheim, I made my first real acquaintance with Wagner, though only, I think, with *Tannhaüser*. But then what a thing was *Tannhaüser*! How I collapsed after it! How somehow Wagner, Shakespeare, Plato, the woods and the views were then all the same thing! And what a wonderful thing! Do young men have these feelings still? Some of them, I suppose, in some analogous form. At any rate, I take off my hat to my then self. It was absurd if you like. But alas, what is later life, except the gradual breaking in of the soul to her prison?

In a contemporary letter, written to Ashbee, I find that what had attracted me to Plato was the curious fraud called Esoteric Buddhism, which had taken hold of me at Cambridge. This is probably all forgotten now with its sponsors, Mr Sinnett and Colonel Olcott, and that brilliant adventuress suspected by the British Government of being a Russian spy, called Madame Blavatsky. I never saw her. But I remember Colonel Olcott visiting Cambridge and addressing the Society for Psychical Research. He told us that he had been visited, when all his doors were locked, by a mahatma, who had materialised himself for the purpose. When he dematerialised again, he had left his turban behind as proof that he had really been there. 'And here is the turban,' the Colonel said, passing it round. I think even my then innocence was a bit staggered by that. I refer to it, however, now only to illustrate that I was led to Plato by (among other things) a belief that there was some supernormal mystic avenue to truth; and that in my mind he was inextricably mixed up, at this time, with memories of Esoteric Buddhism. Thus in the letter referred to I say 'I've taken a new start in the Buddhist line by reading Plato' and conclude 'It's a hopeless matter too, for how am I, a poor unhappy individual, to find this same way, being guideless in the wilderness, unless some merciful Mohini takes pity; and probably there is some insuperable impediment which would prevent him from helping me if he would.' Mohini was an Indian, who had visited Cambridge (under the care of Frederick Myers, I think), and had been watched by me and others with reverence and awe from a distance. Later I took my courage into my hand and asked for an interview with him. He entered, very majestic and refusing to take the hand of a layman and a white man. He told me to read Plato, or to continue reading him. I babbled out something about the argument of the Phaedo, which I don't imagine he knew anything about, but for which he professed approval. He told me, in a general way, to think about Unity, and I retired feeling really that I had got at nothing, but refusing to admit as much to myself. I daresay he was quite genuine. Later, I believe, he gave himself up to social reform in India, perhaps becoming himself disillusioned about the mystic way.

Ashbee had saner and more concrete views than I then had, and he obviously wrote questioning my methods and suggesting that a little work for other people might be a good thing. To which I find myself replying that living for others is a means to mysticism, not vice versa, and continuing to speak of Esoteric Buddhism and Mahatmas. My idea, I believe, was that one must first discover absolute standards of Good and Evil, and then descend (like the Platonic philosophers of the Republic) to govern mankind. One smiles now; but after all, it is the smile of disillusionment; and I must not slander my own youth, since what is my age, or anyone's age?

One other thing I must mention as belonging to this period of my life. At the end of 1884 after my return to Cambridge I was elected to the Society of Apostles, whose official name is the Cambridge Conversazione Society. It was founded early in the nineteenth century by Tomlinson, afterwards Bishop of Gibraltar, and still exists, and a good many more or less famous men have been members of it. It formed for many years a very important part of my life, though not so much at my first election, as in the year or two following, when McTaggart, the philosopher, Roger Fry, and Wedd (afterwards Classical teacher at King's) were the active members. We met, as still the Society meets, on Saturday nights. A paper was read and we spoke in turn, drawing lots for the order. These were, and are, the externals. The soul of the thing, as I felt it, is incommunicable. When young men are growing in mind and soul, when speculation is a passion, when discussion is made profound by love, there happens something incredible to any but those who breathe that magic air. Some breath of it, I almost think, still hangs about the dedication to Cambridge printed in my little volume of verse. I go still to the Society, from time to time, find it of course different from what it was in my youth, in the topics and the opinions discussed, but find also the same spirit of free, candid, uncompromising youth, of all spirits, to my mind, the most beautiful and touching. Oh, brethren, if ever any of you should read these words, be sure that they are written by one who has never forgotten and never been faithless.

In the summer of 1885 I took one of my desperate resolutions. Full of Henry George, of the social question, of the general ferment of things, I determined to go down to Surrey and work on a co-operative farm which had been started there by Harold Cox. This was an odd little bit of experience. The farm was at Tilford, near Farnham, and consisted of so many acres of barren heath, which we were to reclaim. Harold was living in a newly built cottage with a farm labourer and his wife, son and daughter, whom he had imported from Kent. I recall now, with curious vividness, the scent of the country as I got out at Farnham station, the walk of four miles or so up to the farm and my first digging, very incompetent beside Harold. The enterprise, I suppose, was desperate from the first, in an economic sense, but I knew and cared little about that.

I imagined myself beginning to live the right kind of life, manual work on the one hand and intellectual, poetical creation on the other. The manual work was hoeing, digging, ploughing. I really did a good deal of it, though no doubt very badly; and I still recall the back-ache of hoeing and the holding of the plough while Will guided the horse. Gibbs, the labourer, approved of me, but only in contrast to Harold, whom he early learned to distrust. I don't know that Harold had offended, except in taking Gibbs away from Kent. But, further, he flirted with Annie, the rather pretty daughter; and I see as I write a vision of her sitting on Harold's knees, and drinking cocoa, when the parents had retired to bed. That was the manual side of my life.

The intellectual side consisted in writing out lectures, which I was to deliver in the autumn. These were on Carlyle, Emerson, Browning and Tennyson. For all these writers, except Tennyson, I was then what the German would call *schwärmerisch*. To Tennyson, I suppose, I was merely unjust, for I had no sense of and no conscious interest in literary form. My lectures got written and still exist in MS, but I feel no temptation to look at them again. Besides that, I was reading Plotinus, led to him by the mystic side of Plato, which was the one that then attracted me. Plotinus is crabbed enough in form, but if you think, as I did, that he contains the truth about the Universe, experienced in the mystic trance, you will not mind that. How I read! How I thought, or was it rather meditating and dreaming? Anyhow, the great commons with the fern-owls sounding upon them in the dusk, the Frensham ponds, the bracken and the heather were silent witnesses of much passionate brooding in those short weeks; for I append a contemporary letter written to C. R. Ashbee which will give a more vivid picture of this enterprise, and of my state of mind.

Craig Farm, May 1885

You would laugh to see me seated solemnly at meals in the kitchen talking ineffectually to George, Will and Tom about them there peas and how the dung rotted them, but 'arold would 'ave 'is way; and how there ought to be hops here, and beans there, etc etc, with jokes about Annie's suitors and Paget's debts ('Paget calls 'isself a genleman, I dun call 'im no genleman. What does 'e go for etc etc') A slight interval in which I've been fetching beer from the pub in an enormous brown jar; the men all sowing soot for manure, and no one to get them beer so I had to go. It's really very funny. If there were some one to laugh with, I could laugh all day. The family is George Gibbs, silent and humorous (at times), fond of grumbling and hard work: details to me Harold's little mistakes, and has a habit of making the same conversation do several times over, in which case I, of course, make the same remarks, with as much interest as possible. Mrs Gibbs, deaf as a post, with whom I communicate mainly by signs: she, however, converses much, being answered in dumb show.

Then there's Will, fat, stupid, and Alick silently devoted to Annie, who pities him; and Tommie cute and self-assertive, with a dormant propensity to lying and juvenile fondness for a gun: and then there's Annie! . . . Suffice it to say she's superior in culture to the rest, and is considered by some very pretty.

I've just had the sweetest good-night chat with her; but then, she is so catholic. For instance, a minute ago I saw her reclining in Alick's arms, and as to she and Harold! Let us draw a veil . . . Yes, she is pretty . . . Good God, Ashbee, (as Stone would say) there came here the other day one Dr Elizabeth Blackwell! All my ideas of higher education for women and the like are pushed back at least a century by the event! How that woman talked! flowing periods, elaborate parentheses, scarcely a pause for breath, words articulated like the snap of a pistol, gratified smack of the lips at each semicolon! Unfortunate female companion reduced to positive deafness and imbecility by constant association; should think she was paid listener-in-chief. 'Come here my dear and sit by me! Can you give her a low chair?' And we did. And there she sat poor wretch at the feet of the monster! Miserablest of females! 'It is my profound conviction— though mark you I profess myself a land nationalist—that it is idle, nay injurious, to advocate extreme reform before public opinion has duly matured' etc. Ach Gott! Talk of mental diarrhoea! . . . As to Annie's opinion of her, that you may imagine. 'These people have evidently not in any degree developed their intellect' quoth the learned Dr. 'Thank heaven, No!' one felt inclined to say.

Mrs Gibbs is becoming painfully friendly. She bursts at all hours into my studious retirement, crying: 'O Mr Dickinson I've cut open that chicken and its livers all diseased. Come and see. Now what *would* you do with it?' I, good heavens! And the woman is deaf. No getting at her. There's no denying that the family quarrels a good deal. Tom, for instance, 'is such a little beast! I do 'ate 'im!' This, alas, from a sister! And then Will! He will talk so freely at the dinner table about kicking your ass. But these drawbacks will occur. I've tried my hand at ploughing with signal success. What a hardy son of the soil I should have been if I'd been born to it. As I wasn't, I remain a puny son of the pen, much in need of a sleeping draught. But I can't milk the cow. No! It may look simple but I assure you there is an art in manipulating the teat of a domestic cow not easily fathomable. It will ever be a sorrow to me: but the fact remains; I can't milk a cow! . . .

Oh, mein lieber, how I would like to hear that nightingale. But I know 'em of old, and how the chapel sleeps in the moonlit water, and the limes are steeped in fragrance, and all the world asleep . . .

There was a proposal at this time that I should accept a professorship in India. And I write:

> I wait the signal undismayed
> Whate'er may come I ain't afraid.
> India, Nottingham, the States;
> It's all the same, I sits and waits.

'How one gets into this sort of thing. Annie sleeps above me. Beneath me is Tophet and the pit and in the centre, the Ego, mystical, infinite. Only the murmur of Will's snoring disturbs the silence. Will! How fat, how amiable, how childlike. In that rich fairyland of his, where the delusions of childhood are yet unbroken and the Universe appears objective (strange notion! I shouldn't wonder if he really thinks it is an actual solid objective manure he shovels into the cart!) and where Italy is a province of England! Wondrous fairy land! Wondrous Will!

> And Alick had his arm round Annie!
> Enough enough the strain must cease,
> The sweet mad hour has had its lease!
> The snore of William calls to rest;
> William, I answer thy behest.

Leben Sie Wohl. That reminds me that I've read *Hermann und Dorothea*. Sweetest of idylls!'

Opposite the farm house was a cottage occupied by Mr and Mrs Salt. Salt had been a master at Eton, and had recently escaped from that to him uncongenial career. Mrs Salt—Kate—was daughter of the second master at Eton, shy, fugitive, elusive, beautiful and childless. Their house was visited by us all, including the Gibbs; and on its grand piano in the little drawing room Mrs Salt would perform, and sometimes myself with her. I had then, and for long afterwards a very affectionate feeling for her, though quite untouched by sex. She died a year or two ago in Lyme Regis, when I had lost touch with her. Visitors used to come both to us and to them. Among their visitors was Bernard Shaw whom I saw, I think, then for the first time. He arrived on a Sunday pouring with rain, and afterwards wrote an article on his wet walk through the country, passing, as he said, 'from milestone to milestone and cemetery to cemetery', hearing every now and again the cry of an animal that somebody was murdering and returning with satisfaction and relief to London and civilisation.

As for our farm house, it was visited mostly by cranks. Our table manners were not good, and I remember at one of our midday meals, where a lady doctor was participating, Will remarking 'There's worms in my soup'. I don't know whether there was, but the remark put a gloom upon the meal . . . I wrote down an account of this experience next year, in a kind of novel form. It still exists in MS, and has, I imagine, no interest except that of biography. I have never read it through since I wrote it.

In the June of 1885 I left this farm, and shortly after it collapsed. The Gibbs were reimported into Kent, and Harold disappeared from my ken, later to re-emerge, as the most uncompromising champion of political individualism. I have met him since and found he still retains the personal charm he always had. But over the farm experiment a great ox sat upon our tongues.

CHAPTER FIVE

Postgraduate, 1885–1886

The winter of 1885–6 was a rather dismal experience. I was making my first experiment in public lecturing under the University Extension Scheme. My subject, as I have said, was the rather comprehensive one of Carlyle, Emerson, Browning and Tennyson! I had no notion how to speak, and no idea at all how ordinary people felt and thought. My centres were, for the first term, Mansfield (in Nottinghamshire), Chesterfield and Stamford; for the second term Chester and Southport. I lived in the first term at Mansfield and in the second at Chester. I had my lectures written out in full and learned them by heart. They naturally fell very flat and I still remember the cheerful schoolmaster who was my chairman at my first remarking at the end that we ought to be very grateful to Mr Dickinson for 'even trying' to communicate his ideas on these great authors. Worse however than the manner of my lectures was the matter, for I did not conceal the unorthodox nature of my opinions. I also dressed very badly, fed very badly, and was still involved, whenever I had a chance, in my philosophic and mystical studies. I remember that, at this time, I first read Schopenhauer, and also the second part of Goethe's *Faust*. The travelling from place to place was fatiguing, and altogether, looking back on myself, I seem a sad, outlandish, stranded and alien figure. I had no notion how to get into touch with ordinary people, and no desire to do so, for I thought I was the bearer of a message which condemned all actual life.

The following passages from letters to Ashbee will illustrate my condition:

September 1885, Leicester Station

I write en route for Stamford. I have lectured in Mansfield and have every reason to suppose I was wholly unintelligible; having heard no criticism save that the subject is very difficult! And I felt as dull as ditchwater all the time. Still, let us shrug our shoulders and say kismet.

Later:

... going to lecture now, to which I am gradually becoming calm and indifferent. Life is so much bigger than anything one does in it.

In November 1885:

Have been reading hard at Schopenhauer as though I were at Cambridge; and not a pestered foggy lecturer; and feel as if the world were just a great learning school, with really no time to be annoyed or bothered in. Wherefore, I try to say not 'so many dull people to chatter to' but 'so much stuff to experiment on'. And so even election speeches become tolerable. They were at it this afternoon—mass meeting. 'We 'ave the vote, we 'ave our rights, and now lets show 'em we can use 'em, by voting for the grand old man, the people's friend'. "As free trade brought depression?' (Yes)—'*I say No!*'
There were farmers in the train discussing Bradlaugh. 'Oh there couldn't be a worse man: 'E's an 'eathen, a Hatheist.
Goethe I think must be *the* man. I'm kind of bowled over by the second part of Faust: it really seems as though he did take his station among the stars and survey the earth in toto. Such a big world all round one, wild beasts of despair and morbid conscience and cowardice, gaping upon one. And how people fall into scepticism and pessimism and seem to themselves to be wise and deep, when behold they are only weak.

Having just read Wagner's essay on Beethoven, I summarise it to Ashbee and then proceed:

Would that one could express oneself and even see, for more than five minutes. However, I've seen to-night, and do at times have my revelation, and in some future time I'll be a great artist, poet, prophet, anything. Every man that affects me declares in his own dialect, that all have access to the spirit that is behind all art and all heroism: and I think the artist and the hero are those who are more constantly inspired than other poor mortals. I know that all that's worth having in life is comprised in some 'five minutes' which will melt into eternity. I will be patient and proud and soberly acquiesce! I had a vision the other night of the walls of the world falling in, and the perfect man rising out of the ruins. Fiat!
'God or the spirit throws off the world's harmonious systems, as the musician does his symphonies. Heaven is a state of perpetual artistic creation, idea and infinite expression of the idea. We stand to God as a work of art to the artist: only we are essentially both artist and his work.' 'All the world is a festal chamber waiting to receive us when we have learnt to trust our own soul.' 'This is me that speaks to you, not the miserable inefficient me that will be lecturing to-morrow to still more inefficient entities. Leben sie wohl. Isn't Plotinus a poet and isn't a poet a god?'

Later I send a number of quotations from Plotinus, with the odd comment:

Postgraduate, 1885-1886

Happy thought! The whole ideal philosophy is tacitly assumed by every one who admits the joy of poetical inspiration, i.e., by at least a quarter of the race—that's not Plotinus but me, on Tuesday morning.

Chester, January 1886.

How are all you boys? Whirling away the happy hours in blissful unconsciousness of the *Great World* where your unhappy brother is tossing? Tell Headlam I embarked on the *Parmenides* the other night, in a desultory way, and became a little excited. Really with political economy on the one hand, and mysticism on the other, what is a poor fellow to do? Choice of Hercules with modern improvements. That Farrer is a toughish morsel. One thing I learn—never trust statistics. Also, that there may possibly be some dozen of men in the kingdom capable of investigating this awfully complex question and delivering an opinion, and all others presuming to do so should be fined, or in case of recusancy executed. What a nice quiet world it would be then! How I hate popular government just now! Which only means that I haven't the same opportunity of observing the rival forms. I had five mortal hours of Quakers Quarterly Meeting. No more of that, thanks! Is it cant, sincere cant, or truth that they talk? At any rate, it's very strange and corpse-like, dead at least a century, the frivolous observer imagines.

Only one or two positive things I retain from that time. One is almost my oldest friendship, with the lady who was then wife of the rector of Mansfield Woodhouse, and with whom I have kept in intimate touch ever since. She had the perception to discover something behind my odd personality and my peculiar views. The other thing I remember was Chester, where Tom Hughes then lived and with his family treated me with much kindness. It was then that I met again the old boy of my London Dame's school, Pip Hughes, then fresh from Germany and Wagner. My relations with the Bishop, the then famous Dr Stubbs, were unfortunate, for in my contempt for the conventions I wrote to him addressing him as the Rev. Dr Stubbs, and perhaps naturally, though not kindly, received no reply. I also quarrelled with my secretary, a stiff lady, the daughter of the former Bishop, who knew much more about Tennyson than I did and disapproved of my views about him. Finally I gave universal offence by quoting a poem of Emerson's in which occurred the lines

> Kiss and couple and beget
> By those roving eyeballs bold

This sealed my fate as an Extension Lecturer.

When I left Chester in the spring of 1886, I went and walked in the

Welsh mountains, which I already knew from a previous visit with my family. The feeling of relief which I then had at escape from my bondage was passionate and intense. I remember ascending Snowdon, and the great torrents of mist that came rolling up over the summit, revealing and hiding by turns the precipices and valleys below. I thought seriously and passionately about my future life, and came to the conclusion, not on any grounds of felt inclination or capacity, but because of the objective value of the profession, that I would study medicine.

What led me to this was a combination of mysticism, science and humanity. I had already begun studying some chemistry at Nottingham, during my lecturing, and I remember stumping my teacher by inquiring why, when oxygen was a condition of burning, to inject oxygen upon a flame blew it out. He seemed startled and perplexed, and retired for some minutes before he gave me an explanation which may have been adequate, but did not seem so to me. My notion of science, at this time, was somewhat like what I suppose was that of a Renaissance student. Science was to illuminate and confirm a positive view of the world, and culminate in a mystic revelation; and the excitement of my first tentative approaches to it was very great, though invariably defeated. I have understood only too well Shelley's eager rush to the lecture on Geology at Oxford, followed by his blank and disappointed return. 'What was the lecture like?' said Hogg. 'Oh it was about stones stones stones.' So, I fear, were all my lectures and studies in science. The fault, I suppose, was partly mine, partly that of my teachers, and mainly the impossible idea I had formed of what science might give one.

The following letter, written to my father from Pen-y-Gwryd, gives my contemporary feeling about the choice of medicine:

I've been meaning for sometime to write to you about myself, and this seems a good time, after my first lecturing experience. I hope you've not been thinking me very desultory of late. I don't think I have been; I've only been trying to arrange myself, and get clearer before settling down definitely. At present it seems to stand like this. I find that for me, individually, philosophy, poetry, etc. is the real good of life: to be always learning something new about oneself and the world. I believe that is a fact: but also I don't find in myself on the whole a creative gift: i.e. I shan't be an artist of any kind. It seems desirable, therefore, to find some other basis of life; and in fact it is impossible to think unless one is working alternately. I don't find lecturing satisfactory in this way: and the last six months have been rather waste for me. It's too interrupted and desultory and prevents one concentrating. I've all along been thinking of medicine: intending to make enough by lecturing in time to start myself. But it appears that so I shall waste my best years. My head is just in good order now, and I could do good work. Perhaps it won't be, five years hence. So I want to know if you could advance me money for the time I am studying, four years I'm told. I don't want to be dependent on you any more, and we could do it somehow on 'business' principles I suppose. And it isn't necessary: I mean of course I can go on as I am doing and take my chance about the doctoring. Only it seemed worth proposing this, in case it were feasible. But I know you are bothered about money just now, so don't think about it again if it would be a trouble, or perhaps impossibility. I'm in a better position now pecuniarily than when I took my degree, so the time hasn't been wasted, even in that sense. Of course I run a risk in taking up medicine: one runs a risk in starting on anything. But that profession recommends itself to me on two grounds, (1) the humanitarian and (2) the scientific. For as far as I understand myself I want to be always learning with a basis of work among men. It's impossible ever to express oneself, but easier in a letter than in a talk, to me.

My father assented to this plan, and I went back to Cambridge in the October of 1886 to start the medical course. Then occurred one of my right-about oscillations. My friends had gone down. I went into lodgings. The place to me seemed dead, and the beginning of this new course an impossible burden. I got into a state of abject indecision and misery; and wrote a letter to my father saying I wanted to abandon the enterprise. Next morning, as I remember, J. W. Headlam (now Headlam-Morley of the Foreign Office) breakfasted with me, and I told him what I had done. He convinced me that I had done wrong, and I then wired to my father telling him not to open my letter. I should suppose he must already have opened it, but he never said a word to me about it, and I entered duly upon the course.

But the episode shows two things pretty clearly—one the incurable weakness which lies somewhere in my character—lies still, I expect, in spite of a kind of toughness I have grown over it; the other, the uselessness of taking up definite work merely because one thinks it good, in abstraction from one's own qualities. There can have been few people less gifted for scientific research (as distinguished from speculation) than myself; and few less qualified for the observation and manual dexterity that the medical profession requires. My later and more deliberate abandonment of it was already prefigured. I still think, however, that, regarded in abstraction from my own capacities, that profession is the best, and does combine the possibilities of that combination of learning and life which I wanted then and want now, and have very imperfectly achieved as things are.

Having settled down to the study of medicine (or rather of the preliminaries thereto) I became well enough satisfied. But I had no real interest in what I was learning. Here, for instance, are some extracts from letters written at the time to C. R. Ashbee, which show my state of mind about my medical studies and other things:

The Autobiography of G. Lowes Dickinson

October 1886

Fry and I go to a German on chemistry (this was Dr Ruhemann). It's the best fun imaginable. He's dramatic, tragic almost. 'Can we not—can we not—can we not—form also $(CN)_2$? I will show you that this is possible indeed!' (sensation) At the King's debating society is one 'who doesn't believe in 'ell and thinks 'Omer 'umbug'. The secretary tells them in a continuous chant: 'And England does expect that every man shall do his duty and I'm sure if you go home and think about it you'll see it is so, for you must remember that after all we're here legislating for human affairs, and I do believe it'll all come right in the end, and I'm sure you must agree with me that Right must triumph.'

I suppose chemistry *does* call itself a science, and not an agglomerate of facts —but the beginner is apt to be sceptical, especially if he's spending half his time in desperate attempts to arrive at a theory of knowledge.

This letter goes on to comment on Consuelo and on *Wilhelm Meister*, which I declare (in opposition apparently to Ashbee) to be 'the most objective' book I have read, i.e. 'the main part, before he begins bothering with his Lotharios and the like'. It is this objectivity 'that makes it so dull to a man like me, who can't attain the objective heights—not yet'.

I add:

The best thing in the world now is to slip off one's body in the antechapel from 5.30 to 6, and imagine one's a monk, or a saint, or a mystic, instead of an embryo medical!

Really, it's an unconscionable world. I don't object to doing my appointed grind. But that I should be expected to regard it as anything *but* a grind! Why, I solemnly assure you, there exist human beings who take a delight in human dissection; to whom the neat exposure of an artery is an adequate reason for existence. As for me, I don't mind learning anatomy, but I never will regard it as anything but an absurd unnatural employment, which could only exist in a vitiated and diseased society. Mon dieu! Surely to be beautiful and strong in mind and body is the only adequate satisfaction for a man. It's true, that is denied to most, but let us not forget that is what we want. The fact is, I've been reading some more Goethe and he does appeal to me, as the supreme type of the individual (as opposed to the social man perhaps). Have you solved the top hat problem? In other words, ought one to conform and how much? Please reply by wire, in the fewest possible words. I heard from Berry the other day and he says it's difficult to say whether the newness of my opinions or the oldness of my clothes produced the greater effect in Mansfield! Poor me! And I was always innocent of all offence! By the bye, we had the Kreutzer Sonata last Sunday, *I'm* not sure, after all, that Beethoven isn't preferable to Goethe.

While I was working at medical studies I was also engaged in a thesis for a fellowship. I chose the subject of Plotinus, whom, as has been shown,

Postgraduate, 1885–1886

I had been reading for a year earlier. I did two theses, the first, which was only an essay, for the election of 1886, and the second, a rather elaborate study, which was successful for that of 1887. My attitude to Plotinus was not critical but expository. I supposed that he knew the truth. The trouble was that this truth rested on a direct intuition which could not be communicated and to which all the elaborate dialectical preparation led up. Years afterwards Dr Inge published his treatise on the same subject, and I am bound to say that I cannot see that his method was any more critical than my own. Plotinus, in fact, brought me up against a dead wall so far as his route was concerned. But the belief in metaphysics as the method of knowledge persisted with me for many years, and no doubt obstructed any useful pursuit of science. For though I learned what was then taught in Cambridge, and passed the second M.B. examination without difficulty, I really got nothing at all out of it. It did not (naturally) even pretend to give what I really wanted, an explanation of the world; and this I was seeking all the time, and seeking, of course, in vain, in other regions.

CHAPTER SIX

Early Verses

At this point it may be worth while to say a word about my early verses. For though these have, I think, no merit as poetry, they are of interest in my biography, as most young men's verses are. The other day I looked through a collection of mine with very curious feelings. Some I had quite forgotten and could not recall having written them, even when I read them. Some brought back an immediate vision of the place and circumstances where they were written. I had done nothing of the kind all through my school life, nor since my early childhood, when I wrote one or two hymns which were but adaptations of what we sang in church. I laugh even now when I remember solemnly reciting one to my mother which ran:

> Woe unto ye pharisees,
> Woe unto ye scribes,
> Walking in the darkness
> Of your darkened eyes.

Then came the long eclipse of life at school. Then my mother's death. And it was just after that, I think, that I began to express such feelings as I had in verse. One little poem I dimly remember was directly evoked by that event. I cannot now recall it, but I do recall my mood, the twilight in the Backs, the scent of the limes, the curious mixture of pleasure and pain, romance and sentimentality, a world mysteriously opening on me just as it had mysteriously closed upon her.

These earliest verses were written before I had fallen in love (as it is called) and seem to reflect mainly an internal life, dim, confused, excited and chaotic. This is illustrated by the one following, which must belong, I think, to 1884 or 1885, though it may be later. I seem to remember composing it on a bicycle, riding along the Newmarket road:

> I wept and wept 'Alas my sin!'
> I prayed the Lord for pardon free.
> About him stood the seraphim,
> He did not look at me.

The Lord was seated on his throne,
  Beneath him rolled the night and day.
'Dost think' said he 'I sit and moan
  That thou art gone astray?'

Above his head the golden stars
  Circled and sang continually.
'Dost think' said he 'thy discord mars
  Their perfect harmony?'

Beneath his feet the earth was spread,
  The sound of men was in his ears.
'How many are my sons' he said,
  'How manifold their tears!'

The Lord was still and deep in thought,
  The heaven around him silent grew,
He mused on all the things he wrought
  And all the things he knew.

I heard a word—I hear it now—
'He made the world; and who art thou?'

The poem that follows was evidently written in the British Museum, where I spent long hours reading about this time. I used to walk round the galleries in the lunch hour, taken up, not really with the works of art, but with my own dreamings and reflexions. For instance, the busts of the Roman emperors stirred in my mind only the feeling of the transitoriness of history and life, with vague notions about a possible eternal mystical world, somewhere and somehow on the other side. I cite the verses as an example of this, not because they seem to me to have any merit:

The Elgin Marbles
Yes, you are dead, my Grecian friends,
  All dead! 'Twere vain to call you back,
Vain to return upon the track
  To look for you, your kingdom ends,
And so do all, save one.

That frieze of yours upon the wall,
  What eager youths, what strain of men
And fret of horses! How it all
  Pulsates with life! But then, but then
  'Tis dead, like all, save one.

Early Verses

The youth upon the column there,
    The languid limbs, ecstatic lips,
No garment cast about his hips,
    No crown to bind his waving hair—
    A Hermes? Well, he's dead.

That other opposite—you see
    The spread of wings from head to toe,
The dubious look that is not woe,
    And is not hope nor joy—'tis he,
    The Gentle Death—and dead.

Yes, and the scornful Venus too,
    Whose smile convinces her divine,
The Theseus torso there, and you,
    Centaurs and Lapiths mad with wine,
    You are all dead, save one.

All dead save one! And he? Behold,
    Proteus! You see him not? Nor I,
No man hath seen him! Is he old
    Or young, and doth he live or die?
    Enough, he is not dead!

I cannot now remember in what year it was that I had typewritten, and multiplied in a few copies, perhaps 20, the poem called 'Jacob's Ladder'. It must have been some time, I think, between 1885 and 1887. I still have a copy, which I append.[1] It shows the kind of view I was then taking of history, the ordinary (*then* ordinary!) progress idea, but running up rather oddly (as I remember the Rev. Page Roberts remarked to my father) into personal passion. The reason of this is that I was also taken up with McTaggart's mystic view of the universe (of which more elsewhere) and not at all clear (as, indeed, he wasn't and, I think, still is not) how the consummation supposed to be in eternity was related to a process in time. The poem is mainly imitative, as a candid friend remarked at the time, hurting my feelings rather. William Morris and Robert Browning, for example, are obviously drawn upon. And, as usual, it was the idea, not the form that interested me. I wrote it one summer when I was staying for a time at Toynbee Hall, most of it, I believe, in the Reading Room of the British Museum; though also some of it on the Thames near Henley, where my family then were staying, and where I went for weekends. For that reason part of it recalls to me the backwater above Henley on a golden summer morning, and myself lying there alone in a boat in a sort of ecstasy.

---

[1] A poem of nearly 700 lines in various metres, not here reprinted. *Ed.*

The Autobiography of G. Lowes Dickinson

It must have been a little later, I think, that I went to Paris one winter with Roger Fry and wrote while there a drama, or whatever it should be called, round Mirabeau. We lodged in the Rue de Tournon close to the Luxembourg, in one room at the top of a house. We took in rolls for breakfast and made coffee (I suppose) and had our other meals out. Roger used to go to a studio to paint (which studio I forget), and I used to stay indoors during the morning writing at this little work. I presume it has no merit and somehow am unwilling to read it through. I remember my old friend Adolph Behrens declining to criticise it, but saying it was not drama but a dramatic study. The interest of it, biographically, is that it shows me endeavouring to turn from mysticism to history. This movement expressed itself more completely in my first published book *From King to King*. And after that I turned definitely to writing prose history, producing *Revolution and Reaction in Modern France* and *The Development of Parliament* in the years that followed. These books are both out of print, and, though I have often been asked to reprint the former, I have never felt sufficient interest to do the necessary reading and writing to correct and bring it up to date.[1]

I am speaking now of my verse; and all of it that has any merit, or nearly all, is printed in my book of poems, not published but circulated privately among a few friends.[2] These are the record of my love for Ferdinand Schiller, with the exception of the few at the end which were inspired by Roger Fry. Of that part of my life I shall speak in the next chapter. The following, I think, were merely experiments in metre. But, then why these gloomy themes? There must have been some melancholy state of mind which drove me to try expression in verse.

> At height of a melancholy mood,
>   In a wet wild wood,
> Was one who sorrowed and sighed.
>   The last lights of day
> Flickered, and far away,
>   In the darkness, an owl cried.
> And he, the sorrower, sighed:
>   'This is the wood of woe!
>   What dawn will it know?'
>
> Dec. '91.

> The moon had spilt her failing light
> Among the vapours of the night;
> The tempest, like a beast of prey,
> Came howling down the dolorous way,

---

[1] But see, on this, later footnote on p. 144. *Ed.*
[2] *Poems*, privately printed at the Chiswick Press, 1896. *Ed.*

Early Verses

> Or ceasing hissed an undertone
> Known to the wailing owls alone;
>   Wailing owls,
>   Wind that howls,
>   And me, o me,
>   Undone!
>
> Oct. '91.

The following I find in a letter to Ashbee written in 1885. I cite it because it records the kind of insane subjectivism with which I was then afflicted and which recalls the *baccalaureus* in the second part of *Faust*. (I had not, I think, at that time read this work):

> The place is sacred, be thou still!
> A soul is stirring in the hill,
> The lake is conscious, and the sod
> Looks upward, all aware, to God.
> The brooding moon is steeped in thought,
> And all creation spirit-fraught.
> Here lose thyself, and let thy soul
> Assert her kinship to the whole.
> Tell her, though pent in mortal bars,
> She yet shall rule the arching stars,
> Order the change of day and night
> And dominate the season's flight;
> Dim the bright day's effulgent eye,
> And comprehend the circling sky.
> For lo! 'tis she thou hast adored
> So long, and named creation's lord.

The other verses I have date (I think all of them) after my first love for Roger Fry. What I thought at the time worth preserving of these is in my printed book pages 58 to 62. But I have a number of others, interesting to me now as showing the state of mind in which I was living about 1887 and onwards. One of the earliest of these I possess is the following, written during my first stay in Rome in 1887. The little poem that comes after that is more characteristic. And I see, with something of terror and grief, how early I felt and knew the hopeless torturing nature of a love which nevertheless was so absorbing and so dear.

At Shelley's Grave

> 'Twas meet that in the conflict rude
>   Thou heldst against a faithless time.
> No feeble foot should seek to climb
>   Thy frowning tower of solitude.

'Twas meet, nor dare I to repine
  Because I might not see thy face
Nor clasp thee in a friend's embrace;
  My spirit is no mate for thine.

Yet if, secluded from the stress
  Of battle, thou dost mark afar
And pardon, from thy silent star,
  This earth thou once wast fain to bless;

Or if this dome of azure sky
  May draw thee, and this cypress green,
To seek again the sunny scene
  Where twain of those thou lovedst lie;

Then grant that I, in some strange sense,
  May inly blend with thee, and take,
E'en for my poor devotion's sake,
  A portion of thy spirit hence;

Yet not thy wisdom, nor thy power
  To melodise the lightest thought
And speed it down the ages, fraught
  With strength and sweetness, be my dower.

To search the world beneath, above,
  Were good, and good the grace of art,
But ah, be mine the better part,
  A share of thine abundant love.

Rome, April 1887.

When truth forsook me, who had loved her well,
  Crying 'Then follow a shadow if thou wilt';
When poesy forgot her ancient spell,
  Saying 'My cup is spilt';
When faith with truth and poesy had passed,
  And Satan waited, eager for the end,
A voice within me whispered 'Stand thou fast!
  Behold, thou hast a friend!'
'He, loves he thee?' cried Satan, laughing grim.
'What matter?' said the voice 'Thou lovest him'.

Cambridge, May 1887.

The next verses I cite were published, I think, in *The Spectator*. I remember composing them once when I went up the river with Roger Fry to the mill at Grantchester.

Early Verses

Carmen Mysticum

Dear Lord, since thou didst make the earth,
Thou madst it not for grief but mirth;
   Therefore will I be glad
   And let who will be sad.

For if I load my life with care,
What profits me the buxom air,
   And what the sweet birds' choir,
   Or heaven's azure fire?

But if I cannot choose but weep,
Weeping I'll think I do but sleep,
   Till thou shalt bid me wake
   And triumph for thy sake.

Lord, since 'tis thine eternal state
With joy undimmed to contemplate
   The world that thou hast wrought
   As mirror for thy thought,

So every morn would I arise
And offer thee, for sacrifice,
   A spirit bright and clear
   As the wide atmosphere.

For, Lord, since all is well with thee,
It cannot well be ill with me.

                                             Oct. 28th, '87.

CHAPTER SEVEN

Roger Fry and Ferdinand Schiller

I turn now to the curious, passionate, unhappy, ecstatic story of my love and loves. I do so with the feeling that those who read, if they are what is called normal men, will not understand, and if they are homosexual, likely enough will find it absurd. Nothing isolates me more from other men than this feeling that what has been, and is even now to me, so inevitable, so strong and so pregnant with happiness and grief, should seem to them, as it would do if known, merely immoral, gratuitous or silly. The reason, I suppose, is that, normally, passion, leading to physical satisfaction in an easy and simple way, also passes quickly into the substance of life, and there, sooner or later, dies. In my case, owing to frustration, it has continued to possess me without ever being able to fuse with the other currents of life. So that, in this as in other respects, my life has never been harmonised. But then, whose is? I, at any rate, doubt whether I would even wish it.

I have told how in my sixteenth year I had stopped masturbating. No kind of sexual impulse, so far as I remember, stirred in me during the next eight or nine years. For my earlier friendships at Cambridge were quite untouched by that; and my passion was intellectual, mystical, confusedly directed somehow towards the mystery of the universe and of life. In the October of 1886, as I have said, I returned to Cambridge to begin the study of medicine. It is characteristic of me, as I was then, perhaps still am, that I was overwhelmed at first by depression and doubt. My friends had left; my choice of a profession, formed one day upon Snowdon, rested not upon interest but upon an idea that so I could combine science, speculation, and philanthropy. I seemed now to collapse like a pricked bladder. I have related how on the very first day at Cambridge I wrote to my father saying I had made a mistake, and how, when another mood supervened the next morning, I wired to him to destroy the letter unread. I doubt whether he did this, but he never spoke to me on the subject. I then settled down to the first M.B. and continued my medical studies until I passed the second in the December of 1888.

As I have said, I cannot feel that I profited by these studies. But I was not uninterested in them, and I was interested still more in other things. The Society of Apostles began to play a great part in my life, and, in connexion with that, Roger Fry, whom I had met previously in London. My friendship with him began, like other such relations, in a common interest in things intellectual. But by degrees—or was it quickly and suddenly?— it took a different turn. My remembrance is that, though I was at that time in search of love, I expected, so far as I expected anything definite, to find it in some woman. For it must be remembered, I had never yet been in love with anyone of my own sex. Then one evening, in a talk with a student of Classics, I discovered that the Greek love, as I had read of it in Plato, was a continuous and still existing fact. It seems to me, now, odd that this should have been a discovery, and that I should really have supposed that Plato was describing an exceptional Greek phenomenon. But, odd as it may seem, though I was enthusiastic for Plato, it was as a philosopher and a mystic, not as a lover; and I had not grasped the real motives from which dialogues like the *Phaedrus* and the *Symposium* sprang.

The realisation of the facts, I suppose, set free a current of feeling that was natural to me. And the next thing I remember is going one night into Roger's bedroom to say good night, and stooping down to kiss his forehead. This was a decisive moment. I went back to my lodgings strangely excited, lay awake reading (I think, Heine's *Reisebilder*), and said to myself 'I must be in love'. From that time, I grew more and more intimate with him. In the academic year 1887–8, which was his last at Cambridge, we lunched and breakfasted every day together, and every night I used to see him to bed and then kiss him passionately. The feeling of sex was now strong, but I did not indulge it, and should have thought it wrong to do so. There recurred also the old childish, I suppose really infantine, tick about boots, and I used to lie on the floor and get him to put his feet on me. He was fond of me, though in no sense in love. But I did not realise that, for I did not try to analyse either his feelings or mine, except that I knew I was in love and was satisfied to be so. Since then I have seldom been out of love, if the word love may be used of a feeling continually thwarted on the physical side. That question I leave to casuists and medical men, though without much expectation that they will have anything important to say about it. For emotion, which to me is the determining fact, lies outside their province, and usually outside their competence.

Was I happy or unhappy at that time? I cannot answer. My love was certainly happy. But as I look back, the confusion and excitement of my mind, my pursuit of studies in which I performed creditably, yet which somehow I did not really think would lead to a profession, my metaphysics, all the muddle and struggle of youth, extended and intensified by my circumstances, give me in the retrospect a sense of gloom, which may, however, be untrue to the facts. At any rate, it was thus that I passed the year 1887–8. Then Roger went down. He lived at first in his father's house, the judge Sir Edward Fry. This in 1888 was at Palace Houses opposite the Broad Walk through Kensington Gardens. Before that, it was at Highgate, a fact I remember on account of an evening I spent there in the summer either of 1887 or 1888. I went up there to dine; and I remember still with amusement how, while we were having tea before, a solemn footman came up to me and asked whether I had any more luggage coming. I had forgotten a white tie, and this was his way of indicating the fact; and the idea of a special portmanteau containing a white tie tickles me still.

All the evening I had no chance of a private talk with Roger or of any intimacy. As I left, he took me by the arm and regretted this. I went out so disturbed that I had to sit down on my bag in the road to recover. And I think I am right in saying that that night, for the first time since school, I relieved myself by masturbation. For some time thereafter I used to repeat this, though not often, for I had still a kind of ignorant and superstitious fear of it. Later I asked a doctor, who said it was better than going with prostitutes, though of course the proper thing was matrimony. I did not tell him that matrimony was precluded for me, but inferred that there was no harm in masturbation. Nor have I found that there has been. It has neither diminished my intellectual or physical life, nor prevented or tamed down my loves. That it is a *pis aller* is, of course, clear. But it is nothing worse; and better, I imagine, than what, to me, has been the only alternative, physical chastity. Weak-minded people, I suppose, can suffer from it, as they do from other forms of sexual excess. In itself it is merely a relief, and perhaps best called, as a friend of mine calls it, 'tossing oneself off'. It keeps a man of my temperament free from physical trouble, while leaving him open to emotional experience. That, at least, has been my experience for nearly forty years, and I commend it to whoever may have to adapt himself to similar circumstances.

During these early years of my relation with Roger I recall many expeditions into the country. Once I stayed with him alone in the family house at Failand, where Lady Fry, now ninety years old, still lives (1923). It is a lovely place. We sat in the garden and walked about the country. I remember an early morning sunrise, the sun coming up a huge red globe. I remember a hot walk, when Roger, who was afraid of sunstroke, plunged his head into a stagnant and filthy pond. I remember a wood full of foxgloves, which prompted the little poem printed in my book. Another time we walked along the Dorsetshire coast, from Corfe and Lulworth to Weymouth, and back by the valley of the Stour. Bathing at Weymouth, we lay naked on the sand, I holding Roger's hand. We slept in the same bed. And I recollect him saying to me, as we embraced, should we not go further? I said No, and did not want to. Why? I don't know. I believe I thought it would lower our love.

If anyone at all sympathetic will read Whitman's *Calamus*, he may come nearer to what I think was then my feeling than I can easily get now. Talking of these things, men are apt to suppose a continual strain. But in the open air, in health and happiness, that strain, though present, is subordinate—a background and condition of emotion, but not a tyrant, as it may at other times become. Then I remember, after a long day's walk, supping out of doors at Weymouth and realising, what so often I have felt before and since, the perfection of happiness given by physical and emotional wellbeing—a happiness which the young, and even the older, are apt to interpret, as I did then, as somehow revealing the nature of the universe. Alas, it is but a moment casually permitted to one of the little creatures meaninglessly produced in a world indifferent either to their happiness or their misery.

This first love of mine lasted, in this form, a year or two. That phase was ended by Roger falling in love with a woman. That led to explanations which had not before been desired or sought on either side; and I learned, what I had not known, yet also had not not known, that his feeling for me was different from mine for him. I still recall the conversation we had, late at night, in the house where he was then living, in Beaufort Street, Chelsea. I was unhappy, yet not very, nor lastingly. For Roger did not cut me off from anything I had had. Later, he became engaged, then married, and I saw less of him, yet still a great deal. All our life we have been friends, and I have indeed a kind of married feeling towards him. Now, when age is coming on, we seem to have less in common in our interests, for he has become more, and I less and less, interested in art. Still, I think our affection will last as long as we do; it rests on an intercourse so long, so continuous, so varied. At Dorking, at Hampstead, in Italy, in Switzerland, I see myself with him, and always happy with him. *That* love, at least, transformed itself into a perfect friendship.

This relation with Roger overlapped another, more passionate, more harassing, and more persistent. At Clifton School Roger had been contemporary with McTaggart, the philosopher, and one Ferdinand Schiller. I became intimate with both, McTaggart being, in those years (1887 and 1888), the principal inspiration of the Society of Apostles. Schiller I came to know well, after he had left Cambridge and was for a time resident in London. My first recollection of him as one for whom I might possibly feel love is an evening we spent together at All Souls Place. And it was, I think, in the summer of 1888 at Cambridge that my feeling became set.

Roger Fry and Ferdinand Schiller

He came up in June, for a few days. And what I remember now is going round to his rooms in St John's (I have a kind of idea they were in the first tower) and waiting for him in a curious (or perhaps not curious) state of excitement, reading poetry the while. I do not think he came. I think he was playing whist somewhere. And there is something about this typical of all my relation with him. For, though certainly he was, and is still, deeply attached to me, he never needed me as I needed him, nor understood fully what was going on in my mind and heart.

Then next, later in the summer of the same year, McTaggart, Roger and myself went to stay with him and his family at Gersau on the lake of Lucerne. His mother was the kindest, humanest, most pagan woman I have ever known. Her husband being in India, she had brought up her sons at home in England. Her devotion to them and to all whom they cared for was her almost exclusive motive for living. I remember as though it were yesterday our first arrival at Gersau, Max (now a K.C.) and Canning (now the pragmatist and don at Oxford), on the tennis court, and the dear lady overflowing with gaiety, kindness and shrewdness. There was a tennis court behind the house, a bathing shed in front. Close by was the church, with its clanging, pitiless bells. The house is now the Pension Fluhegg. How it lies bathed in sunshine and gaiety in my memory! There was a largish party in the house, and I shared a bedroom with Roger outside. We walked, played tennis, bathed, chaffed for a happy month. Then came the end, and Ferdinand, that autumn, left for India.

I was not then very unhappy, for, though he attracted me, he did not possess me, and I still felt more closely drawn to Roger. I returned to Cambridge and lived, in the following years, a curiously solitary life, working at the history of modern France, which was later to make my book. It was in 1893 that this passion fixed itself. Ferdinand returned for a holiday, and we went again to Gersau. He acted as host, and I can still see his eyes and teeth gleaming at the head of the table. It was that year that I wrote the poem about the ascent of the Rigi, and also the first of the two hymns to the Heavenly Love, which are in the printed book.[1] Both these are pretty faithful records of my then feeling, better than any I could now give. The kind of mysticism I then had I derived from McTaggart, but my love for Ferdinand gave it body. I cannot now recover it; cannot understand how I thought that this personal passion in transitory individuals could be the key to the universe. But the mood is, after all, well known and constantly coming up, at any rate in Europe, since Plato. So does a strong and passionate personality stamp itself on the centuries!

Well, that delight of Gersau ended like the former. Ferdinand returned

---

[1] pp. 241 ff. and 236 ff. below. *Ed.*

to India; and this time left me far more forlorn. It was in the following two years that I wrote the sonnets which are my best poems and which have, I think, really some permanent value.[1] They are the best record of my feeling. Every week I wrote to Ferdinand, and every fortnight he wrote to me. I have his letters still, and very melancholy they are, for he had the habit of reserving for them all the moods which found no expression in a life described by others, from the outside, as cheerful and sociable. To me these letters, coming upon my then solitude, were the principal events of my life. I waited for them, week by week, and often have let them lie upon my table, while I worked, postponing the pleasure of opening them that it might not too quickly pass. Then in the winter of 1894 or 1895 he fell dangerously ill. I waited some days fearing the worst, then heard he was better, and coming home.

That summer (1895) we went to Kandersteg. It was less happy for me than the time at Gersau, for I wanted more and got less of him, and I was often disturbed and bitter. I left Kandersteg in August or September, to go to the Wagner festival at Munich. And it was there that I wrote the poem beginning 'If in this house of music', printed in the book.[2] All my passion, frustration, aspiration, mysticism, is there expressed better than anywhere else. I will not here comment on it, for I am removed far away from it; and yet so easily get back again to it, when I read what I wrote. I will only say that at Kandersteg I had done my first climb, the Blümlisalp, and also walked, through the night, to the top of the Gemmi pass; and these experiences are reflected in the poem. I remember how I wrote it, sitting out of doors in an avenue at Munich (I could not recognise it last time I was there); and how all my passion, grief and mysticism blended with the music of Wagner.

That was almost the last poem inspired by that love. But the love went on, in the same way, for many years. Ferdinand returned to India in 1896 and came to Europe again in the summer of 1899. We then went for the first time to Sils Maria, in the Engadine, where the Schillers took a house at the end of the village as you come into it from Celerina. That summer seems, looking back, all happiness. We climbed a good deal. The air made me feel well, as I have never felt elsewhere. Ferdinand and I sat on the balcony, our arms round one another, reading Dante. And following him up the mountains in the dim dawns seemed to me the culmination of joy. Every night he kissed me good night. And that little ceremony, nothing no doubt to him, was a kind of sacrament to me. That place hangs all in a golden mist in my mind.

In 1904 Ferdinand returned to Europe for good, and lived with his

[1] pp. 250–63 below. *Ed.*
[2] pp. 244 ff. below. *Ed.*

mother and Max at Esher. I had hoped from that the consummation of my wishes, for I had always dreamed that, with Ferdinand at Home, I should have nothing further to desire. It did not prove so. His life in India and mine at Cambridge had led us on very different tracks. He was busy and constantly fatigued, and we had little in common to talk about. Gradually I found that my passion was waning, and we meet comparatively seldom now. Yet we are good friends, as we could hardly have been but for the long past, and I think we shall never cease to be that. It is curious to think that I do not really know whether he ever understood the nature of my feeling. The passion in it I am sure, so far as he felt it, worried him. He has never married, but his feelings of sex, so far as I know, are directed entirely to women. His not marrying is due, perhaps, to his pessimism about life, and a determination not to add new victims to it. His strongest feeling has been for his mother, and after her death I think he has thought nothing worth while, though he has appeared cheerful enough. He is an able business man, now fairly rich, and a collector of Chinese porcelain. Behind that sinister, enigmatic face what memories, what love, what sufferings, what joys, lie hidden away from me!

The poem that follows I wrote in 1904, and at Esher. It reflects accurately my feeling then, and, off and on, for many years; and for that reason I insert it, as it is not included in the book. Has it any merit? I don't know: I can't stand apart from it. It is, in some profound and intimate sense, *me*.

> By that bright soul within you that I find
> Beyond the self you show me, and behind,
> By the strange light that harbouring in your eyes
> Betrays your habitation in the skies,
> By that which, unintended of your tongue,
> In every word you speak is undersung,
> And by the touch of that indifferent hand
> That utters more than you can understand;
> For that soul's sake that, prisoned in the flesh,
> Grows consubstantial with the nerves that mesh,
> For that love's sake that, fluttering like a bird,
> Even from the cage makes the blue heaven heard:
> By all of you that is not all you seem,
> For sake of all of me that does not dream;
> Take of me what you will! And what remains,
> This element of earth with all its stains,
> This husk of love he hastens to disown,
> Though it be that wherein his wings were grown,
> This passion that, rejected of the soul,
> Is yet the deep whereon her billows roll,
> The sense that is the body of desire,

> The flesh that is the fuel of the fire,
> Yea, all of me that daily dies to live,
> I do not say accept, but oh forgive.

I have found one more poem, which is undated, but which must, I think, have been written later:

> Was it I, oh, was it I,
> Claiming intemperately
> What nature, who freely gives to all,
> Denied to me at my birth,
> Claiming of you what you could not give,
> What you loved too well to give?
> Or was it rather you,
> You who gave to the world
> What should have been given to me,
> Pouring out on the desert sand
> What my heart was cleft to receive,
> Till you were left barren and dry
> As I, as I?
> Was it I? Was it you?
> No matter whichever it be,
> For now irrevocably
> My heart is yours.
> Cast it away if you will,
> Tread it down in the dust;
> From that dust, when all is dust,
> You will pluck forget-me-nots.

CHAPTER EIGHT

Ferdinand's Letters

Since writing the last chapter I have re-read Ferdinand's letters to me, extending in a continuous series from 1888 to 1904, and after 1893 written fortnightly, a post card being sent almost always in the intervening week. My own letters to him, from that year 1893, were, I think, weekly.

According to his own account, he went to India to make money, not so much for himself as for his family. 'Frankly,' he says, 'we are all paupers and it is evident that a family of paupers can't live on each other's contribution to the family washing.' This word 'pauper' must be taken with many a grain of salt. I doubt whether there was ever any real reason for Ferdinand's anxiety. At any rate the result is rather ironical. For both his brothers are well off, and so is he himself; and as none of them have children there is no one to leave the money to. And, so far as I know, all this would have happened, whether or no he had gone to India.

If he were right in his constant judgment of life there (and of its effect on himself) it would have to be said that he had sacrificed his life to no purpose. But whether that really is so, who can say? For in some sense India made as well as marred him. And no one can say what England might have done.

However that may be, the correspondence seems to me to have an interest other than the merely personal to him and to me. There emerges throughout a character very marked, very consistent, very faithful and affectionate. I shall try to give an impression of it by a selection from his own words.

First, then, there runs throughout a pessimism which was not inert, nor passive, but defiant. This colours his view both of Indian life and of the world. Already in 1888 he writes from Paris just before leaving for the East:

I have been brooding over things in general with the usual result—utter disgust and mental prostration. Things seem altogether 'flat, stale and unprofitable', for I am damned if I can grasp this sorry scheme of things in any way whatever. I have been repeating to myself over and over 'Du bist am Ende was du bist' and that it can't really make any difference. I am almost beginning to believe it. Confound it! I am as savage and sore with the world at large as a bear with a broken head and my principal feeling just now is that I don't want to make any new friends. No man having tasted the old desireth the new.

He adds immediately, 'no doubt all this is very young and foolish'; but it continues over fifteen years. And though to infer a complete character from such letters would be an error, for Ferdinand is an active business man, and commonly charming and even gay in company, yet the deepest thing in him is this constant and, I suppose, inborn mood.

His first letter from Calcutta records his father's disappointment with him that he had not a moustache and, generally, seemed to have learned nothing of importance at Cambridge. He complains of the assiduous attentions of his servant, and finds that the only interests of the population are 'horses, racing, cigars and women'. As to his new work (bill-broking):

it seems to be absolutely indispensable that one should run about the city and grin like a dog. But there is a good chance of making money in twenty years or so; the fallacy being that by that time you will have lost the capacity for enjoying it when made. As for the place and climate: The gorgeous East indeed! Ha ha! It's one of the biggest frauds going. Any man who cares two straws about things in general must, in his heart of hearts, curse life under conditions such as hold out here. So you see it's a jolly prospect and by the time I see you again we shall probably be as far asunder as the poles.

Later he writes:

About the number of lies one has to tell I can't give you any statistical information, for the whole system is one vast lie. I admit at once that my professional work has great possibilities in an artistic way, for we don't deal in vulgar straightforward lies, but chiefly in the more delicate and refined kinds, such as the lie by implication.

He describes his life thus:

I rise at seven, dawdle till 8.30, breakfast at nine. 9.45–2.30 run about the city grinning like a dog, tiffin, and, till 5.30, a repetition of the morning's performance. Then to my suburban home, where I read or sleep till dinner time, 8 o'clock; then a game of billiards and bed early. So you see it's an absolutely colourless existence, without change, without end, day after day and year after year, it's always the same, and by the time one has saved sufficient money to retire one is about fit to step into one's coffin.

Whenever he speaks in general of his work in India, it is a variation on this theme. Thus, once when I had said that 'all men are merely fragments of man' he comments:

Perhaps you are right and let me recommend you to come here if you want anything in stomachs, livers, reproductive organs, etc, as we have a large selection always in stock.

This view of life is supported (whether as cause or consequence who can say?) by a view of life in general which is well expressed in the following comment on his brother Canning's philosophy:

I wish I could make out where Canning gets his faith in the sanity and rationality of the Time process from. In fact I want to know where anyone gets sufficient faith to attempt to universalise the bits of our experience. It's quite a small order, I doubt not, but somehow no one seems to be able to find time to give a really convincing explanation. . . . And please don't say that it's irrational to want to know, for it is at least as rational to have the desire as to want to content it by imagining that there must be an extralogical or suprarational method of disposing of it.

So, of McTaggart's philosophy, which believes that the Universe is 'really' (whatever it may be apparently) a company of pure spirits, related to one another by perfect love, he says:

I wish I were like Jack whose philosophy very largely consists in persuading himself and others that 'I want what I get' is the same thing as 'I get what I want', and the ridiculous feature of the whole situation is that he generally does get what he wants. It's preposterous, but I suppose the G.A. hasn't succeeded in classifying him yet and allows him to kick up his heels till he finds an appropriate rope to tether him.

In 1892, McTaggart visited him in India, and on that he writes to me in a tone I recognise as characteristic:

In a way I was glad when he departed. It was really too high pressure, and the machine might have burst. But one thing seemed clearly proved, that the stars in their courses are powerless to influence the immutable laws of sympathy, and however much one had always dimly perceived the truth of this, it was exceedingly pleasant to find one's instinctive gropings confirmed.

Of McTaggart's philosophy he adds:

We discovered a complete and most perfect specimen of a Hegelian category in Jack and his pony. As a student of Hegel you will scarcely need to be told that Jack represented the thesis, his pony the antithesis, and the 'ard 'igh road the synthesis, and that the two former inevitably resulted in the latter, as every well conducted category should.

He also cites the following two lines for a parody from the philosopher:

> When the Frys shall cease from Rogering
> And the Dickers sod no more.

Canning Schiller, now the leading English exponent of what is called pragmatism, was indeed a curious example of the contradiction of temperament by ideas. His temperament, I should say, is naturally as gloomy as Ferdinand's; but his philosophy is meliorist. What discussions we have had, Ferdinand, Max, Canning, and myself, in Switzerland, up and down mountains, or in the little sitting room, while Canning garnered flies from the ceiling. How forensically Max has argued, in his best barrister's manner, interrupting the flow of his eloquence only to beg poor Canning to allow him to speak for just one minute; how Ferdinand has sunk, after one or two passionate outbursts, into sardonic silence. How Mrs Schiller has protested against the noise caused by the slaughtering of flies with the newspaper—'Ach Gott, Canning, bitte, bitte'. How we have dissolved in laughter at the end, only to begin again. One little touch I always remember. Challenged by Ferdinand to explain why, on his pragmatic view, we cannot control the weather, Canning replied 'We can. We have made umbrellas'. And the indignation of the brothers! Or 'Is it not a fact that either the sun goes round the earth or the earth round the sun, quite apart from how we think about it?' Whereto the reply: 'It depends what you mean by going round.'

But I am digressing. Ferdinand's own attitude towards life is expressed poignantly in such passages as these:

> I had a curious waking dream the other morning. I had been reading Fitzgerald's letters overnight, and got to the closing years of his life, and in the morning I woke up, and as I lay half dozing, half-dreaming, the conviction suddenly came to me that I was dead. It was a most delightful sensation, and I congratulated myself and reflected 'Well I shall have no more worry and bother and can go and have a good talk with old Fitzgerald and a lot of good fellows on the other side'. When I awoke and found only the status quo you may bet I was precious disgusted.

Or in this passage of July 1897:

> I meant to have written you a longer letter but I did not sleep much, chiefly because a deaths-head moth made such an infernal row beating its wings against

Ferdinand's Letters

the panes that I could not sleep till I had expelled him (I know it was a deathshead by the feel of his clawed feet on my hand in the dark); and after I had got rid of the august spirit, my mind would not calm down, and so I lay awake a long time, thinking and wondering about this incredible Universe, and our life therein. I often wish I could pray.

This attitude was accentuated by the climate of Calcutta, which never suited him, and by the accompaniment of those more tragic and terrible events from which England is comparatively free. In June 1897 Calcutta was visited by an earthquake, of which he gives the following account:

The Earthquake June 1897

I was talking to . . . at the time, and the first thing we heard was a sudden low rumbling. Whereupon he said 'It's an earthquake' and we rushed out on to the flat roof and witnessed a most astounding spectacle. The house on which we were is surrounded on all sides by houses, and when we got out it seemed as if the houses all round us were going to fall in on us. I couldn't help thinking of the last verses of 'Childe Roland to the dark tower came'; for the houses seemed to be really squatting round us, chin in hand, preparatory to falling upon us. I had, as usual, any amount of black bile on tap, and I remember distinctly protesting against the unfair and ungentlemanlike fashion in which one was to be done to death. Like a modern Ajax I stood defying the forces of nature, watch in hand to see how long it would be till the whole thing collapsed. It is no exaggeration to say that the houses oscillated like swinging lamps in a ship on a strong sea; and in addition to that awesome spectacle the movement of the ground on which we stood was so violent that we were seized with most terrible nausea. Presently I heard a voice, as from a great distance, shout confusedly 'Run, run, man and get into the open'; but by the time I really was able to pay attention and recover my selfconsciousness the whole thing was over. . . . When I got to my rooms they had the appearance of a moraine to a first class glacier, and I immediately sat down, like another Priam amidst the débris of Troy, and indited a letter to my mother.

The same year, Calcutta was attacked by the plague and he tells the following anecdote:

Here is a little gruesome incident connected with the plague. At one of the houses visited a party of natives were seated on the floor playing cards. The inspector was struck by the rigidity of one of the players and on touching him with his stick the corpse suddenly fell forward. The other inmates of the house had arranged the little card party, in order to conceal the fact that there had been a death from plague in the house.

In 1900 there was a flood:

The Autobiography of G. Lowes Dickinson

It's a great pity [he writes] that you were not in Calcutta during the last week, when you would have seen an impressive spectacle of the 'might, majesty, power, and dominion' of the beneficent Being that rules this universe. What the Hell he was playing at he presumably alone knew; but he poured down 31 inches of rain in 58 hours, then paused for a bit and piled on another 89 or so in the next 72. Not a bad record, only it happened to swamp the place beneath. Really the quality of this mercy is rather more than we can appreciate. The streets of the greatest city of India presented an extraordinary appearance. Owing to the overflow of the numerous tanks which abound, whole streets were converted into swirling streams, which swept along, pell-mell, rats, snakes, birds and fishes, the while the melancholy lotus-eaters stood waist deep in the stream and grabbed at the fishes. Altogether about 100,000 natives are homeless . . . already cholera has broken out and there have been several cases among the Europeans, one or two of which have ended fatally.

That was and is the undercurrent in Ferdinand's life, and the deepest element, I do not doubt. But it is not pessimists who are either the most inactive or the most depressed of men. Ferdinand, who hated business in his soul, has always done well in it. And the more superficial stratum of his life—on which after all we all have to pass most of our time—was gay and cheerful enough; and that in the ways usually considered manly and sociable. Thus, in 1892:

I am brutal, athletic, horsey (haven't I just bought a mare which will buck you over a five-barred gate as soon as look at it) in fact everything that is requisite and appropriate to this land.

But he adds:

Somehow or someway, my dear old crock, when one has a body as inadequate as mine one doesn't quite get the satisfaction out of the pig and the pigskin which makes life in the East enjoyable to most of us.

This ironical reference to his body is characteristic. He was always lamenting over the inadequacy of *ours*, especially of McTaggart's, and adding that his own, 'though not much good, won, by comparison . . .' In the same letter:

Calcutta society has been suffering very badly from an epidemic of skirt dancing (you will find a full, perfect, and sufficient satire on it in a series entitled 'skirt dancing in a verandah. Vignettes.' by one F.N.S.) and at present a lady who calls herself 'La Belle Siffleuse'—better known as the syphilous one—is giving us an entirely new conception of the limits of classical music.

I am still engaged in a multitude of tasks such as re-arranging and bringing out a new catalogue of the books in the Bengal Library, stage-managing a play to be enacted in the tongue of the Fatherland, and worrying round to settle up a few of the rather complicated business affairs that my father has left on my hands. But when that is over I intend to be lazy and go out snipe-shooting every Sunday. It's not half a bad programme, I can tell you, and if you have never had a tub in the open, under God's sky, you don't really know bad from good, and without that the beginning of knowledge is not even possible.

Even business could be made the occasion of jesting; and he writes:

> Times is bad, master, and one is reduced to all kinds of shifts to turn an honest penny. e.g. I offered the other day to stand outside the banks with a placard placed round my neck 'we have better-looking men inside' . . . the only comment on the proposal was that it was rather unnecessary to have a placard.

The above illustrates a kind of wit, and humour, he had which seems to me —no doubt a partial judge—rather amusing. Thus, after a serious illness, returning thanks to a toast of his health, he said that the reason he had not died was that he was a man of the world, and death would have shown a lack of 'savoir vivre'.

In another letter written from the Riviera, I find the remark: 'Did you know by the way that, when Lord Ducie vacated his villa to place it at the Queen's disposal she wrote to him

>> Linger longer Ducie
>> Linger longer DU

(some read *Do* which is obviously corrupt).' I suppose no one remembers now the exquisite irony with which Yvette Gilbert used to parody the sentimental English song 'Linger longer Lucy, Linger longer, do'. 'As to the soul,' he adds, 'it's very quiescent just now. Somebody (a woman of course) asked me to lend it her, but I declined on the ground that it isn't negotiable.'

This kind of gaiety, in his more genial moods, extended to his relationship with me. Thus he writes from Paris, on one of his visits to Europe:

> My sister wrote to me that you were looking quite aggressively smart and wide-awake the last time she saw you. But then women have no eye for the really picturesque. On the whole I am of the opinion that to 'restore' you would only result in something absolutely inartistic and incongruous. You can no more become a man of the world by taking thought than you can add to your stature or—well, learn to serve at tennis. Anyhow I hope that by the time I come to London you will be wearing the right kind of hat, of which I append a sketch for your information.

This last extract reminds me of what too seldom appears in *my* letters, the gay and cheerful side of our relationship when he came back on leave. His letters and mine speak rather of that fidelity in absence, that forced abstention and loneliness which intensified, no doubt, on both sides, while it saddened, the friendship, and which, in my case, and very likely in his, had a powerful effect on the whole development of the emotional life.

I have already spoken of this, but these letters tempt me to dwell on it a little more. Ferdinand's own attitude to sex I have never felt that I understood. Some women certainly attracted him and he has usually had about him one, at least, who was devoted to him and he to her. I do not think he was ever homosexual, in the sense of feeling physical attraction to those of his own sex. I find in my letters only one passage which suggests anything of the kind. Speaking of faces, he says, of a friend, but not a very intimate one:

> He is one of the people whose faces I feel in love with and curiously I have never had that experience except with men's faces.

He adds that there is only one face he likes when he takes an 'objective view' and 'as for my own I simply loathe it'. His dislike of the faces of his friends he constantly recurs to! But if he had not himself the temperament called homosexual, he of course knew about it, and speaks of it sometimes as if he did not particularly reprobate it. Thus at the time of the Oscar Wilde case, he begins a letter: 'My . . . (mustn't use the words since the Oscar Wilde trial).' And he says that his mother 'is much exercised about Oscar's case and she has already determined that his plays ought to be withdrawn. What impartial juries we should have when women are eligible!' Again I find that he read Carpenter's little pamphlet on 'Homogenic Love'. Carpenter is not very explicit in this, but leaves no doubt what he is dealing with: and Ferdinand writes:

> I have read it and I suppose it's all in order, though I have a kind of feeling that these things are better left unsaid. Perhaps it is just because science has a way of treating these things as phenomena merely, that I think they should not be printed.

This expresses, well enough, what I have always felt, that the medical way of dealing with these questions concentrating on physiology omits the element of passion which gives interest and importance to the whole subject. But I think Ferdinand's distaste was stronger than mine, and it may have extended to the facts as well as to the treatment. Indeed, Carpenter's treatment *is* not, in that sense, 'scientific'. He goes on:

Ferdinand's Letters

On one point I think Carpenter is wrong. I don't believe the 'outward and visible sign' is necessary and essential, or even stimulating, except at very rare intervals. I have a kind of notion that you and I don't agree on this point, and it is I think very likely that my asceticism (which is constitutional) is au fond responsible for this. . . . Only, my dear, if we don't agree about this I don't see that it really matters. Besides you must partially believe it too, if you can say that you would 'buck up' all right without me. Unfortunately, I don't feel at all sure that you would, and it is rather too late not to feel responsible for you now. After all, it is much more endurable and perdurable than most of one's responsibilities.

This passage shows clearly that Ferdinand knew that my feeling was, on the physical side, more urgent than his. When, however, he refers to the 'outward and visible sign', he is, I am sure, not thinking of more than kissing and embracing, which in fact we used to do. I did not myself, at that time, desire anything more, or think it would have been right. But I desired that more than he did, and it, or rather interruption or suspension of it, disturbed me more than it did him. For what I needed and received was physical gratification, and I think he did not.

The key, indeed, to Ferdinand's attitude is given by the word asceticism. This, I think, must have been constitutional, though it received reinforcement from his whole attitude to life. In an early letter from Calcutta I find him saying 'I can hardly hope to escape my fate' (meaning marriage) and adding: 'It's a horrible possibility to have to contemplate, and hence my excessive bitterness to the other sex.' This I should not press, for young men have a way of so talking; but in Ferdinand's case the attitude persisted, and in spite of strong friendship with women he has never married. Later he says: 'One will always somehow, I think, be able to summon up sufficient resolution to pull oneself up, should one ever begin to drift towards the abyss which ends in matrimony'. But also he writes:

I cannot help thinking that I am unduly ascetic and I'm pretty sure that my views on the relations of the sexes are morbid—only as they are instinctive rather than rational it is rather difficult to change them all at once. But please believe that I am trying very hard not to be afraid of letting myself go; and that I try not to be appalled at the occasional glimpses that I catch of the 'abysmal depths' of personality. I daresay I should be quite sane on this point if I did not have such persistent attacks of the utter illusion of this existence. The other night I awoke from a dream of that kind which has vaguely recurred for several years now, with the intense conviction that my existence was not bounded by the turn of its present earth-life; and oddly enough it was a very unpleasant sensation.

That interests me, because, more than once, I too have had the sensation (not the thought, but something much more convincing) both that this world was unreal, and that reality was something very terrible, in which I had missed my way.

Characteristic, too, of us both, is the following:

You say you had rather that I were in Calcutta than living in domesticity with you. . . . True, O sage, but yours isn't a really domestic nature like mine (there's the pity of it that I am prevented from marrying).

Why 'prevented'? I know of no impediment, other than his own choice based on his own temperament and convictions. However that may be, our relation was very passionate, on my side, and very faithful and affectionate on his. As I have said in the previous chapter, it assumed its closer form in 1893, when he was home on leave for the first time and we spent a month together at Gersau. He writes after I had left:

I am glad you said what you did say, and I need not hesitate to tell you how much and how often I have been wanting you ever since your departure. I wonder if you can guess how often I went up the road and looked at old Pilatus, who immediately came out in his true character as a hoary-headed old sinner, now that you have gone; and I asked him a good many questions, some foolish and some wise, which he treated, however, with the supremest and most implacable silence. . . . Well, it is a satisfaction to me that one never somehow grows the crust that one dreads.

Then comes the rather revealing sentence:

Sometimes it really makes me quite afraid when I realise how much more love other people have for me than I for them, and then it always seems to me that I have somehow obtained it by false pretences.

The closer character which our relation had assumed, during this summer and autumn of 1893, is indicated on my part by the sonnets I wrote (printed in the book) during the following two years, and on his part by the fact that his letters now usually begin 'My beloved'. In the first of these he says: 'I wrote to you from Brindisi, and immediately after the despatch of that letter received one from you, which was a great comfort and yet greater grief. I wonder how often I read it during the voyage.' He goes on to speak of his mother. 'My parting from her was a terrible one—the worst because the most hopeless—and coming at the end of a series I'm afraid I broke down rather badly—for which I loathe myself.' He goes on, however: 'I have already plunged into the inevitable whirl of social gaieties.' In the next he says characteristically that there is a 'bruit' at the base of the aorta and that he is 'rather annoyed that I should not be without spot or blemish as it interferes with my idea of one's body as a temple'.

In 1894 he is saying:

I can't conceal from myself, confound it, that my letters mean much to you, so much indeed, I fear, that I almost think it sinful that so great an influence over another should be given to a mortal like myself.

Another letter ends:

If it is any mitigation, I will tell you that I want you almost as much as you want me, only, as I am ascetic by nature, the provocation keeps me going.

In the summer of 1894 he had dysentery and ceased writing for a while. I suppose I must have reproached him, for he writes:

I don't pretend to excuse my silence, though it will perhaps gratify you to know that I quite realised what that silence would mean to you. It ought to be both a comfort and a grief to you, this admission—a comfort that my moral nature prompted me to perceive the particular issue; and grief, that, having perceived it, I should have refused to face it. Tant pis pour moi, my dear, and you will, I hope, put it down to the diabolical side of me which is always prompting me to inflict needless torture on others because it imagines that the scheme of things demands thus much of co-operation.

Then later:

Seriously, however, I don't feel that it matters very much because I have moments when I get the kind of sensation that you are mysteriously present, or rather that I am with you, and then I realise how futile letters are.

Meantime, I was writing the sonnets, and I sent them to him in 1894. They are, at least, genuine, and in those years were my principal comfort. They are only what is called a 'cri du coeur' and no proof that I could have been a poet. But they are raised, I think, to poetry by the passion they express, and so far bear out Shelley's

>   Most wretched men
>   Are cradled into poetry by wrong,
>   They learn in suffering
>   What they teach in song.

Acknowledging them, Ferdinand writes:

Of course, and you will understand me, I read them with a great pain at my heart . . . for a man who though 'steering with a shoreward gaze' misdoubts of the existence of a harbour or an end—to borrow one of your similes—the knowledge of these things is bound to make him afraid. For myself, I think I can honestly say that I don't care what comes, but for the other people I do care most emphatically and more intensely with each year that passes in separation from them. At the risk of saying what sounds rather ridiculous and absurd, I will tell you that I only began to realise how intensely important my own existence was when I saw how much it meant to three persons in the world, my mother, yourself and Canning. . . . I feel that it is somehow wrong for them to care for me as much as they do. Really, my dear love, I am not worthy and I always feel a great fraud. . . . I believe I told you before that the chief reason for feeling that I am deceiving my friends is that I recognise in their love for me the element of passion which I cannot detect in my love for them. I do believe that I have a nature in which the ingredient is missing, and therefore the loss is smaller on my side though it fills the whole of one's being. At all events I cannot help thinking that a universal pity, even though it include the object of one's friends' affection, is not an adequate return for that affection and that is all that I as a rule manage to give.

This passage is revealing. It shows plainly that Ferdinand was aware of something in my feeling to which he could not respond. His, for all I can say, was better, and I do not know that it was less keen. But it was less passionate, if what passion contributes is the physical element.

In this connection I will cite a passage from a later letter, where, speaking of moments of strained relations between himself and his friends, he writes:

The bitter truth was that I did not care for them more than for my own soul, and that I knew that I was unable to clear the shadow that threatened to destroy the whole relationship.

He concludes:

And you will go on writing sonnets, won't you? and grow wiser year by year while I continue to tread out the daily measure appointed by the commercial mill, and we shall come out under the stars at last, though it may not be till 'that to-morrow when we are counted dead'; Amen.

As I am speaking of the sonnets, I may as well add here one that was not printed in the book but that I wrote in a copy of Shakespeare's sonnets which I gave him. He cites it in a letter, adding:

Ferdinand's Letters

It's very beautiful my dear, ain't it? In its way it's almost the best thing you've written.

It runs thus:

> Could I but sing, my love, as I can feel,
> I would not turn to Shakespeare for a tongue,
> Nor to an alien music make appeal
> To sing the love that never yet was sung.
> But of a thousand poets who have praised
> The softer love that hath a fleshlier end,
> Since he alone a manlier note hath raised
> To tell the finer passion of a friend;
> Take from his lips the prelude of a love
> Faithful as his; but not as his betrayed,
> That moveth not, though all the world remove,
> And in the teeth of death is undismayed,
> Writ in the blood that binds, the tears that part,
> Sealed with our lips, and treasured in our hearts.

Ferdinand's return to Europe, in 1895, had been a consequence of an abscess on the liver of which he nearly died. Naturally we were all, and I in particular, distressed more than usual by his insistence on going back to India; and I was no doubt very importunate. He suggests to me that my letters were somewhat depressing, as I am sure they were; but adds, writing from Gersau:

I'm not bucking up myself much. Somehow my departure this time is so much more harrowing than before and I really find it so difficult to leave the people I care for that I am tempted to wish this might be the last occasion.

> Better oh better cancel from the scroll
> Of universe one luckless human soul
> Than drop by drop enlarge the flood that rolls
> Hoarser with anguish as the ages roll

And yet of course as you have so often insisted one can't help enlarging the flood, both by abstention as well as by action.

But he adds that he would feel a coward and a shirker if he did not return. 'I don't put it on personal grounds, but though, God knows, I am ready to settle my account at any moment, I want to honestly and fearlessly try to live up to the beliefs and hopes that my friends have in me; not that I for a moment imagine that I shall succeed, but I mean to have a try, and if I fail I would like at all events to sink with all colours flying, so to speak.'

After his return to India, in 1895, it seems clear that he was continually struggling with ill-health. His letters become more constantly, I will not say depressed, but defiant and more seldom illumined with the kind of malicious gaiety which was also in his nature. In September 1896, he was laid on his back with a bilious attack, and was sent up to the hills, where he seems to have been able to walk and climb. He writes:

When I take an objective view of myself I get a picture something like this. On one side mea mater murum suum aedificavit and completely hemmed me in on that side: then came my friends and each pegged out his little claim on the other sides; and finally the devil and the deity came and hedged me in on the side of my physical health, so that now I have about as much scope as a yellow monkey on a purple stick. Not that I complain in the least, I hope I am obedient to the laws 'whose strength I own, whose justice I arraign.'

He goes on to speak of the 'immature warriors and the mature matron' who frequent the station and quotes a schoolboy's remark that it had an 'embracing climate'. Receiving my book *The Greek View of Life*, he makes, among others, the remark 'By the way, the Greeks must have been thorough men of the world, this world, Mr Dickinson, not the next, as you and Jack are always trying to be': a remark in which I recognise a good deal of truth.

From this date, 1895, it seems to me, from the letters, that he was carrying on a continual struggle against ill-health. He becomes more continuously gloomy with fewer intervals of gaiety. Such passages as these are common:

November 1896

No, my dearest crock, I shan't treat the recording angel's account as one does that of an inn-keeper. He can charge any items he likes, for aught I care, seeing that I shall have to pay both for what I've had and for what I haven't had. That's the beauty of the thing, you pay either way.

The longer I live in this world the more I find myself in direct and violent antagonism to all that is generally by common consent held to be desirable, and I sometimes tremble to think what the end of such persistent opposition must be. It seems to me that madness lies that way.

What a mess I seem to have made of my life when I look back on it. But oddly enough I cannot now feel the least little bit distressed at the fact.

Meantime, of course, social life continues as before, and he reports that he has found his true vocation as referee at a prize fight! Moreover, his years of return to Europe, 1899 and 1902, gave us our happiest times of all. It was especially in the latter year that we did, if I remember right, most

Ferdinand's Letters

of our climbing; though I had begun in 1895, at Kandersteg, and had also climbed in 1899.

It was in 1902, that I wrote, in Lugano, on my way home from Switzerland, a letter to Ferdinand which I never sent, but which I will here cite, as a contemporary record of how I felt. I quote without selection or modification:

Dearest and most competitive of pig dogs, I've written a long letter to your mother, but I have such a desire to talk to you, I must do the next best thing—quanto intervallo! which is to write. I find, on reflexion, that only two people have given expression to the experiences which to me are intimate and profound. One is Plato in the 'Phaedrus' and the 'Symposium', both of which works you ought to know better than you do. There's a metaphor in the 'Phaedrus' about growing wings—how Eros caused them to sprout—and how only the presence of the *eromenos* softens the skin, so that the feathers can come through and in his absence the orifices close, and get clogged with hard wax, whence irritation and trouble of all kinds; well, I know all about that, it's hardly a metaphor. The other chap is Shakespeare in the sonnets. And the one especially that begins:

> When in disgrace with fortune and men's eyes

and ends

> For thy sweet love remembered such joy brings
> That then I'd scorn to change my state with kings[1]

is so absolutely true to my feeling that I might have written it myself.

It's a curious thing to have a woman's soul shut up in a man's body, but that seems to be my case. And if you consider it in that light, it may explain to you some things that perhaps worry and perplex you. It has its advantages too. Only it's damned hard to manage; because the woman's instinct is to expatiate and abandon herself, and that's what you hate, and I don't say you're not right. Anyhow, out of the two elements there has grown, in these years—15 isn't it?—a kind of feeling to which I find no parallel except those I have mentioned, and which it seems almost trivial to call love. But the bother is, that the woman in me is always wanting to lose herself in you—and understands, to a discreditable degree, all the phrases about 'worshipping the ground a person treads on'. She wants to say things she has no business to; and the man knows jolly well he's got to have a life of his own, if the whole thing isn't to go to pot, and so he ups and flogs the woman, and so it goes on; and perhaps, if you look at it so, you may more easily forgive some of my extravagances. I have a body that loves you, as well as a soul, that's the crux of it all. You know that, of course. But you have no similar feeling yourself; and it's difficult to understand what one doesn't experience. For instance, to kiss you is to me a sort of opening of heaven; and to you I imagine a rather tiresome formula, or at most a convenient symbol of intimacy. I don't refer to that as regretting or complaining or anything of that kind. It's a constant wonder to me that, feeling as you do, you give me so much as you do. But I'm trying to state some of the truth with an even brutal literal-

[1] The misquotations are as it was written, and so I have left it. *Ed.*

ness—partly to clear my own mind, partly because I hate to think that there should be anything you don't know of on my side. Some things there must be—some things need not and ought not to be said. But I'm trying to give you a sort of key, and you can construct the rest for yourself. The other curious and provoking thing is, that our lines of life and our characters have shaped so differently, that we only touch, as it were, at one point of the circumference. In a way it doesn't matter because there's a kind of infinity where one does touch. But in things temporal it dislocates life in a rather distracting way. You care, I think, every year less and less for the things on which I spend all my time—literature and philosophy and such matters; and I, of course, understand nothing about business. So that we can neither of us associate our feeling for one another with our daily task. This gives me a curious feeling of living in two different worlds, one of which—the world with you—contains all the good I know, and the other all my duty. And that, of course, explains the shock and the break of leaving Sils and returning to Cambridge. That is, I think, the worst element of parting from you—that one goes into a world which you do not know, about which you do not care, which is, so to speak, cut off from you; and vice versa of course.

The letter breaks off at that point. And I add:

The above I wrote and did not send, but kept for my purposes, as a partial record of what is really all my life. But it is the merest adumbration of what I really think and feel.

I have no doubt now that I was right not to send the letter; just as I doubt whether all that I have written here should or will ever be shown to Ferdinand. For the truth is, I do not now know how much he realised, or what he would think if he did. After writing the letter and waiting a day or two in Lugano, expecting to hear from Roger Fry, who had proposed a tour with me, I put myself on my bicycle and rode on, and over the St Gothard pass; that is to say, I pushed the bicycle up those interminable windings, slept at the hospice, rode down to Fluellen, and so by boat to Gersau, where I broke in unexpectedly on Ferdinand and his mother. I remember then, as at other times, how his face looked different, more beautiful and more dear, than I could recall in absence; how glad they both were to see me; and what a happy few days we had, in that mild and sunny autumn strolling and sitting about the little village. Once too we got up and climbed the Rigi again at night, ten years after I had written the poem printed in the book. Nothing in my life with Ferdinand lingers more sweetly in my memory. He returned to India that autumn, but came home, in 1904, for good. He got work at once in the city, and is now, as I have said, one of the directors of the Credito Italiano in London. He lived in Esher with his mother and Max, first at a little house called Parkfield, later, and still, in what is called Esher House. I stayed down in the neighbourhood during the summer of 1905, I think it was.

Ferdinand's Letters

But Ferdinand's return, to which I had looked forward so passionately, meant the end of the passion that had desired it. I say, of the passion, not of the love. For I feel that, behind walls, the old feeling still exists on both sides. For we both have faithful natures. Still, for many years now I have not craved for his presence, as I used to. And when we meet, we seldom talk very intimately. His mother, after a little time, found the complexity of English life intolerable, and returned to Gersau. She died, later, of cancer, in the house at Esher. My last remembrance of her is an afternoon in the garden there, where her nieces and nephews and others were assembled, just before the operation, to take leave of her; for so it proved. She was as cheerful, as selfless, as thoughtful of everyone, as I had always known her. Walking round the garden with me, she begged me always to keep in touch with Ferdinand, for he would need me when she had gone. I have done so, and should have done so anyhow. But the memory of that most human, loving, humorous, pagan woman, is one part of the tie that binds us together. I have now, and for many years, no kind of physical feeling for Ferdinand. My love for him, I suppose, is more what he would always have wished it to be. Is it better? I do not know. It is certainly less violent, and less full of pain.

CHAPTER NINE

Some Letters of 1896 to Ferdinand

June 1927

Ferdinand gave me the other day a batch of my letters to him for the year 1896. That was the year after his return to the East in October 1895. In illustration of some of the points made before it will be interesting to put down some of the contemporary evidence, since it serves to correct or reinforce memory.

First as to our relation itself. On June 30th I write:

I'm writing in my little top room in All Souls Place. And do you imagine I'm not thinking about last year this time, when I jumped every time the bell rang, thinking it might be you, damn you! Well, well, well.

In October:

It's peculiarly cussed of the G.A. to give you the worst possible season and the hardest possible work in your first year out. I sometimes think, with a sort of incurable optimism, that some day some peculiar insight will be vouchsafed to you as the result of those unutterable external conditions. This day last year I said good bye to you. It was Friday and I saw the last of you from the top of a bus at Hyde Park Corner—a thing which often recurs to me when I pass there. I was wondering dismally whether I should ever have a glimpse of you again. Qui sait? Many things turn up in the 'changes and chances of this mortal life'. I had a letter this morning with the motto 'per incerta certus amor' which I like.

In December:

There are such gulphs between us. And though I believe, if we met, we should bridge them as we have done before, meantime we seem to talk through a constantly thickening mist. And you look only for indifference or cessation, while I look more and more for fruition with less and less hope to achieve it. At least I know it can be given to us, as we are, without looking to other worlds. Well, good night.

This last sentence interests me, but I can't now say what was in my mind. It certainly was not physical fruition, to which I never looked from Ferdinand. Oddly, as I write, it comes over me that some fruition there has been, in the fidelity of our friendship through all these changing years and moods and feelings—as though somehow we were indivorceably married.

This same year was the one in which Roger Fry became engaged to his wife—a thing which was to end so tragically in her madness. To this day, after thirty years, she still lives in an asylum—that brilliant beautiful woman. But it is idle to digress on that. I seem to have made, and indeed still remember, various excursions with Roger, bicycling in the country. That was the time when bicycling could be a pleasure, when railways had taken the place of coaches, and automobiles had not begun, and the roads, even the great high roads, were more or less deserted. In July I write after one of these little outings:

Just returned from Heathfield. Imagine, my dear, a tract of heather and beech and pine woods, and then the line of the South Downs with their eternal sleep upon them ('the sleep that is upon the lonely hills' Wordsworth says—but specially on the Downs, with the shadows in their hollows) and a peep of the sea beyond. And close at hand a great lake, down among the woods, where we walked till it was dark, and then came out upon a tower and saw, right across the night, the revolving light on the Eastbourne coast. I thought of Kipling with his 'song of the coast lights'. Then this morning we rose at 4.30, and rode up to Croydon—but that's all indescribable. More beauty in five minutes of it than in all my early walks in Switzerland, snow and all! That's the country I really love—still left to this dear England, and the best thing left to it. And so back to town and a swim in the Westminster baths just to remind me that we are learning how to make even our cities tolerable. Heathfield was the place of the Eliots, and the tower I spoke of is in honour of the Lord Heathcliffe who defended Gibraltar 'talis defensor' and for such country one understands how a man might fight.

This bit of patriotism interests me, for the only patriotism I know is one for the English countryside, now rapidly disappearing, I suppose, for good and all. But the Empire! What is there about that to be patriotic for?

In August we were cycling in East Anglia, and I find a letter from Woodbridge:

I write to-night merely to indicate the address—Fitzgerald's home. And for the last hour we have been contemplating his estuary under the full moon. More tomorrow, when Roger leaves me, and I shall have only too much leisure to use or abuse. Good night dear boy. Why are you not here? Why are you never here? By the way, Mrs Meynell has the phrase 'affection made vulgar by undemonstrativeness'. Just put that in your pipe and smoke it.

Some Letters of 1896 to Ferdinand

I go on, from Aldeburgh, next day:

Roger left me to-day and I have been feeling a little as I did when I left you at Kandersteg. Quelle vie! Who knows whether we shall ever have another of these expeditions which have been my chief delight for many years past now. Well, we have had a lovely day, a bathe in the sea after an early start, and ended up in the Dedham valley, Constable's country, whence I proceeded here.

It must, I think, have been a little earlier that I wrote the following from Cambridge:

It's 10 p.m. and I've just returned from bicycling. I started at 6 p.m. and rode to Overcourt, where there is a ferry over the Ouse and a little pub—sleepy river choked with reeds, watery sunset over the lonely flats, and one church spire in the solitude. Voilà, for repose! And all the way home a great tawny moon. I had supper at Overcourt and mouched about conversing with you. Mein Gott, how glad one would be, at times, to swap one's intellect and all the fever of this racing life for mere animal passivity. The river Ouse has done so. It used to be a great waterway and now it lies idle, swamping in weeds, its locks broken down, and has forgotten there is such a thing as commerce. This is the companion picture to the Thames in London, which has a greater poetry. But when one's tired one prefers idylls to epics.

This of Overcourt (now, I observe, written Overcote) is a recurring 'theme' in my life. Only a week or two ago I bicycled out there with an undergraduate. We crossed by the ferry and wheeled our machines along the green road on the dyke that leads to Holywell, and had tea there, sitting out and looking at the slow river. The meadows were full of buttercups and the hedges of hawthorn. The young man, charming as they always are, faintly stirred my sensibilities, and interested my mind. We rode home to a late supper, and smoked for an hour in my rooms, looking at Japanese prints. 'And so to bed!'

This same summer I was visiting various towns and inquiring into the working of local government. Thus I find myself at Sheffield and Manchester.

How and why it is [I write in September] that busy men will give up so much of their time to public work gratuitously remains a mystery to me. If the University world and the practical world could but come more into contact, how good it would be for them both. That's the question that's always exercising me. Jack regards it as a vicious heresy. But what's the good of thought unless it's energic and operating on stuff? The Spirit really does move eternally on the waters, and inspires every little fat-cheeked mutton-chop whiskered grocer who sits on a board of Guardians, whether he knows it or not. Perhaps it ain't so bad after all to die *épicier*. Well, my friend Doncaster here, late undergraduate at King's, will be a University leaven in Sheffield. And no doubt it's worth while continuing to 'cast one's bread on the waters'. I shall think so anyhow and not 'consider too curiously'.

From Manchester I write:

Yesterday I had a sort of field day. Went to the meeting of the corporation, and then was taken to lunch with the Lord Mayor and various aldermen and councillors. I assure you I'm becoming quite a man of the world, and learn to adapt myself to my company. The Manchester councillor is the most admirable of men, excellent at business, conscientious, contemptuous of culture, though partly pretending not to be (because perhaps he has a son at the University) aware in a kind of irritated way that society is not perfect, that there's a Labour movement etc, but regarding such things on the whole as the product of ignorance and of men who have 'no experience of business on a large scale'. Add the native northern self-conceit ('we don't know when we're beaten in Manchester') and stir the whole with a spoon of imagination—and you have the article. On Tuesday night I spent the evening at an alderman's house and we played whist—such whist as would have made your hair stand on end. My partner (a woman of course) habitually trumped with the wrong suit. However we all became very friendly over it. The alderman had been 40 years on the Town Council, and given far more time to public business than to his own, which is what 'makes us what we are', Mr Ferdinand Schiller!

This interests me, looking back on it after thirty years, because it is so characteristic. I don't know that anything came of these efforts to penetrate the practical; probably few men ever had less faculty for that than myself. But always I have hankered after it; always refused to confine myself to what really interested me most. I believe the reason for this to be that what interested me could not be fructified without mixture with an alien element, as I felt with more or less clearness. What we call genius or (in the case of failures) incompetence etc, implies a savage unthinking pursuit of the one thing; this gives us art or literature or science, but seldom a man. The man is the sacrifice to the work; and what profits is not he but his appreciators—if they do profit.

But I was and am always calling in question what I most like, driven by a feeling that one must somehow expand, and break the mould. Yet the mould none the less has been obstinately set, and I feel pretty much the same person as when I was 20. Love, literature, natural beauty, are the things I really care about. Yet I have spent most of my life in writing and thinking and inquiring into political facts and tendencies; with no result I imagine! So Wordsworth (si parva licet etc.) tells us that he had spent three times as long thinking about politics as writing poetry. And who cares now for his politics? But then there is this other thing, the making of the soul and the concern with the world, and its problems and labours.

I should add that my political opinions at this time strike me now as odd. I was still in a kind of Socialist-Tory condition, induced originally by Carlyle. Thus I find myself writing in October, half humorously I suppose:

The British Empire trembles in the balance and the Liberal Party is in the very act of disintegration, leaving a clear field for the Socialists. Rosebery's speech on Saturday stirred my blood. That's the man for me. I believe in the aristocrat; and if the democracy will believe in him too (which is a very different matter from licking his boots) why, we shall get along. A propos, half the mayors in England are now peers. Do you think men will ever learn that there is nothing heroic in declaiming humanitarian sentiments from platforms? Have 'em by all means and sit tight on them till they're wanted for action. Them's my sentiments. Jack has returned, as absurd and ebullient as ever. Wedd sardonic but not yet depressed. Berry overworked of course. I sybaritic with a chronic intellectual fever, and plenty of leisure to feed it fat. And so good night.

As to literature and my own writing, I find various remarks. One which rather interests me is:

Literature goes all wrong when it tries to criticise life instead of interpreting it. You will find someday that that is a profound remark.

I don't know whether it is or not, for I don't know what was in my mind. Or rather, I think I do know, and I agree. The profoundest literature has got past criticising. In that same letter I refer to a question set in the Higher Local examinations (for which I was invigilating) which seems still worth recording: 'Answer the following objection: Some particular dispensations of Providence seem to show a deficiency of goodness.' 'I guess they'll have their work cut out!' I comment. 'This is education.' In June I write, referring (I imagine, but am not sure) to the first idea of what became 'The Meaning of Good':

I wish you to note, my dear, that I began this morning my next 'great work'. This is to be a philosophic treatise on the theme 'the profoundest principle in man is that of activity directed to an end'. Doesn't sound very profound, did you say? Well, you wait and see! Meantime it's such a pleasure to me to get to writing again (in spite of the torment of it) that I begin to think it's necessary to my salvation always to have some writing on hand. To-night I'm going to try and squash in to *Tristan and Isolde*, with Macnaghten. Do you remember Macnaghten? I'm now off to read blue books in the British Museum.

The Autobiography of G. Lowes Dickinson

Macnaghten is now a Judge (I think? But how inaccurate I am!) Anyhow last night, at the Society's dinner, I sat next to him; always one of the most charming of men, and a great friend of McTaggart and his widow. I remember that night at the opera. It was the time of life when *Tristan* shattered me to pieces. We sat, I think, on the left side of the upper gallery, having squashed in more or less successfully. Later I sat there with Gilbert Cannan to see the *Meistersinger*. Cannan, I believe, after a career erratic in every way, is now in an asylum. How the world is strewn with wrecks!

Another reference to this book occurs in another letter:

My metaphysical book, which I'm trying to get on with, will be a sort of *Athanasius contra mundum,* except that Jack and Canning ought both to be with me. It runs counter to the method in vogue for every department of inquiry, a method which insists on endeavouring to understand by eliminating everything that is intelligible.

I suppose that this remark refers to a belief of mine, which I am still heretical enough to hold, that the most, not the least, intelligible thing is the human mind. Science discovers sequences of events by ignoring it. But nothing is more unintelligible than science. Psychology, on the other hand, begins to be intelligible, whether or no it begins to be a science. In philosophy I have always been a natural and instinctive Platonist in the sense that I would like explanation and think no explanation to be possible except in terms of Good. If anyone objects that this is chimerical, I don't know that I have much to say. At any rate, I shan't say it here, where I am concerned with stating the course of my life and thoughts, not with defending it or them.

These same letters Ferdinand himself reread after I had returned them to him. And he writes to me thereon, on 18 June 1927:

Esher House
Esher
Saturday

Dearest Goldie:

I spend a good portion of this afternoon re-reading your letters to me. What wonderful and delightful letters they are! And how poor and inadequate in the known conditions of my life in India the response must have been! Apart from the incredible malice of circumstances that condemned us to 'such an ought as never was, And such a Was as will be never more',[1] what a waste and for what purpose? Looking back I of course see that I really had it in my power to end the frustration and torture that it involved, although at the time it seemed to me that I was caught in an iron coil of circumstances. I ought to have burst through that bond and counted the world well lost for love, yours and my mother's. The torment of that thought I must carry to the grave, and no tears can wash out

---

[1] A quotation from Sonnet III(A) in *Poems*, 1896, p. 251 below. *Ed.*

what Fate has written. But though—as you say—you never influenced my conduct, you all the time moulded my soul, and whatever of virtue it holds is due to you and to my mother. And believe that, however undemonstrative I may have seemed, it was not really so, and I want you to know—if indeed you have not known it all along—that I always realised—from my undergraduate days—that your love was an incredibly precious possession. I well remember that when I first read the sonnets they took my breath away, and it seemed to me incredible that they could have been written to me, as I could discover nothing in myself that entitled me to such a great and overwhelming affection. Well, all I can say is that that feeling is true and alive today, and that it is the only comfort and solace that I now have.

For ever your affectionate devoted friend
F.

I replied saying that, as I looked back, I did not regret the absence, so far as our relation was concerned; since my physical feelings towards him might have caused a breach. He did not reply to this, which I daresay was not new to him, but the importance of which to me he probably never understood. I take this letter of his as the last word about our friendship. Nothing now, except death, is likely to disturb it. And though it runs underground, it is real.

But for him another episode has begun, on which I may have more to say.

12 July 1927

With regard to Ferdinand, another episode has begun. This year, a month ago, he met Miss Susan Ertz, a novelist. After a few meetings he was desperately in love with her. The first time this has happened to him. He is now 61. This passion is fixed in his mind by a curious fact on which he insists. He says that, for years past, every year, he has dreamt, and dreamt often, that a woman came to his room and said, when questioned, that she had come to marry him. He said 'Nothing of the kind. I don't know you, and anyhow I'm not marrying'. She replies 'Wait'. This dream-woman, not at first but presently, he identified with Miss Ertz. He says he never saw her face in the dream, for it was always hidden in a kind of mist. But he saw her dress (evening) and throat. He asked her to dine; and when she took off her cloak, recognised the dress and throat. This does not seem to me convincing. But the curious thing is that the lady was born in 1887, and that it was in that year that he first had his dream. Of that he says that he has written proof, or at any rate proof that satisfies him. She, however, is in love with another man, and does not offer any hope that she could ever marry Ferdinand, though she likes him much and they are always about together. I met her the other day and had a talk about the whole thing. She insists that there can be no idea of her marrying him. He is unhappy, and yet, of course, more alive than he has ever been.

The episode continues, but has led to nothing further. 1931.

CHAPTER TEN

Oscar Eckhard and Peter Savary

I will add here, as belonging to the same theme, an account of my last and still active passion, the only one with regard to which I feel I have something to reproach myself. The reason for this is the difference of age. Roger and Ferdinand were practically my contemporaries. Oscar Eckhard, the subject of this one, is a full generation younger. He came up to King's in the year 1908, when I was 46, with an introduction to me through his mother. I asked him to lunch, and there peeped round my door a fair head with tousled hair and blue eyes on a very small body. I took to him, and we arranged to ride together that afternoon. That was the first of many rides, for he had at that time almost no acquaintances among undergraduates. I thus came to see a good deal of him, without any idea of anything more than a pleasant companionship. I was, however, almost without knowing it, becoming more and more dependent on him during that academic year.

In the December of 1908 my father died, and in the spring of 1909 I went to America. I remember parting from Oscar with affection, but quite cheerfully, and carrying a pleasant remembrance of him throughout my tour. Our relation was renewed in the autumn of 1909, but as it grew more important to me, he began to sheer away. This distressed me, and my feeling, which I could ill disguise, more and more distressed him. We parted, in much agitation on both sides, at the end of the Lent term of 1910, and I wrote to him from London explaining my temperament and my feeling. I then went abroad with my sisters to Italy and Sicily, and got a reply to my letter, some weeks later, at Taormina. It was a short rather stiff note, which I, in my then condition, interpreted as an indication that we could resume relations as before, whereas he intended it to indicate the opposite.

In consequence there was much miserable misunderstanding and friction in the next term, complicated by the fact that Oscar had fallen in love with a Newnhamite and wanted from her the feeling which was forced upon him by me. Our relations became more and more strained, and on my side more and more unhappy. I behaved in a way which I cannot defend, writing him continual notes, worrying him constantly, and in fact behaving with all the absurdity of younger lovers. In the September of that year I joined his party (which included the lady) at Munich for a Wagner festival, and afterwards at Diessen in the neighbourhood. Oscar avoided me all he could, and I endeavoured not to see it. He was particularly unhappy, because the lady had declined at that time to become engaged to him. I went on with him and his mother to Baden Baden, and after a few wretched days there, he sent down to my room a note breaking off our relations. It must seem absurd to any outsider, as it almost seems absurd now to myself, but I was more overwhelmed with distress than I have ever been in my life. I left Baden Baden by the next train and arrived shattered in England.

On reaching Cambridge I wrote to Mrs Webb and cite here the letter which has recently come back to my possession:

I have returned suddenly. I am in great trouble. Oscar has broken off all relations with me. Nothing new has happened to cause this and I don't think I am to blame. I'm all broken to pieces.

I got into communication with his mother, who throughout showed me extraordinary consideration and comprehension. This was some comfort. He returned to Cambridge in the October term, and through a common friend we had a kind of formal rapprochement, but saw little or nothing of one another during the year 1910–11. The year after, we began to come together again, and in the Easter term of 1912 I first kissed him. The remembrance of that still moves me. But he, though meeting me in that way, had no answering passion and was constantly swept back by strong reactions. There was a good deal of friction in the months that followed, and a good deal of unhappiness and distress on my part. But in 1912–13 I went away for my journey to the East,[1] and the tension was relieved.

I thought of him continually during my absence and we corresponded. On my return, I found him very unhappy, owing to the unfortunate course taken by the love affair to which I have referred. I did what I could to comfort him, and we met from time to time pleasantly, though there was always the danger, or the fact, of friction. Then came the war, and he went into the army. The misery of this to me, the almost certainty I felt that he would be killed, is something I cannot even now dwell upon. I visited him while he was in training, and remember dreary walks in the wet, sleeping together in a wretched room in a miserable pub, the slipping away of the embarrassed and encumbered time, the chill of parting, the sense of despair on my side and of embarrassment on his. Before he went to France, we met at Winchester, and drove in a car to Micheldever, where I remember sitting

[1] See pp. 177 ff. below. *Ed.*

with him in the churchyard and strolling down a grassy track, very affectionate and friendly.

Then France, the uncertainty, the waiting, the brief returns, the passion of meeting, the horror of parting. I write to Mrs Webb on 8 January 1916:

I have not seen Oscar and I fear I may never see him again. How these personal things still tug at one's heart, in the midst of a world catastrophe! We're poor small creatures. As Goethe said, 'Man is weak and fate very pitiless'.

I was living at that time almost alone at Cambridge, dining in my rooms, for I was out of touch with the popular feeling. I used to write to him weekly, and think of him almost hourly. It was my one comfort, a comfort now mixed with terror and gloom. On his first return he came into bed with me, and we embraced with a passion of happiness on my side and with content on his.

He escaped alive from the war, and when the armistice was announced, by the booming of a gun, on 11 November, it was of him that I thought first. I wrote a letter, from the 'Nation' office, to express my feelings. He was then in England, having been wounded, though not seriously, in 1918, and not sent back to France. It was a month or two before he was released. We then began to meet again from time to time. He came several times to Cambridge, and everything seemed to go well. Then he had one of his miserable affairs, with a typewriting girl, a flirtation without her becoming definitely his mistress, absorbing all his energies, making him wretched, yet also tying him fast. Under these circumstances he was always impatient of me and my affection. I should add that, according to the tick I have referred to, I liked him to stand upon me when we met. I think this rather bothered him, though he used not to seem to object. We usually also went to bed together. And he was certainly kinder to me than, I suppose, I could rightly rely upon his being.

At any rate, last year (1922) after parting with me affectionately as usual, and even kissing me in the street, he wrote later saying he could not see me any more, and giving no indication that he ever wished to. I waited six months without replying; and then wrote saying I took him to mean that he wished to break off relations, that I consented, but that I wished to do so without bitterness, and hoped he would write me a word of farewell. He never did. And I have not spoken to him since.

I suppose this is the best thing that could happen. But I am pretty sure that, if he gave me the chance, I should welcome a return. I am sometimes angry with him, and often think he must be heartless. Perhaps he is. But more likely he is egoistic (that I have always known him to be), hypersensitive, and very unhappy. I remain on good terms with his sisters and mother, and so hear of him. He is in business, and apparently happier. I expect that really he was never easy, in face of feeling like mine, and I cannot blame him. Most people, indeed, would blame me, and perhaps rightly. But I cannot take any interest in these blamings and approvals. We are in the hands of something deeper and more violent than all that.

May 3 1927.

Taking up this story: Oscar is now married, apparently happily, and a baby is expected in the autumn. He is farming in Gloucestershire near Lydney. Last year he was in Cambridge studying agriculture, and I saw something of him. He was quite friendly and is still, and I shall probably go and stay with him this summer.

Looking back on all this, it seems, of course, silly and disproportioned, as I always knew it would. But I don't know that the old man's view is truer than the other. It is merely different; in other words, one is a different person. I can hardly imagine now being once more in that state of mind; but one never knows, since men seem to be never free from these onsets, at any age. I find myself, also in accordance with expectation, thinking the whole business of passion a kind of lunacy (*mania*, as Plato says), obscuring and interfering with the real business of life, which is knowledge and action. This is, so far, like Shaw's view. But Shaw appears to me never to have been in love. That is, he reduces it all to the illusion of lust, and one would suppose, from anything one can read in his plays, that love, as known to Plato or Dante or Goethe, was unknown to him. Perhaps it is.

What I feel at the moment is that this love business is at once important and significant, and also illusory, because no person can be sufficient to fill and satisfy the infinite desire of the soul. Which may lead to the Platonic line of development. Only the fallacy there, as it seems to me, is the use of the same word, and the implication of the same passion, in love for a *person* and love for *Good* in its various forms. There is no *bodily* passion except for persons, and the involving of the body makes all the character, the complication, the confusion and the tragedy of love, in the common significance of that word.

I should add that the morals of men or of society about this subject seem to me always merely foolish or cruel. But I expect I have said all this elsewhere. There is nothing more discreditable in loving a man than in loving a woman; nor in such physical acts as may seem appropriate to both persons. On the other hand, there is no superiority in the homosexual to the heterosexual love as such. Both are capable of all the depths and all the heights. It is only on what appears to be the Shaw view, that love has no point except for procreation, that homogenic love can be logically condemned. But nobody really believes this, as their whole conduct shows. Else, e.g., why prostitution? And why any copulation, except with a view to children, and limited to that?

On the other hand, as I say, I see well enough now how mistaken was my own early view, finding expression in Plato and appealing to me there, that the love for men is of a higher kind than that for women.[1] It may be, but it seems seldom to be so. What is perhaps odder is that it seems so seldom to work out happily, although in some ways conditions for its doing so are favourable; since society does not condemn or suspect the common practice of men living together. Much of the difficulty, of course, is due to affections which are ill-matched; some, I think, to the sense of social condemnation which disturbs and bothers so many people. But also it requires rather rare gifts to conduct a great passion. And then everything changes, tout passe, tout lasse, tout casse, in personal relations, as in other things. Broadly, I think that friendship, where there is no physical attraction, makes a better, because more permanent and disinterested, relation. For that only does not crave and does not importune. But that is all discussed in the *Phaedrus* of Plato, and even as I write these words and recall that dialogue, I see how hazardous are these generalisations. At bottom, perhaps there is nothing to say, except that there is one law for the young and another for the old.

I may as well add that I still feel an attraction and sympathy with male youth which I have never felt and never shall for female. Last night I spent the evening with some undergraduates listening to the gramophone. I am not the least in love with any of them, nor likely to be. But the subtle charm of them to me pervaded all the atmosphere. It is only when this mild radiance blazes up that trouble begins.

I conclude this chapter by referring to another affair which occupied me this year (1922). During the war, I met at Roger Fry's a boy called Peter Savary, a nephew of the Swiss lady who was then teaching his children. Peter, then sixteen, was sent to the Friends' school at York, and I used to see him from time to time. After finishing at school he came to town, and tried various experiments in dreary and ill-remunerated work. Finally, he was employed by the Friends' Relief Committee. This year, in the spring, he fell ill with influenza, and I took him away to the Isle of Wight, at Brighstone. We had a very happy time. After a brief explanation, he was willing enough to let me kiss him and embrace him, though he was averse from any further intimacy. He always took my arm when we walked out; and seemed quite happy and unembarrassed. But the affair with Oscar has made me nervous, and I dare not count on that. At present he is away in the Haute Savoie for the summer; and when he returns he may be on my

[1] It seems Plato abandoned this later. See the *Laws*.

hands; as the Friends are closing down and have paid him off. So that must wait. I am not worried about him, and perhaps, at my age, should not mind much if he wanted to break with me. But one never knows.

This story also I will take up again, 3 May 1927. It developed in a way that surprises and rather disgusts me in retrospect, since it shows how little one knows how one may behave in these matters. In 1923 Peter accepted the post of secretary and guide to conduct parties going out fortnightly to Samoens in the French Alps, not far from Geneva. I was at the League of Nations that summer, taking Murray's place on the Committee of Intellectual Cooperation. When that was over, I went out to Samoens for a month or so. I then began the old business, as with Ferdinand years before. Excitement, worry, delight, peace, torment, and all the rest of it. However, en somme, all went well enough. I returned to Geneva for the meeting of the Assembly in September, and, while there, was able to help Peter to get the place in the League of Nations Office in London, which he still holds and conducts with much efficiency and hard work.

After the Assembly closed, we went down to Italy together (Italian lakes) for a week or two. In the course of this I had one of my absurd fits which ended in a row. I am naturally willing now to attribute all the blame to myself. But once more what does that matter? What surprises me is the despair that overwhelmed me. It was as bad, I think, as my feeling after the break with Oscar at Baden Baden, described above. Fortunately, however, on this occasion it lasted only a few hours, and we continued our little tour without further trouble. I have been since then on very good terms with Peter. He is a curious boy—one calls him 'boy' though he is 28, because he has something so boyish about him. He is tiresome, teasing, but very affectionate.

I have just been away with him and my sister to Lyme Regis. We played a great deal of chess, at which he always beats me. He has no physical feeling for me, being entirely heterosexual, and having in that matter a good deal of unsatisfactory experience, against which he is in revolt. But he will kiss and embrace, though always in a teasing way, combined with a real affection. This particular relation does not now bother me at all, and I suppose is not likely to again. What does bother me is his future, and especially how and whom he is to marry.

So that's that, at the age of 65.

The following passages, being written in the year 1923 when I was at Samoens with Peter, will serve to illustrate my then state of mind:

I. August 6, my birthday.

61, older, but it seems not wiser. For two days ago, arriving at Samoens from Geneva, I met Peter—his face, so pale by nature, burnt red, his hair, that in the spring was a tangled mass of yellow tow, cut smooth and plastered down, as young men wear it now, but still the grey eyes, a little too close together, and the smile that suddenly illuminates his face, as the sun a landscape under flying clouds. He was friendly, as always; yet, as I write the words, a tremor seizes me. For was not Oscar friendly? And did not that end? And yet, even now, is not ended for me. For if, suddenly, he were to come, here and now, down the path under the checkered light, should not I . . . ?

Peter is kinder, simpler and more honest than he. That first night he came to my room, sat on my bed, let me take his hand and kiss him, kissed me. But that I know he does to please me, not to please himself; and, though he likes me, he would like me more if I did not love him. And now that we are together, and yet so far off—for he is crowded with people and business—I feel that old tossing of a sea within, and see nature as a curtain that may at any moment roll up on the drama of him and of me. Meantime, I will describe the curtain.

An ancient village in the Haute Savoie; in the centre a huge tree shadowing a seat around its trunk; the church with the columns of its portal standing on basalt piers; little shops; paths that lead out to the meadows and alps; where stand the chalets, brown beams on a base of stone, story piled on story, gallery superposed on gallery, the hay above, the living rooms below; a pot or two of flowers; goats and a barking dog, or a cow; in the shadow within, an old woman; outside, a man sharpening a tool. Away they stretch, up the green pastures, among the oblong patches of yellow corn, sparsely scattered on the slope that rises to a beechwood, where the old trees shadow, and make cool, grass and rocks and flowers. Beyond that, higher alps, then cliff upon cliff, and at last the first patches of snow. But in the valley and meadows everywhere are flowers, pink and yellow and blue, cups, wings, clustering tubes, while here, where I sit, cool under the sun-shot screen of leaves, murmurs unceasingly the turbid stream that flows from the glacier.

All this is real, determinate, independent of me; so that if I now fell dead, it would know no tremor or shock. Yet, for me, it floats like a curtain and suddenly will draw up, when a sunburnt face, two grey eyes, and a yellow head shines upon me, making my only reality walks with him, talks with him, and scenes that have wrapped him round; not here, but in England, the downs, the white cliffs, the sand hills and rabbits, of villages yet unvisited by tourists, in the Isle of Wight.

As I return from my thoughts that fall, a curtain upon a curtain, over the scenes of nature, what comes back to me first is the sound of running water, the great stream over the stones booming like a ground bass, and the rivulet beside me splashing counterpoint. Then I see grass, yellow in the light, green in the mottled shadow. The patch of shade in which I lie falls from a clump of pines, behind which, at its very top, shines a huge diamond which would be, but for the foliage, the intolerable sun, hung naked in a pale sky. Near by is a mountain ash, and other trees and bushes enclose the meadow, save at one spot, where, through a rent, shimmer below the stones of the glacier torrent. The meadow falls steeply, and over the green hedge at the bottom rises the mountain opposite, patches of trees and corn on the pasture, then, as the slope grows steeper, bare rocks and falls of stone, till all ends in a rounded peak, green under the azure sky. My eyes return and fix on blades of grass and three-leaved clover. And still the glacier torrent roars, and the little stream beside me ripples along in tinkling counterpoint. Next moment I am in another world; and in that, always beside me, one dear figure. An arm in mine, through lanes and over downs; a flash of white teeth; an arm about me and my lips upon a cheek; chess in a cottage garden; meals; the sea, and the cliffs, the downs and the rabbits, and the thrushes singing. Nothing more, nothing worse or better. But, of all the heavens, I would choose that one ever and ever.

Here, through no fault of his, how different! All day long I walked in the mountains under the shade of trees, and out on the burning pastures where they are making hay. What things I saw of beauty! A corridor of water in a wooden trough rushed down the valley, foaming along in a swift clear stream, while a rain fell from its interstices over the mossy ground. The woods were pines, one in chief, a deep dark green hanging from its drooping twigs like icicles, or falls of water arrested in the air. There were beeches too, and the ground was strewn with last year's brown leaves. Flowers were everywhere. I noted their forms and colours, sometimes their names—old names like harebells, buttercups, campanula, and others I did not know—all staring silently, in the shade or in the sun, waiting perhaps for the wings or feet that would brush the pollen to their pistils, or, fertilised already, letting their petals fall that their seeds might grow. Infinite life was there, I knew; and feeling, I could not doubt; and, for these hours, by chance I too a part of the life, yet merely an episode to it—like all the others, waiting to fall for others to take my place. I did not resent, any more than I comprehended. I was at peace.

Only, behind all this was that heaving sea. Shall I see him tonight? Will he come to me and kiss me? And 'pleon hemisu pantos' I said; that, rather than aught else, and the waiting for that more than the having it. But night came, and its stars and the glow in the west, and he did not come, and in torture I drugged myself to sleep. And now I sit writing this in the garden. He is in bed and needs his sleep. He does not get too much. The tall pink flowers shine, lights vibrate on the hills, and I, as always, wait, wait, wait, the same at 60 as at 25. Do we never learn and never change?

He came at 12. I said something of my night. He said gaily 'you ought to be spanked for it'. And so we strolled to the village and he saw me off to the hills, where all day long I have wandered, and sit now in the woods while he climbs in the heat some far mountain; as I did once, happy with Ferdinand. And now I am half happy, half disturbed. Does he care for me still? Do I bore him? How foolish to care! For the shade is about me, the insects hum in the silence, the sun declines, no soul is near. And what am I, alive for a moment, with this spread before me for a festival?

II. The meadow, as far as I can see, is a forest of hemlocks. A forest, for these flowers are like trees, except that their stems are green. They run up very smooth to the point where the first branch springs, so that no pigmy could climb them, though a fairy squirrel might. Where the branches spring, the green bark opens and spreads in a fan, out of which grow great leaves, deeply indented, as though they would branch too if they could, but flat and thin and pencilled with runnels for sap. The branches end in a great blossom, and the greatest of all crowns the summit. The blossoms are made of bunches of green twigs, bearing, at the end of each, a cluster of flowers, green in the centre, where they are still closed, but white all round where they expand in the sun. Of these white flowers three of the petals branch into double horns, the other two are small and oblong; and fine stamens, one for each petal, cluster round the pistil, bearing their ball of pollen at the tip. The whole cluster spreads in a plain of white light. About it the bees hover and hum; below lie the prairies of green grass. The sun is hot, and the plain pulsates with life. To the tiny insects it must seem really a forest; and what sense they have of it we can but guess, who have our own scale of size and our own colour vision, as they have, and not truer than theirs, nor than that of an archangel. How strange it must be to see trees bearing umbrellas of flowers, and to journey among them perhaps for many days! As for me, I rise, and in a few minutes am out of their wonder and in another.

III. Kant said that the feeling of the Sublime arises when we contemplate the force, the enormousness and the terror of nature from a position in which we ourselves are safe. I think he was right. For let the sense of personal danger arise and pass a certain point, and fear drives out aesthetic contemplation. This I felt the other day when I had lost myself on a steep mountainside with precipices breaking below me, and some doubt whether I could hold my footing, and by grasping bushes and trees and grass haul myself up into safety; or whether I should slip into the abyss. My heart beat violently, my lungs panted, not altogether, I think, from exertion. The instinct for life took hold of me, though I have not much reason to wish for life or to avoid death. But reason in such cases has no weight at all. Fear sweeps it aside, and fear is nature's device to tie us to life till she chooses herself to destroy us.

Today, on the other hand, and here seated calm and safe in a great wood, the stream foaming below, and the cliffs shining through the trees above, I feel the sense of the sublime. I seem to identify myself with nature, approve her terrific and inexhaustible life, admire her beauty, and forget that she has neither heart nor morals, even if she has intelligence, which is doubtful. Some think, as I once thought, that the inference to be drawn is that our 'real' self is identical with Nature's, and the shrinking, fearful, sensitive soul somehow an error or illusion. I cannot think so now, if only because I have learned to love and to pity just those individual shrinking selves. And what is all the majesty and indifference of nature weighed against the impotent undeserved woe of one of these little ones? Let me be frank! What is it all, compared to Peter?

IV. On the top of a hill a green knob. Green everywhere, falling down and rising up, in mountain, pasture, firs, shadows, the whole valley with its stones and its torrents. Patches of snow here and there. Eastwards, grey cliffs and one tremendous peak of Mont Blanc, blazing white. A fresh west wind; goats in a neighbouring chalet; voices calling from far away; else silence and peace, on the grass, and the great ox-eyed daisies, and the gentians tossing in the breeze. A few years, a few months perhaps, and I shall be dead. Others will see the pageant that still delights me as though I were twenty, or immortal as it. When I descend, I shall see Peter, seen perhaps better from here, and loved as though he were a spirit, not a tired overworked guide.

V. At six in the morning the valley and the hills were still in shadow, though white rays shooting up behind the eastern crag showed that the sun was hurrying fast upon his way. The village was still asleep, and, in the upper road I followed, the chalets stood still, their geraniums shining only to the dawn. In the upper village a figure or two was seen, a dog barked, a few fowls strutted and pecked. But after climbing the pastures one came to the great wood, and there for hours it was still and shady and cool, along the watercourse; and no sign of life appeared except a black squirrel chattering in a spiral up the stem of a pine. Only on the upper alp did one come into the sun's blaze. There the peasants, man and wife, were mowing the grass, and all the air was full of the bells of wandering cattle, while voices called from heights and depths. On the ridge, cliffs and tumbled rocks descended sharply. Suddenly there was a blaze of golden flowers; and at last, from a green knob, one saw Mont Blanc, the white domed summit and the long lines of piercing needles. There it was very still. Tiny crickets jumped so thick that the meadow seemed to vibrate. Two large ones were tied tail to tail on a blade of grass close by, in pleasure so intense they had no power to be afraid, and two swallow-tail butterflies pursued one another like flames.

Long I gazed, not in thought, but bathed in a sea of sense. Then down to the shade, where, lying still, one saw, from time to time, the figures pass that had passed for centuries—an old man on an ass, a woman with a basket of linen, a little girl carrying a cake from the village below to the lonely chalet where she lived. The illusion of peace and permanence was irresistible. Man, it seemed, was joined with the flowers and the insects and the cattle in one vast harmony. So have the singers of idylls seen it and sung it in the past; and so, for a moment, in the solitude and sunshine and peace, can the most disillusioned modern see it.

Then thought awoke and the tyranny of truth. The cattle with their bells are feeding; the crickets and butterflies copulating. Driven by those instincts, they prey, up and down the scale, on one another; and man the same, till his preying becomes the oppression called work, and the suicide called war. He may think, imagine, what he will, he can never deliver himself from those instincts that drive him from behind as they do the animals. And what that thing is that drives behind, or why, we ask in vain. The answers are our religions and our philosophies, which hang like a huge cloud, glorious or terrible in colour, in our sky, form and reform, disappear and gather again, and are but vapour over a solid world. Believing them, we are intoxicated; disbelieving them, we are sober; but in either case ignorant and slaves. For much though we may learn, we take no step towards learning the secret. Well and variously as we may swim, the current none the less sweeps us on. In science, in art, we may seem to escape, to look into the life of the world, to refuse to be the individuals we are. But the first toothache disillusions us; and pain, madness, torpor, ends at last, for good and all, the genius no less than the peasant.

That is no reason why we should not pursue science and art; they are our noblest dreams. But the stuff of our lives is not they. They control nothing, and explain nothing. IT sweeps us indifferently along, if any IT there be, for its own ends, not ours. We are no more to IT than our blood corpuscles are to us. They serve us, whether or not we know that they are there; and they do not know that we exist, still less know why. If they have purposes, their purposes are not ours. They are instruments to us, as we to IT. Perhaps there is no IT. One thing, however, is certain. If there is an IT, our beliefs, our morals, our aspirations have no validity for it. It says simply 'Feed and multiply; and, if you will not, perish sooner than otherwise you would. For you perish anyhow, sooner or later. What you do with the leisure chance may give you, here or there, is matter of indifference to me. Pursue science, pursue art, if you will, as once men built the towers of Babel. But be well assured there is no escape. There is distraction, if you can find it; and I do not grudge it, till the moment comes for the crash and the end.'

There is one other thing left, perhaps the best. We may be kind to one another, within the limits set by the prior satisfaction of our own needs; since we must live before we can be kind. This, which is Christ-ian, though not Christianity, and for which it would seem the peoples called Christian are less able than others, this seems to me, in my old age, the best thing there is, the source of the purest joys. It alters nothing that I have said above; but, within the limits allowed to some individuals, it seems the best way of spending freedom. Evidently it is not the *nature* of IT. Evidently, it is, if not contrary, yet merely casual and accidental to IT. But for us it seems the best thing, and some are capable of it. There are, first, the rare saints. But others attain a little. And even Goethe, the artist and man of science, said that he himself, one of the pagans, was the only true christian he knew. And perhaps he was. Those months or hours or years of kindness are the best way of spending the little leisure granted us between our birth in blankness and our death in catastrophe.

Yet I must add that to me, even now at 61, one thing blots out science and art and kindness; that is Eros. And one face, one laugh, the pressure of one arm, intoxicates me still. All I can say is that I know I am intoxicated. I dare not add that I wish to be sober.

Comments 1927

If I read such passages as these in someone else's works, I should probably be unsympathetic; as I imagine most people would be in reading these. I am still very fond of Peter, and he has developed and improved since those days. He has worked hard and well in the League of Nations office in London, to which I helped him to get a post that summer. I see him often, and we are on very friendly terms. But looking back, the feeling represented in the above seems extravagant. It is the nature of feeling to be such, and not less, perhaps more, in old age than in youth. I can only leave it at that. The trouble about Peter is that he would be better married, but has not the means and has not found the right person. I don't know how that will shape in the end, and can do little or nothing about it. His surface gaiety conceals a very hopeless view of life; but he is curiously boyish for his age. He is not in the least homogenic, and needs women. But he is disgusted or discontented with casual relations, and finds no permanent one. He is thoroughly 'good' and kind, as I know from many instances, and especially from the trouble he takes to make pleasanter the lot of Lizzie, the elderly maid of the lady where he lodges. But he makes no friendships with women of his own class. He has also no definite prospect of advancement in the League, and no effective power to push himself. These things worry me, but I can't do much, or anything, to help.

As to the views of the universe expressed in the passages cited, I have not much to say. As views go, mine are much the same now. But it is curious how little one's views affect one in comparison with one's interests or moods. It is an obvious error to suppose that a pessimist is a gloomy person, or an optimist a gay one; and I can still be interested in much and enjoy much. Also, although that view of the world seems to my reason the only plausible one, yet I don't see that I do effectively believe it. All sorts of half-beliefs, hopes, guesses etc. continually come up. Looking forward to death, I do not permit my thoughts to suppose anything but the end; yet I know that there is a feeling that it is all an open question, and that it may be quite different from what reason reasonably supposes. I have no belief in the hideous Christian mythology of hell, nor hope for its dreary heaven. In fact, I cannot fill my vague sense of possibility with any plausible imaginations.

I am still interested in the stuff that appears in the publications of the Society of Psychical Research. But I get no conviction, and doubt whether conviction is attainable, considering the different explanations possible for even what looks like good testimony (e.g. the wide extension of telepathy). Nor do I think that survival would be necessarily a good thing. It might be very bad, if, for example, it was at all like this life, as ignorant, painful and insecure. I can only record that my philosophic pessimism is much contradicted by opposite and incompatible moods, and that I don't see how it could ever be stabilised by incontrovertible demonstration. I am four years nearer to death than I was when I wrote what I have cited, and cannot reasonably count on any future. Yet I go on as if I were to live for ever. And I suppose so does everyone. What else indeed can we do?

I wrote the above at Lockeridge, Marlborough, 30 June 1927.

6 July 1927

This last weekend I spent with Oscar at his farm at Aylburton near Lydney, on the borders of the Forest of Dean. I found his wife a pleasant, friendly, competent woman, running the house well and cooking well, Oscar himself tired, and, if not overworked, over-busied; but certainly happier and more self-dependent than I have ever known him. It does not seem to me likely that he can make farming pay, and perhaps he will have to give it up, though I hope not. A baby is expected in October, and Doris is going to Lockeridge to prepare and recover. All that is good. It seems to me, then, that here too my troubled and at times very distressing relation has subsided into a friendship. This cannot be, with Oscar, as deep as with Roger or Ferdinand, because he himself is not as deep. But at bottom he is a nice nature, much obscured by various 'complexes', but emerging now into some stability. I find fortunately that I can see him without disturbance and leave him without grief. Here too is something saved; at any rate no angry scar left. And I am content about it. This, I should think, may conclude that chapter.

Oscar is now living at Chiddingfold near Haslemere, has two babies, to whom he is devoted—but no work!

1931.

CHAPTER ELEVEN

Young Don and Writer, 1887–1897

The account of my passions has led me away from the normal course of my life. For though these things evoke and possess so much emotion and therefore bulk so large in the memory, they really occupy very little time. And the impression inevitably given, in an account of them, that one's whole life was passion and distress or ecstasy is very far from the truth. My own life has been mainly one of work and thought, and I now return to that aspect of it.

In the year 1887 I was elected a Fellow of King's College, on a thesis I had written on Plotinus. I have already spoken briefly of this. It was never published, but is preserved with others in the library of the College. I don't think it can have been very good, in one sense, because it was quite uncritical. I imagined myself to be dealing with a man who knew the truth by some extra-rational supernormal experience. In fact, Plotinus does claim to have had this experience, and I daresay he did. The question would be, what value has it as truth; and that is a principal part of the whole question of mysticism. Mystics, so far as I know, have all clothed their experience in the form of the religion or philosophy they have been brought up in. The Indians are Brahminical, Plotinus Platonic, Boehme or Blake Christian, and so on. Whether, behind this, there is a common element in all the experiences I do not know; and I doubt whether anyone could profitably consider the problem who had not had the mystic trance. But those who have had it do not analyse and criticise. The question whether the trance is really a revelation of truth or merely subjective appearance would, in any case, remain.

I cannot claim that my thesis on Plotinus throws any light upon it. I wrote as a disciple, expounding the master; but as Plotinus is a logician and thinker, as well as a mystic, there was plenty to be said. Granting my standpoint, the dissertation, I expect, is pretty good. Anyhow, I had read all my author, and thought much about him and about his relation to Plato. I should say that there was as much in my treatise as in the book which Dean Inge has since published. I may add that he applied for and read what I had written when he was working at the author. For the reason given above I doubt if I shall ever look at my work again. What I recall now is the curious state of mind in which I was when I wrote it. It was written mainly in the reading room of the British Museum; in one sense not a bad environment for this oriental-italo-egypto-greco writer! But I really think that, for the time being, I was almost abstracted from the actual; and I mooned about the wintry and foggy London with a feeling that it was all an illusion and that some day, any day, I should awake into the real world. From the moment I finished the dissertation to the present time I have hardly looked into Plotinus. I wonder whether I ever shall again, and if so, what I should make of it?

On being elected to my Fellowship, in March 1887, I went for the first time to Italy. My companion was C. R. Ashbee, and we joined, for purposes of visits to the ruins, a party conducted by Professor Middleton. This visit made an extraordinary impression on me. The sunshine, the beauty, and romance (as it then was to me) of ancient and papal Rome, the marvellous country, the long trails of oxen in the Campagna, Tivoli with its garden and waterfalls, the Boboli gardens, the Pincian at sunset, worked on me like an intoxication. Then, as often before and later, the illusion possessed me that somehow life might, and could, be something far more pleasurable and passionate than it ever seemed to be to modern men, as it had been (I thought) to Virgil or Horace, and in modern times to Winckelmann and Goethe. I had not then, and never have had, any interest in the details of archaeology, and was mildly amused by Middleton's solemn enthusiasm over 'the largest block of travertine in the world'.

But an antiquity that was also an ideal and a provocation brooded over the place. I felt something still of that, when I was last in Rome, and perhaps should feel it even now. Rome appeared, and appears still, the true capital of civilisation; whereas London or New York are mere noisy crowded mushrooms. One remark made to me by Middleton still remains in my mind. He said to me once in a restaurant in Rome, that one really needed two lives, one to find out how to live, the other to live. Perhaps on that principle we need hundreds.

Middleton himself impressed me in those days as a kind of fascinating but inaccessible rosicrucian. He looked, I thought, any age, and always wore a black scull cap. His language had a frankness which offended our more squeamish Fellows. I remember him once referring to someone, in our combination room, as a 'bumsucking pimp' and repeating the phrase loudly to a Fellow who very hastily escaped from the room. He used to tell extraordinary stories which perhaps were the inventions of opium dreams, for he was supposed to take, or have taken, some such drug. He told us he had stayed in bed two years, and during that time accomplished his enormous reading. He had travelled, according to his tales, much and romantically, and expected to be burnt by Indians, and read Lucretius as a consoling preparation, and had called on a pasha in Turkey only to find his head affixed to his own door. He used to have stories also of China, but those ceased when Sir Thomas Wade, our late Minister there, joined the college. He had been a friend of W. Morris and the Pre-Raphaelites, and I have sometimes wondered what Morris thought of him. He left us later, to become head of the South Kensington Museum, married a Miss Stillman, produced a baby and shortly afterwards over-drugged himself to death; or so at least I have always understood.

It was in the winter of the same year, 1887, that I decided definitely to abandon medicine. The reasons for this choice are sufficiently shown in what has already been said. My Fellowship made me independent of my father, and I embraced the opportunity. My father, I think, was disappointed, but did not reproach me; he never did.

That Christmas, for the first time, I went up to the Lakes, with my friend Grant. We were to have started, I remember, at two o'clock in the morning; and I waited in the sitting room, dozing in an arm-chair, for my friend's arrival in a cab. He did not come, the cab having failed him, and I crept rather miserably to bed. We got off next morning. It was bitterly cold and foggy, and the railway carriages were not warmed. We reached Windermere, however, that night; next day saw Wordsworth's cottage at Grasmere; and then walked over Helvellyn to Keswick. The lake was frozen hard, and there had been no snow; it lay before us, a great extent of clear black ice. We put on our skates and enjoyed precisely what Wordsworth describes in the *Prelude*, though he is speaking of Windermere, cutting across the ice in the evening glow and under the first stars. The next day we skated along the lake to the far end, and went up into Borrowdale, where we climbed some of the mountains. One day, laid up with a sore foot and left alone at the inn, I read the *Prometheus* of Aeschylus and Hardy's *Tess of the D'Urbervilles*.

I recall this little expedition because it has left so vivid an impression in my mind; for though I never cared for outdoor games, having an almost preternatural ineptitude for them, I have always loved walking and climbing, and certain physical feelings on such occasions have given me more happiness than anything else, and, indeed even at my age, still do. Moreover, though I have now seen much of the world, I have never seen anything that seems to me more beautiful than the Lake District. The mountains look, one might say, as high as those of Switzerland, but are far more beautiful in form, and are also on the proper scale for human faculties, not over-arduous, and offering constant changes of beauty in a very small space; whereas Switzerland, like America, just goes on being the same, till one tires of it.

The Autobiography of G. Lowes Dickinson

It was, I think, in the December of 1888 that I went for a few weeks to Paris with Roger Fry. George Graham, an old family friend, was then studying art there. We went straight to his studio where I, still suffering from seasickness, lay down to sleep on his bed, in a gallery, and waking heard him talking below to his French maid. He was, I believe, no use as an artist; but he had the artist's temperament, and had wandered much about the world, spending some time in a monastery in Japan. By this time, I suppose, he felt dissatisfied with his life, for shortly afterwards he went into the Diplomatic Service (his skill at languages, I imagine, helped him) and finally became British Consul at Teheran. He was there during the war, was shot at, and nearly killed, and had altogether agitating experiences, which told upon him, so that on returning to England he had to go to a private asylum, where he died the other day. His constant friendliness, and his elaborate and courtly manner, are well impressed on my mind. He looked after us, on this occasion, most kindly, and introduced us to his friends, among others to Darmesteter and his English wife, who was also a minor poetess (Miss Robinson, if I remember right).

Roger and I took a room in the Rue de Tournon, close to the Luxembourg. He was studying art and I visiting museums and galleries, attending lectures at the Collège de France, and writing a kind of drama on Mirabeau. This I still have, though I have not the interest or patience to read it through, and I daresay it has no merit. Still, it interested me at the time. I used to write at it in our untidy attic, after we had had our roll and coffee and when Roger had gone out to his work. I should think that few young men ever got less out of Paris than I did. For to get anything out of it, it seems to be essential to approach it by the route of women, and that was no route for me. I am amused, as I look back, to remember a visit to one of the dancing places (was it the Moulin Rouge?) and my boredom for the short time I could stay. And also, how a very ugly old prostitute came up to me once, in some eating place, and began fondling me. I fairly ran away. Paris, to me, at that time, was merely a place where one continued one's own thoughts, in more or less discomfort. But, of course, I liked being with Roger.

After this I settled down at Cambridge. And as my income was small (a Fellowship at King's was then, and for many years after, worth only £80 a year) I started once more to lecture in the University Extension scheme. I now worked the lectures from Cambridge, travelling one term every week to Newcastle and back. Besides Newcastle I lectured at Leicester and Norwich, and, I suppose, some other places; but of all that I have a very vague remembrance.

The principal change that was taking place in me was, that I was shifting the centre of interest from a supposed perfect and mystic world behind Appearance (that is, behind the world we really know) to a possible perfection in this world, in a temporal future. But this shift took place slowly and confusedly. It was connected, I think, with my studies of Hegel, though I cannot remember exactly when these began. The inspiration to them was McTaggart, who, as I have said, became a very intimate friend from the year 1885 or 1886 onwards. To him, I believe, Hegel meant a release from his then empirical realism to the idealism he has since pursued. We used to read him together, in the English translation—mainly the Logic, both the great and the small. This, indeed, from the beginning was, I think, the only part of Hegel that interested McTaggart; and I was interested too, though in my usual way; that is, in a vain quest for some road that would take me into a mystic world, of which this one should be only the shadow.

Our reading, however, seems to me, in retrospect, to have been very unprofitable. We never really discussed the difficulties. McTaggart was more bent on getting through so many pages a day; and the whole notion (so preposterous, as it now seems to me) that the world can be deduced from abstract logic, and that, being so deduced, it somehow changes its whole character by merely becoming what is called rational, we accepted as a kind of article of faith. I was, however, myself really more interested in the applications of the Logic, though I was compelled to admit that they were not logical. Nevertheless, I believe that the real merit of Hegel is in that extraordinary survey of the life of man, his history, his art, his religion, which brought it all into a seeming concord with the postulated laws of thought. I remember sitting down, with a sort of intoxication, to a book like the *Aesthetics*, and I know not how long it took me to discover that this fascinating rhapsody omits altogether the thing that is specifically art. But in that it resembles most other treatises on aesthetics; and I did not then care about that. I wanted to see Reason progress magnificently through the panorama of life; and so she did, in the crabbed, cunning, imaginative works of that pedantic and poetical enchanter.

As for McTaggart, if I may digress for a moment about my old friend, at one time the most intimate and most frequented of all, he was, from the philosophic point of view, quite uninterested in the concrete; for he did not believe that philosophy could handle it, except—important exception —at one point. He held then, and I suppose does still, that in the relation of love we come into the closest contact we can attain with Reality; that Reality is an eternally perfect harmony of pure spirits united by Love. This idea is the key to McTaggart's philosophy, and the real thing that drove him to pursue it. The rest has been a continuous and (I suppose) vain effort to prove it by logic. The concrete and phenomenal world being excluded from philosophy, he was able to submit frankly to his prejudices, as something, so to speak, too low to be taken seriously. But if he did not take them seriously he took them very violently.

The Autobiography of G. Lowes Dickinson

When he first came to Cambridge, he was then an unkempt young man, thin, crooked, walking always with a twist of his body towards the wall because, as was credibly affirmed, he was always being kicked at school; and with amazing grey eyes, through which his soul shone. He was a follower of John Stuart Mill, a radical, and an empirical realist. But after a year or two at Cambridge, having discovered Hegel and become an idealist, he became also, for most purposes, a conservative. He has been, ever since, an imperialist, a believer in public schools and universities (of the older type), a lover of all ceremonies and traditions, of feasts, port wine, scarlet robes, professorships, mayors and corporations, bishops, the House of Lords, and in fact everything English except the House of Commons. One of his suggestions for the reform of the Upper House was that those bishops should be added to it who were excluded under present rules. He became, in fact, and is the most curious combination imaginable of Dr Johnson, Hegel and Robert Browning. He was at this time the most intimate friend of Schiller, Fry, and myself, the inspirer of our thoughts; witty, profound, sentimental, absurd, everything in turns, at once exasperating and delightful, and never more delighted than when he exasperated.

When I see him now, with all that shut in under so thick a veil, when I consider what he was to us and compare what he now is for younger generations, who hardly take him seriously, I could weep or I could laugh. Yet both attitudes probably are irrelevant. For the same man, I believe, is still there, behind the mask; and sometimes even now in the Society of Apostles, the mask lifts, and astonishes the young men with the vision of something they cannot understand or accept, yet cannot fail to be impressed by. The war broke off my intimacy with him, and I suppose it will never be renewed. But there are few men to whom I owe so much, few who have been more part of my life; and I salute him here, in words that he perhaps will never read, but that spring from a depth below our estrangement, from that common fountain in which once the springs of our youth were mingled.

To resume, it was not the Hegel of Eternity, but the Hegel of Time that inspired my historical studies. And an attempt I made to describe the Puritan revolution in dramatic and poetic form shows how convinced I was that history should be a form of art. I am inclined still to think so, and to maintain that it has never been better treated than by Shakespeare. But I also thought that it should be philosophy; and I spent much time, in these years, in reading the various philosophies of history produced in the 18th and earlier 19th centuries.

My book *From King to King*[1] was the result of all these influences. I

[1] *From King to King: The Tragedy of the Puritan Revolution*, published by George Allen, 1891. *Ed.*

started writing it one summer, 1889, I think, when I was staying at Thames Ditton with Roger Fry. This place, which is now almost a suburb of London, was then a small village, and very pleasant with its meadows, the Thames, and Hampton Court close by. The lines in that book of mine:

> This blessed isle, with all its congregation
> Of friendships made and making, this Elysium,
> Whose willow-glassing streams and flowered fields
> Invite to love and contemplation, this,
> Which like a spirit sings in the cuckoo's voice

and so on, recall to me now the early summer meadows, a young foal in the grass, Roger himself and thoughts of Ferdinand, and then, a stroll in the moonlight and Milton's *Penseroso*. I have still a weakness for that little book, the first I printed; for I believe it was a good idea of handling history, that the moments were well chosen, and the drama succinctly unrolled, from Eliot in the Tower to the execution of Vane. And the words of Mr Pepys introduced at the close of all still strike me as an admirable ironic commentary on the whole. I suppose, however, that the execution was inadequate. Anyhow the book excited no interest; it was not long before the remainder copies were distributed, and it has never been reprinted in England, though there was an American edition, brought out some years ago, which, however, had no sale.

While writing this little book, I was also beginning to study the French Revolution, which led me on to the later history of France; since I wanted to see what had come of the Revolution, and to test (or ought I to say, to impose upon history?) my rather vague and tentative theory of progress. I lectured on this subject—at Norwich, I think—and then put my results into a book which afterwards appeared under the title *Revolution and Reaction in Modern France*. It is written in a very odd, and I should say not very satisfactory style. I had not written any prose to speak of, and had to learn how to do it. And I well remember sitting a whole morning at my table trying to write down the first sentence, and dissatisfied with every attempt. I record this only as an example of the way not to do it. My advice to any young author would be now: 'Begin anyhow and get into a swing. You can always return later and correct your opening sentences.' But such advice, of course, would be useless, for everyone has to find his own way, and make his own mistakes. The style I evolve in this book, a series of very short sentences, grouped into paragraphs and unconnected except by the colon, which I misused for the purpose, is not good. But it was sincere, in the sense that I was determined to avoid all mere talk and meaningless empty phrases, such as fill so many textbooks of history. I finished the book in the summer of 1892, going over for week-ends to Blythburgh in Suffolk, where Roger Fry and my old friend Wedd were then staying.[1]

This was a welcome change from the depressing climate of Cambridge, which I have felt all my life to have a pernicious influence upon me. My book was well reported on by Lord Acton. But when the renewal of my Fellowship came up, it was defeated by one vote. I remember how I was sitting in my rooms, playing the piano, when my friend Laurie brought me this news. I think I was more excited than distressed; for in fact I rather liked the idea of going to town and being thrown on my own resources. What would have become of me in that case, for good or for evil, it is idle to speculate. In fact, the afternoon meeting of the Governing body solved the question by appointing me librarian, a practically sinecure office which carried a Fellowship. So I remained at Cambridge. This occurred in the November of 1892.

I stayed on, then, at Cambridge, and at first there was little difference in my life, which was more solitary then than it has ever been since. I sat down to study the Parliamentary history of England, from the first Reform Bill onwards; still with the idea that the history of the recent past would give guidance for the future. I ploughed through debates, pamphlets, histories, innumerable "dry as dust" stuff, which ultimately turned into the book *The Development of Parliament in the Nineteenth Century*, which was published in the year 1895, but has long been out of print and never reprinted. As may be seen from this book, I was then, in my political opinions, a kind of Socialistic Tory. This was due, I suppose, on the one hand, to a contempt for the House of Commons as I imagined it to have become, a contempt really based upon Carlyle; and an absurd belief in the House of Lords, based upon nothing but antagonism to the Commons. I am bound to say, however, that both Houses during the war did much to justify that opinion. On the other hand, I had become a kind of academic Socialist, partly from my reading in French socialism, partly from the writings of the Fabian Society.

About this time I had arranged that the then leaders of that Society should come to King's College and lecture. There came Webb, Shaw, Clerk, Bland, Olivier. Webb I remember becoming involved by McTaggart in philosophy, and scored off in a kind of debating way which did not go deep but naturally rather annoyed him. Bland talked football to the young men. But the real event was Bernard Shaw, the most amusing of men, whom, I fear, we treated rather badly, for after a long evening in my then very cold rooms we saw him to bed about 2 a.m., and after that, I rather think, he was visited by some drunken revellers. At lunch next day he described inimitably his Irish relations, especially an uncle who thought

[1] This book I have now (May 1927) agreed to reprint substantially unaltered.

he was in Heaven, and hung himself up in a basket from the ceiling dressed in gauze. Seeing we had pianos in our rooms, and shared one another's commons, Shaw pronounced that we were already Socialists, in his sense. His lecture was brilliant. It was attended by Professor Westcott, afterwards Bishop of Durham; and he requested me to find out from Shaw what his moral basis was. I inquired, and received on a post card the following message: 'Ask the old boy what his is, and tell him mine's the same.'

To return to my book, if I was not then a fully convinced Socialist, I saw at least that the question of labour and capital would overshadow all others in the future. Of foreign politics and war I was not then thinking. This is expressed in the book, which was at any rate genuine and sincere. Its weakness was that it was written from a place so remote from the actualities of politics; and from that point of view the annoyance or contempt of such practical radicals or socialists as attended to it was probably justified. Here I am concerned with it only as an indication of my attitude at this time. I had had, since my early youth, the double impulse, both to deal with contemporary problems and to maintain detachment and impartiality. Perhaps this is really impossible. But the impulse kept me, through all my Cambridge life, in a state of tension and unrest. In some ways Cambridge suited me extraordinarily well. The stream of young men, the good talk, the speculation and metaphysics of my particular friends, the beauty and leisure, and gaiety attracted me. At the same time, I always felt that the 'real business' of the world went on outside. I wanted to bring the two things into contact, so that our thought should influence events, and events our thought. This kept me then, and indeed has kept me all my life, in a kind of tension. I could never 'plunge', so to speak, either inside or outside, and my position has been like that outlined in one of my early poems:

> Not wholly from the world withdrawn
> Nor wholly to its service sworn.[1]

I suffered in this way from a continual restlessness, which, even in later years, still haunts me, and which belongs, I suppose, in some way to my character. It was, however, more marked in these earlier years, when I was constantly thinking that I should end in leaving Cambridge. The character of my books is partly to be explained by this condition. I never wanted to write learned or scholarly works. I wanted to influence opinion and the course of events. I cultivated therefore a style as succinct and lucid as I could, and chose my subjects with great care, with that end in view. Whether I have been at all successful I doubt. Events can be influenced by thought, but only if the thought is more original than mine has ever

[1] This is very bad verse, but very true psychologically.

been, and the personality behind it more massive. Voltaire and Rousseau did for France, and Marx for Germany and the world, what I should have liked to do for England. But have we any real parallel to such writers in England? I think we are too indifferent and too averse from ideas.

In the year 1896 my position at Cambridge changed. I resigned the Librarianship, and was made an 'Annual Lecturer'. I was to take essays and to lecture on what was then known as 'Analytic and Deductive Politics'. Previously I had been getting more and more solitary, spending whole days at work without any engagements, and seeing very little of any company. My teaching work now brought me into touch with undergraduates. From that time on, till I resigned my lectureship in 1920, I had a set of men assigned to me for the two winter terms for essays. I liked this work. It brought me into direct contact with individuals, and though these were not commonly remarkable, and sometimes stupid, there were always one or two who were clever and alive. I usually managed somehow to get into touch with, and to feel an interest in, even the comparatively stupid.

To this I was, of course, helped by a temperament which was always ready to go out in sympathy to any young man. There are, I believe, in Cambridge, from the nature of the case, an unusual number of such temperaments, though they may not always be aware of themselves; and I have no doubt that, next to the intercourse of the young men with each other, their intercourse of a personal kind with sympathetic teachers is the best thing Cambridge has to give. Probably, or possibly, future reform will abolish this, without knowing what it is destroying. For the best things are always imponderables, and the imponderables, by definition, cannot be weighed. Year after year this stream of young men poured in on me, and, though I did not "fall in love" with them, yet that feeling, very much in the background, kept me young and in touch with them. I think, at least, that many of them would say so,[1] after making all allowance for the deceptions to which, in such matters, one is liable.

I should add, to obviate any misapprehension, that I never had any affair with any of these young men, except Oscar, of whom I have spoken, and that I see clearly, if only from that example, how unfortunate such relations may become for the young men, who must be, to any teacher, his first concern. Yet even here I may be wrong. For there is one of my colleagues who manages to have romantic episodes with his pupils without apparently any injury to them. On these questions, involving personality, it is hazardous to generalise. But, at any rate, my practice was as I have described it. (No, I am wrong. There was one other case, long before Oscar, in which I fell in love and betrayed the fact. But that was ended by the action of the young man, before any disastrous complications ensued,

[1] I wonder? (1927).

and since then our relation, very friendly, has been entirely without that element.)

As to my lectures, those I continued, two terms every year, until I resigned my lectureship. My business was to enlarge and concretise my subject, which became, in fact, a general discussion of modern political problems. I came in time, I believe, to lecture well, in the academic way. I spoke always from notes, added continually, from year to year, to my matter, as was natural in a subject so continually developing, not to say bulging and protruding outside all skins of general theory. I was interested myself, and I think I interested my pupils, most of them. At any rate my audience always continued to the end without any defalcations to speak of, and varied round about a hundred in the later years. I had a quite definite idea of what I wanted to do in lectures—to stimulate the students' interest so that they should feel they were dealing with a live subject, which was going to be of interest and practical importance to them all their life. I used not to conceal my own opinions, but also not to preach them unfairly, having, in fact, in many important questions, a very open mind. I lectured in this way for some twenty-five years, never losing my own freshness and interest. Whether I produced any result, or what, who can say? The parable of the sower applies to all such work; and a single teacher is rather a light makeweight against family and social interests and preoccupations. Still, I expect I helped to wake up some minds. What more can a teacher do, or what better?

Meantime I continued, in my leisure, my literary work. My opportunities were particularly favourable, for I lectured only in two terms, leaving the Easter term and the long vacation free. This is an arrangement, not, I think, very common even then at Cambridge, and likely, with the development of organisation in education, to become impossible.[1] It was, of course, open to me to neglect my chances and produce nothing. But I think it certain that to leave such chances of neglect is better than to tie teachers to a life in which all their time and energies are absorbed in teaching. At any rate, I was only able to produce my books by devoting to them a considerable part of the time which was paid for by my Fellowship and Lectureship.

In the course of some thirty-five years I have written a dozen or more books, and I may have received for the whole of them, in money from publishers, something round £1,000.[2] It is clear, therefore, that it was only my position as a teacher that enabled me to write them and live, and that I could not have written them if teaching had claimed all my time. In that

[1] (The new statutes, however, are intended to secure leisure to lecturers for research and writing. 1927).
[2] Must be more—1931.

case also I am clear that my teaching would have become stale and burdensome, as, in fact, under the conditions granted me, it did not. The arrangement, clearly, is one which no commission would ever approve.[1] It slipped through under the freedom of the old Cambridge, and I am glad to have been the lucky man to profit by it.

The next subject to which I devoted myself in my leisure time was Greek civilisation. I remember how the idea came to me one day in our dining room at All Souls Place, in the old arm chair, now long vanished from my life—(who bought it, I wonder? Does it still exist?)—that Greek life and literature might be made available to those who could not learn Greek, in some really human and interesting way. I began writing the book at Kandersteg in 1895, and it consoled me there through some bad times. This book, I often think, is really the most useful I have written.[2] It continues to sell, both in England and still more in the United States. Scholars I daresay, so far as they look at it, would find much to criticise. There was, of course, much in Greek life which I omitted. But I still feel that I have got hold of what may be called the central thing, the thing that makes Greek of permanent value to civilisation. And that thing, if it is to have any wide influence, must be given through translation. That is why Professor Gilbert Murray's translations have such value, even though they have, as it were, the wrong colour. They are readable, and read.

I was myself brought up almost exclusively on Latin and Greek, until I took my degree; and I have borne witness to the incredibly stupid and wasteful method, or lack of method, which was applied to me. It was not till I had got right away from the Classics, that I really began to see what they were worth. I now think that Greek literature, because of the language itself, the most expressive we know, and because of the perfection of form and variety of content, is the greatest of which we have knowledge. Some classical scholars feel this so much that they take either no interest, or a subordinate one, in any other literature. I cannot understand this, seeing that every age needs to interpret and express afresh old truths, however perfectly they may have been expressed at other times, and in other languages; and seeing also, that the actual context, if not the underlying profundities, alters and extends from age to age. But I know nowhere else such a combination of beauty and depth, of wisdom and wit, of gaiety and insight as Greek literature provided. My object in my book was to make known to a public not educated on Greek, the character and environment of these treasures. I think I succeeded, and perhaps that book will be read still when everything else I have written is forgotten.

---

[1] See note above—p. 147.
[2] *The Greek View of Life*, Methuen & Co., 1896. *Ed.*

CHAPTER TWELVE

Mrs Webb

3 May 1927

It is, I think, a year or two since I have written at this biographical account. I shall now say something of what is almost my oldest friendship, with Mrs Webb. She is now, and has been for fifteen years, living in Cambridge. She is 87. Only the other day she had a fortnight's illness from inflammation of the bowels, with acute pain; yet has recovered. She has suffered from gall stones more than once (the worst pain, I suppose, that there is). She used to have constant headaches, influenza, heart-attacks and dizziness. But all this left and leaves her as it were unsullied, uncomplaining, the most beautiful soul perhaps I have known or shall know, except, it may be, my sister Janet and Mrs Moor. She has also a strong and sincere mind, which prevents her swallowing any humbug. She is a member of the Church of England and the widow of a parson. But what she believes now I do not know, nor I think does she. But she has 'faith' in the sense of courage, love and hope. Those are the last great qualities that abide when all other things go, and we can but wait our passage to annihilation or whatever else there may be.

I met her first, as is mentioned above, when I was lecturing at Mansfield Woodhouse. My lectures were very bad in manner and very unsuited to my audience. But they interested her and so did I. We quickly became intimate and I used to pour out to her my crude ideas. She has lately sent me a packet of my letters to her, which I propose to use as contemporary evidence of what was going on in my mind then and in successive years. It will be remembered that my lectures at Chester in 1886 terminated in my dismissal from that occupation, and that I then determined to study medicine. In May 1888 I find myself writing that I am shortly to be examined in anatomy, and that 'as you hint, anatomy is not fascinating. But I'm often very thankful to have it to do, else I should speculate my head off, and when I had bust it produce not Athene but a cloud.' 'There's more interest in physiology,' I add, 'but then it's such an infant science and consequently a chaos of incomprehensible and contradictory facts.' This was forty years ago, and I need not add that physiology has made enormous progress. Whether it has become more coherent I am not in a position to say. When I wrote it was certainly in a very rudimentary condition. I go on: 'I look out on the Backs and enjoy my "learned leisure" but am thinking there's rather more of the "leisure" and less of the "learned" than might be of late—for I don't regard anatomy as serious work.' I did not. I never knew it well, nor had I any skill or interest in dissecting.

In 1891 I find a prophetic forecast: 'Just imagine a man of brilliant abilities deliberately sitting down to invent a flying machine that shall be the most destructive weapon of war ever conceived. Some Frenchman's doing it. He ought to be hung. But it's no good hanging people. These things are in the grain of mankind.' 'But so,' I conclude, 'is St Francis of Assisi.' This still seems to me the last word. In 1892 I write from Paris:

We (Roger Fry and myself) are four storeys up in the noisiest street in Paris (this is a figure of speech, but the pavement is rough cobble and the buses very large), close to the Luxembourg, which indeed closes the south end of the street.

I proceed with miscellaneous remarks about Parisian architecture and pictures, not of much interest. For, in fact, as I have already said, I did not really see anything of Paris, since I was hermetically sealed in my own thoughts and literary efforts, and since the principal interest of Paris, women, was no interest to me. You may take a horse to the water, but you can't make him drink. And my impenetrability to my environment has always been, and still is, scandalous.

In 1892, as related, my Fellowship at King's was renewed, and before long I was teaching. I write in 1898:

With me things have been going well of late. The undergraduate continues to delight me. I like my pupils and in my small way I think I am useful to them, though no one can ever do for them what they do for themselves. An unspoilt youth of twenty with his mind just waking up and his feelings all fresh and open to good, is the most beautiful thing this world produces, I believe. The only atmosphere I'm really at home in is that one of the Platonic Socrates.

This extract about Cambridge is, of course, the complement and explanation of the one about Paris. What I say about the developing English youth at his best I still hold to, and last night was saying, as I remember, the same thing to Kennedy, the architect. Au fond one changes very little.

Cambridge, on the other hand, was not then, and never has been, altogether congenial to me. I find a passage in another letter (undated) which gives the other side:

Mrs Webb

The spectacle of learning gets more depressing to me every year. I care only for fruitful and vital handling of the eternal commonplaces or else for a new insight that will really help someone to 'internal freedom', as Goethe said. The German accumulations of research are intolerable burdens. These being my sentiments, I don't feel quite comfortable in a university. But must stay there as long as it seems better than other alternatives.

In these two extracts is the whole of me, so far as Cambridge is concerned, and it is as true now as then. It occurs to me to add that in the English universities, at any rate Oxford and Cambridge, there are two types of people, those who like young men and want to teach them, and those (much fewer) who want to research. There is a veiled and often an avowed antagonism between them, which is apt to express itself as an antagonism between 'science' and 'classics'. For those who like young men, and have the maieutic faculty, Cambridge, and especially King's, is ideal. But the position is precarious, and it is not very likely that even a pale adumbration of Socrates will long be tolerated in an age at once scientific, utilitarian and unimaginative. The much abused, much laughed at, but always victorious Oscar Browning is the largest figure Cambridge has known, in my time, inspired with the maieutic passion. But as a researcher! The two things seem to be hardly compatible.

I have, however, in my old age, produced one book, my *International Anarchy*, which is a sound book of 'research' as well as one of propaganda.[1] So far as that is concerned, I say 'nunc dimittis'. In the same letter quoted above, I say:

I don't believe God (or whatever may be the boss of the Universe) is so stupid as to judge by results—that is, external products. He judges, if he has any *nous*, by the quality of souls.

Perhaps, however, he expects souls in universities to show their quality by researching!

The clash of feelings which I have always felt at Cambridge is perhaps only the reflex of a more fundamental internal discord. In another letter (1909?) I write:

No, I'm not at all in harmony with myself, and I doubt if I shall ever be—it's the nature of the beast. Fact is, I mistrust harmony—till we are all perfect in a perfect world.

I do. And I can't imagine anybody of any perception feeling harmonious. It could only be done by ignoring most things in life.

[1] See pp. 198–9 below. *Ed.*

The Autobiography of G. Lowes Dickinson

In the year 1901, as I shall relate in a later chapter, I paid my first visit to the United States, and I find some letters dealing both with this visit and with my later one in 1909. One dated New York, 8 December 1901, says:

I write in a very cheap condition. I was given supper at 12 p.m. on terrapin and duck and champagne, and kept up till two, and I have to go out to lunch with some perfect strangers on top of all that. This is a very hard life, and I wish it was over.

But my persistent priggishness adds:

I believe it is very useful and informing to me. It has cleared up to me wonderfully my own point of view and shown me how deep-seated is my antagonism to the whole type of civilisation which America represents. But I have said all this ad nauseam.

This is, in fact, the constant refrain of all my letters from America. Probably fatigue has something to do with it, and the mere fact of being a wanderer instead of settled among friends has more. I continue:

I never knew how dear to me is England and my friends. Seems to me there's nothing like the best type of English men and women, their breeding, their tenderness, their perception, their intellect. There may be such in this country too, but naturally one doesn't find them out in a few months.

My second visit to the United States was in the Spring of 1909, after my father's death. In a letter of April from New York I say:

I'm in a fearful bustle of lectures, dinners, lunches, etc., but am getting on pretty well so far. I have much the same impressions of America as before, but I doubt whether the impressions are of what is most important here. What is most important lies out of my ken—the material development of the country and the immense energy and force brought to bear in the doing of it. Naturally I don't get into touch with that. It's like laying the foundations of a city, and my interest is in the songs that are one day to be sung in it—when? Generations hence, if ever. Meantime, I am surprised at the number of people who have read my books and speak to me with apparently genuine enthusiasm about them. I think I am better known and count for more here than in England.

This latter remark I fancy is true, though in neither country have I ever been or ever shall be a 'best seller'. In May I write from Colorado, in the accustomed splenetic way:

At this moment, being surly and irritable, I see America at its worst. One never seems to see a face which has been touched by emotion or illumined by thought. Always the same cheerful effective types, male or female, large white teeth literally stopped with gold, perennial hard smiles, hard voices without any rhythm or subtlety, great arid mouths and chins, pretentious flashy dress. The only people who look human are the European waiters and the negroes. They're all so disgustingly at home in their environment—so completely 'at ease in Sion'. Well, this is mere ill-temper I suppose. At least, it's all true, but ill-temper makes me emphasise it. Then the relations of men and women. I rather sympathise with the Scotchman who said he would like to see 'less chastity and more delicacy'. Co-education, as I saw and heard of it at Madison, made me shudder. The young men go 'girling' or 'fussing' and the young women say 'our fussers are coming to-night'. Isn't it indecent? And of course there's no real sentiment in it, nothing beautiful or passionate—only this eternal barbarian girl and boy game, which doesn't even come to anything. It is a coarse, tough, ungracious plant that grows on this soil. The people are good—yes, good-natured, yes—but, well thank God I don't have to live here. I wonder whether England would look the same if one saw it as a stranger from outside? Perhaps it would. Essentially I feel the whole thing just as I did seven years ago—only, in calmer moments, I try to see it, and not merely feel it. To-night I'm just letting myself go.

But I break out at once

And I'm missing the cuckoo and the lark and the nightingale and the hawthorn; and there are so few Springs left in one's life! Here there's practically no vegetation (6,000 feet up), and one hears only an occasional shrill chirrup by way of a bird. It really is a God-forsaken and man-polluted continent! Perhaps I'd better stop.

Two days later the weather clears, but not apparently my mood. For I write:

The hideousness of the town surroundings! An immense black gasometer is the foreground of my view. The railway runs just in front. Long lines of sordid little wooden huts and hovels, planted down anywhere, disfigure even the dreary red mud of the soil. What a country!

A little later I am at Niagara, having visited meantime Plump Hughes at Topeka (see above). I speak of the rapids 'like a chain of alps, set tossing and flowing thirty miles an hour down the narrow ravine'. In a previous letter, in 1901, from the same place I said:

Niagara is impressive, but neither attractive nor beautiful. It gives me the sense of tremendous force and bulk, but those are things that I am coming to hate. For the question always arises—is this force good? And nature gives no answer, or not a hopeful one.

The Autobiography of G. Lowes Dickinson

This reminds me that I have just finished *Moby Dick* for the first time of reading. It is a great epic, (apart from form) as great as Homer or Shakespeare. And no one ever realised before with such candour and truth the fact of Evil. It is the world-hymn of Evil. Niagara is its riddle, or indifference. Lear is its tragedy. We aren't fit to probe those regions. We have to go on and (as my father said in his old age) 'turn to good where we see it'. We have not the organs nor the brain nor the courage to probe the world. Our religions and philosophies are all apologetics or lunacies, ways of going round the fact. Even when we are in the power of Evil, as in acute physical pain, we cannot see or know it, we can only endure it till it destroys us. Against that last fact we are all flung, sooner or later, like drops of rain against the window pane, to run down in tears of blood.

Some of these letters deal with my travels of 1912–1913, which I speak of elsewhere. I shall use the letters there.

Turning now to more personal matters, I was in the habit of confiding to Mrs Webb my feelings, happy or the reverse, especially in reference to Ferdinand and Oscar. In 1905, I write, on the eve of starting for Switzerland to join the Schillers:

I don't think that the worth of one's personal relations can be measured by the pleasure or pain they bring. They have a sort of absolute value. And the more and the stronger the better. The only thing I fear is the growth of indifference and self-centredness.

Already, in 1888, just after my return from Gersau and before Ferdinand's first going to India, I write:

I don't know when I shall see him or how again. I think the one immortal thing we are given in direct experience is love; I don't believe it goes when it seems to; it only gets hidden.

I feel, at this moment, forty years later, that this is probably true; and that, in spite of the illusions of desire, the changes of time and space, the alienations, and all the rest of it—in spite even of the fact that no one should, and few men can, devote themselves exclusively, or even mainly, to love—since it is one of those things that eludes or corrupts when pursued, and surprises by its arrival when you turn away from it and renounce it. Sometimes now, when I see Ferdinand, and he kisses me with that old fidelity of his, I feel that something is there achieved which goes deeper and is more immortal than all that fills our time and thoughts on both sides; but that 'something' cannot be seized and exploited. It waits and abides. Except for that, we have hardly contacts, so far has life swept us apart.

In 1899, I write, after meeting Ferdinand in town on his return from India:

I have been trying to realise in a dazed kind of way. After all these years the effect of his actual presence is a thing that sort of 'bowls me over' as they say—so unimaginable and unaccountable and altogether wonderful.

At that time there was some idea that he might not return to India. When the decision was made the other way, I write:

I feel really—well, there are no words. But it's terrible to find myself so wrapped up in him. I could say it wasn't right—something in me tries to say it—but how idle all that is. The bottom is knocked out of everything—my work, my writing, it all seems so footling. Well, I know—I believe it *isn't*. I know, to an outsider, it justly seems contemptible to be so absorbed in one's personal life. But there it is—the war (Boer war) and all the rest of it, is like a pale indifferent spectacle. Well then, time comes in and restores the balance, and so on. But it's just that one hates. Time wears one smooth and one congratulates oneself on getting 'peace' or on 'healthy activity' or whatever it may be. But at bottom it is feeling I value, not activity. Is that all wrong? And is one taught 'as by fire?' I don't know. If anyone told me so I should resent it. And all this isn't for you to answer but to give me relief. Dear lady, this is a *deliberately* selfish letter.

So it was. But those are the letters one likes to get. This, looked back on in cold blood, seems to me to express very well the dual quality of love—its egotism (of which I was clearly aware) even its absurdity—and yet its importance; so that the altruistic or social things may seem only pallid ghosts in its presence. My essential Platonism evidently still haunted me. I was moving towards his later pre-occupation with political and social fact. But I have never, even now, when almost all my time and thoughts are given to those things, felt that they are substitutes for love—that they are the 'real' thing which love only misconceives. *They* are purposes in time. *It* is a partial breaking through of something on the other side of time, as poets and mystics have always felt. I recall one of my own early poems:

> Oh many a year must pass and many a pain
> And many a sorrow run its purging course,
> Ere she may hope by patience to attain
> What never yet was yielded up to force,
> And unimpeded clasp the sister soul
> That rounds her broken crescent to a whole

This at sixty-five! It's a queer world.

The Autobiography of G. Lowes Dickinson

In March 1913 I write from Hong Kong:

If there is any significance in this life—as I believe there is—it lies in what people have made of their souls more than in what they have otherwise achieved.

Perhaps. But one should add that they ought never to be thinking about their souls. I go on

Now *you* have made a very nice white clean beautiful soul. So don't worry.

This, at any rate, is true. And truer than ever now, this summer, when at any moment she may die. She has made her soul, and never thought of it. And she bears out an observation I find in an earlier letter of 1901:

. . . that the soul does not grow old with the body is a belief of mine which I am glad to find your experience endorses. Nothing except the spiritual is real. That is an increasing conviction of mine. And I find it in all people who have had profound experience—especially of Evil.

I have had more experience of Evil since I wrote those words. Are they true? Upon my word I don't know. Evil is incommensurable to our powers, and therefore to our judgment. We can only 'turn to Good'.

In this correspondence, I find references to various people of more or less note which it may be interesting to preserve.

Thus, in 1891 I write:

I have been seeing something of Westcott this term. Do you know his books at all? I don't, but he himself is a most interesting person—a mediaeval mystic, or rather a very modern mystic, who sees the finger of God even in the Stock Exchange. He is a great lover of Browning, and a great believer in (ultimate) socialism, the consummation of Christianity. . . . One would like to see the finger of God everywhere, but how can we—in your neuralgia for instance?

Westcott was the Professor of Theology in Cambridge, but shortly after became Bishop of Durham.

In 1890 I write of my old friend Edward Carpenter, whom I had met earlier:

He has been staying with me a few days. He's the only young man of over forty I ever met. He's kept so by renouncing everything most men desire. And, as you suggest, he is always positive—full of the possibilities rather than the failures. The slightly aggressive partisan tone of his book is quite absent in his conversation. He has a way of sinking himself in the person he's talking to, which makes one feel one has a second self confronting one. He suggests that, when two people love, one is the mirror to the other, and he likes the mirror part the better of the two.

I remember that visit very well. I have kept in touch with him more or less ever since, and now that he has removed to Guildford, go down from time to time to see him. He is now 83 or 84, has had a slight stroke, but seems to have recovered pretty completely, though he cannot walk much. He is himself the completest contradiction of the popular view that homosexuals are decadents, sensualists, etc, etc. And that, in spite of the fact that he believes in and practises the physical relation very frankly. How it is that public opinion' hasn't managed to get him into prison and murder him, is a mystery to me. We must be thankful for small mercies!

A once famous man of genius who died young and tragically was J. K. Stephen, of this college, author of *Lapsus calami*. In 1891 I write:

We had a debate here on the proposal for an Agricultural Tripos, in which Stephen made a speech surpassing even himself in brilliancy of phrase. He drew a pastoral picture of Oscar Browning and myself brushing away the dew on upland lawns, clad in smock frocks, and driving before us the peccant sheep, or the docile pig: 'That' he said 'would be ornamental; it is what I should like to see, what I hope I may see. But it would not be *useful*. Better would it have been for the docile pig to abide in its congenial sty, etc. etc.'

The Agricultural Tripos is now, I suppose, the principal contribution of Cambridge to civilisation—or rather, the agricultural experimental farm. It is useful, whatever else it may be, or not be. And it looks at the moment as though that is the most a university, in modern days, can hope to be.

In the same year, I write that I am about to pay a visit to Robert Bridges; Roger Fry (a cousin) had sent him my early poem 'Jacob's Ladder' (see page 83 above). I say that he approves of it, 'especially the Greek part, which he says "gives promise of poetry of a rare and original character".'

In this letter I find also an emphasis on my constant and now more intensely than ever held belief, in 'a devil for all practical purposes':

There's a weird shrieking November wind in the Backs to-day. Only a few red beech leaves left, and the yellow from the elms strewn on the ground. But as Shelley says—'If winter comes, can spring be far behind?' '*Can* it, *can* it, *can't* it?' Humanity goes on saying, half believing and half despairing, and very much conscious of a 'devil for all practical purposes'. You see I'm rather proud of this exceedingly original discovery of mine, which doesn't affect my general speculative optimism.

The Autobiography of G. Lowes Dickinson

In January I write:

Last Sunday I spent with Robert Bridges, poet. I like him. He was particularly kind to me, and we talked much on poetry, metres, etc. and agreed a good deal, though he's not interested much in some things which are the most interesting to me. He was very encouraging about my poetry, and I begin to be surer myself that my faculty is in that direction; certain, by a negative exhaustive process, it appears demonstrably not to lie anywhere else!

These remarks interest me. If I *had* been a poet, I should, I suppose, have *had* to be one. But I had, it would seem, some justification for my experiments in that direction. Anyone who reads this memoir will quickly perceive that I had no overmastering impulse at all, but a wide range of sensitiveness.

In a letter to Mrs Webb of 1891 I find:

It's a hard world to find one's way in, and not made easier by the natural instinctive intolerance of men. No one can be patient with Smith because he isn't Jones; forgetting that it's a third-rate Jones at best that Smith would make of himself, if he tried. But all men, more or less, carry with them the curse of limitation, which gives them all their powers, and all their defects. Some few (Caesar perhaps) approximate to universality; that's one kind of genius; another is merely emphasised limitation (say Poe). But the grandeur and deliverance comes from that part in a man that rebels and claims to shatter limits sooner or later.

'I hope this sort of thing doesn't bore you' I add, pulling myself up! I recognise now the quintessential 'me' in that passage. And still I—I will not say I believe—yet I do not disbelieve that death might be liberation into a larger life—that of what we now call the 'Subconscious', the 'universal consciousness' etc. But one talks idly, and had better be silent.

I have already narrated how I first met Bernard Shaw. In 1892 I tell how I went to see his first play *Widowers' Houses* at its first appearance; and I am a little surprised at my verdict.

It was a socialist tract against slum-landlords and possibly effective from that point of view:—as a play miserably dreary and unconvincing, all the personages unintelligible and repulsive caricatures, and even the dialogue not very clever. I don't like my powder and jam mixed in that inartistic way.

This sounds like the sort of criticism I am always hearing from intellectuals and lovers of the drama. I haven't read the play in question, or seen it, since, so I don't know what I should think now of my comments. I remember, however, one thing; that after the performance there was a great deal of noise and hissing, and that after some time the manager appeared to say that Mr Shaw had left the theatre. Whereupon Mr Shaw appeared upon the stage, very pale, and began a speech: 'I hope' he said, 'that the time is coming when a play like this will be impossible.' 'It's impossible now' from the gallery. 'It's not impossible now, for it's just been performed' from Shaw. And so on. It's possible that Shaw has sacrificed permanent fame for propaganda. If so, I am the last man who would count it against him. What the devil does 'fame' matter, or living through the ages? It is one of the greatest illusions men have.

At some time before the war—the letter is not dated—I heard Bryce speak at the Liberal Club in Cambridge. He referred to 'the great Liberal Party with its character behind it and its future in front'. The only person, except myself, who seemed amused, was Jem Stephen, who guffawed. I comment: 'It was a nice lecture, but Liberal principles as defined by him are also the principles of most Tories'. Later, during the war, I saw a good deal of Bryce. I liked his unceasing vitality, and the wide range of his knowledge and experience, as well as the incorruptibility and courage which, in politics, appears to belong to the middle of the nineteenth century. It is rapidly disappearing now. Otherwise, his mind didn't interest me. One wonders, indeed, whether a mind can be interesting in itself, if it gives itself to practical purposes, which after all is its main business. 'It' (whatever 'It' is) says, in effect: 'I intend you to become instruments; and if you insist on remaining ends, I shall give you beans—futility, insanity, etc. etc.'

I find also, in this correspondence, some remarks about my literary views and projects. In 1891, I talk about my *Mirabeau* (see elsewhere) and my idea of representing the French Revolution in a series of dramatic studies (cf. my *From King to King*): 'What I want to do in the French Revolution plays is to approximate to the Greek manner, introduce lyric interludes and set the whole against a background of fate (or Providence you would prefer).' And I go on to refer to 'my growing conviction that such dramatic treatment is the only way that really represents truth at all, and most history books and chronicles are mere stuff and materials for books'. I find myself essentially believing the same now.

In 1903 I write about what was to become my *Modern Symposium* that it's 'in rather a problematical condition and I hardly know how it will come out'. I add: 'It seems to me I'm a born writer and born for nothing else'. And then characteristically:

I would rather have been many other things, if I could have chosen, but the calling of literature can be an honourable one, if one takes it properly. I am often astonished at what I write myself. Something takes hold of me, and I am possessed by a kind of passion and inward freedom that seems to have no relation to the other 'me' or to the real objective world. The dualism—I might say pluralism—is almost intolerable at times. And I have to take refuge in the dullest of work, in irony, in anything! How mysterious everything is, how terrible and how sublime, when one has the courage and power to look into it. But it's so little I shall ever be fit to see and know.

That last sentence, at any rate, is true!

Another passage written in 1891 rather interests me, as showing how continuous one is:

I'm becoming more and more possessed by admiration for the Greek art; that is, not only for their work, but for their magnificent detached, controlled and unsentimental attitude, which a modern man (while imagining that he admires Sophocles) calls 'coldness' etc. I believe romanticism might be defined as the abandonment of reason; whereas the classics set reason to passion (that's meant for a musical metaphor). That view runs through all Greek work—their architecture, which depends on definite measured proportion, which is apparently exhaustible at the first glance and yet is never exhausted; their drama, where the passion is informed and controlled by general conceptions, instead of the anarchy of Shakespeare, etc. etc. The real passion is Plato's not Swinburne's.

CHAPTER THIRTEEN

Greece and Writing, 1897–1901

The Greek View of Life was published in 1896 and it must have been some time between this and 1899 (1897, I think) that I first went to Greece. My companions were three men of whom I will take the opportunity to say a few words.

One was Nathaniel Wedd. He was two years junior to me, so that we had been undergraduates together. In those days he had been notorious for blasphemy (so called) and the reading of Baudelaire. He was elected to the Society of Apostles and with Fry and McTaggart was a principal attendant from 1886 on. He is, I think, one of the ablest men I have known. He became a Fellow and Classical tutor at King's and his teaching was universally admired by his pupils. But he was more than a teacher. He gave up all his time and energies to undergraduates, was at home to them at all hours of the night, stimulated, comforted, amused, and generally maintained the best tradition of King's, that of friendship and intimacy between undergraduates and dons. But he overworked and over-smoked himself, so that in the end he fell seriously ill, and many years of his life have been thus frustrated. During all that time I never saw him cast down, nor did his mind or memory ever seem to weaken. He is now back at King's and in better health than it ever seemed likely he could achieve, though not able to do any teaching. I was very intimate with him for many years, and still am, though the difference of opinion about the war has caused a certain reserve.

The second of my companions was Robin Mayor, ten years my junior, now a high official in the Education Office. He had joined us on some of our expeditions on the Thames, and I recollect how, at one of the inns, being a little drunk, he held forth on the desirability of marrying and reproducing so good a stock as his own. This ambition he fulfilled, and has now a charming little family.

The third member of our expedition was A. M. Daniel.[1] At Cambridge

---

[1] Now Director of the National Gallery, 1931, having previously been a Trustee.

he had been a football blue and a medical student. He took his medical degree, but did not practise, as he had plenty of money. He then turned to philosophy, and for many years read hard in Aristotle and Kant and Hegel, returning, after his football matches, to his solitary rooms and this, for a footballer, unusual occupation. He removed later to York, but continued his studies, becoming at last almost incapable of society, and suffering from indigestion and such-like troubles. Then, after some years, he turned from metaphysics to art, by the route of Hegel, from whom he had learned that works of art constituted an 'organic unity'. He thought he would like to perceive organic unity, and proceeded to do so with his usual thoroughness, becoming a connoisseur and a buyer of pictures. About the same time he took to riding, and pursued that art with his customary deliberation, combining theory with practice (I have heard him quoting Aristotle to his groom) and becoming in the end a fearless cross-country rider. During the war he was Mayor of Scarborough and did good work unifying all the charities of the city. I know no one more intelligent and more delightful.

The visit to Greece with their company was a revelation of what travel can mean. I had been depressed and worried. But from the moment of landing at the Piraeus life renewed itself in perpetual interest and delight. The Acropolis at Athens revealed to me the meaning of the architecture and mouldings I had seen parodied all over Europe. It was like hearing music at last played in tune, after a long perversion by slight discords. Even more wonderful than the architecture was the sunshine and the country; bare hills and plains clear cut, exquisite in form and colour and indented everywhere by the shining sea. The view from the Acropolis, with the hawks hanging before one; Pentelicus and an eagle sweeping round its summit; the line of the sea against the shore in the bay of Marathon; the plain of Eleusis; the ruined temple at Sunium rising from a sea of red poppies over the sea of blue waves; bathing at Aegina, and the scent of the pines; the spring gushing from a plane tree at Delphi with its shining peaks; and that bronze charioteer seen with the hard and clear beauty of Greek youth—these things still flicker, though far too faintly, before my memory.

But above all I recall an evening spent at Mistra, above Sparta. We rode through the little village, for such it now is, hidden among orange groves, and then up the slope of Taygetus to that deserted mediaeval town of whose very existence I was unaware. There we stayed the night in a monastery inhabited by a single monk, strolled under the full moon round the deserted streets and churches, and heard from below the chant of the frogs, the *'brekekekex koax koax'* of Aristophanes. It was here on this night that there occurred to me the idea of writing a dialogue on Good, which I carried out in the following year or so.

Greece and Writing, 1897–1901

Later, I paid a second visit to Greece, and on that occasion we went round the islands in a steamer chartered for his party by Professor Gardner. We then saw, in pouring rain, the remains of the nine cities of Troy, the crater of Thera, and many lovely sights. But it was the first visit that renewed my life, as once had done my first experience of Italy. On both occasions it seemed as though a door swung for a moment ajar and showed one what one might conceivably have been under the influence of a southern climate and a more passionate beauty-loving society. In Greece, in particular, I felt as though my dull senses were being stimulated into life, and trying, as it were, to throw off the long incubus of thought and books, to live by feeling and perception. I understand how Goethe must have felt both when first he saw Italy, and when, under a sense of duty, he left it to return to the unfriendly north. Only with what organs, what knowledge, what genius was he equipped compared to me!

In 1926, I made my third visit to Greece, this time with Raisley Moorsom. We went through by train by the Oriental Express, and stopped at Larissa to see the vale of Tempe. Then on to Delphi and to most of the places I had visited in 1897. The country still seemed to me the most beautiful I have visited, though of course there was no longer the enthusiasm of youth. Where I had travelled before on mules we now went by motor car; except for the Langada Pass, between Sparta and Kalamata, which we crossed, as before, walking and riding; the most enjoyable part of the trip. We also visited again the little town of Mistra, but this time in the afternoon. It was much lower than my remembrance had placed it, and the wild romance of the moonlight night was not there. But still how beautiful it was and how solitary! At Athens (always a disagreeable city) the atmosphere which I remembered so pellucid was thickened by smoke from factories at the Piraeus; but the Parthenon and the Erectheum more rather than less superb. We went once more to Sunium, but this time by car instead of ship; and still it was one of the loveliest places I know:

> Place me on Sunium's marble steep
> Where nothing but the waves and I
> May hear our mutual murmurs sweep.
> There let me live, there let me die.

One re-echoes to that subtly false romanticism, but it is a travesty of Greece, which was a realistic passionate civilisation, combining poetry and intellect as no other has done, and free from all false archaism. What a civilisation! How still it shines upon us like a star out of the murky train of history! We returned slowly up the Adriatic, stopping at the wonderful islands and towns, and seeing, with a mixture of amusement and disgust, the attempt of the Jugo-Slavs to blot out the Italian Language from their Italian towns. Nationalism is certainly the silliest, as it is the most pernicious, of human follies. And Italy herself, once free from it, has caught it worse than anyone else. And so back to England, precisely at the close of the 'General Strike'—the 'first' as the militarists say of the great war!

My next book was *The Meaning of Good*, the idea of which, as I have said, came to me at Mistra above Sparta. I wrote it, I think, in 1900, some of it when I was staying near Thursley (Surrey) with Roger Fry. Some, in particular the myth at the end, in the garden of my lodgings at Westcott. (I looked for them the other day among the new houses, but couldn't find them.)

I was impelled to use the dialogue form for the same reason that it was used by Plato, or by Berkeley, because I was dealing with matter very controversial and confused, and because, though the method must endeavour to be sound and argumentative, it must also be flooded with that passion which is the condition, in such matters, of the object existing at all. For (so it seems to me) in most ethical treatises the object fades away like seaweed left dry on the shore, and one seems to be elaborately dissecting a corpse. There are, I think, too many personages taking part in my dialogue, and probably it is frigid in parts, but on the whole, last time I reread it, I was surprised to find how good I thought it. While I was writing it G. E. Moore's book *Principia Ethica* appeared and made a kind of furore among my Cambridge friends. 'The age of reason has come,' Lytton Strachey said. I remember that it appeared to me, on reading that book, that I had been guilty, in my own dialogue, of what Moore called the 'naturalistic fallacy', a phrase which always amuses me, for it suggests some kind of unnatural vice. I tried to dodge this error in my book at the last moment, but I expect it is there, and also that it doesn't much matter. Moore has probably long ago altered his position, on this as on other points.

What I believe to be true, in my own book, is the tension of experience, the quest of Good, the perpetual dissatisfaction, and the knowledge therefrom derived. When I say this is 'true', I mean that it is true of those who count in such matters, of Goethe let us say. What is more questionable is the mysticism which still haunted me, as it haunted Plato, and which appears in the concluding myth. The terrible events of the last few years and the horrible spectacle at present shown by the world have made me more sceptical and despairing. But it is possible that, in such matters, youth sees better than age. One thing further is perhaps worth noticing in this book, that, while I was still influenced by McTaggart's idea of an eternal perfection of spirits related to one another by love, I also suspected that this might be illusion, or (perhaps I should say) an imperfect parable. For my myth, though it does not go beyond that conception, yet suggests that there *is* a beyond.

At the same time that I was writing this book, I was also making my first acquaintance, through translations, with Chinese literature. It was the time of the Boxer riots, and the European expeditions to suppress them. I suppose it was that that gave the stimulus to my reading, though Trevelyan tells me that I expressed myself as unable to take real interest in a civilisation so unhellenic as the Chinese. At any rate it was this reading, and especially a book by Simon called *La Cité Chinoise*, that gave me the idea of the only book of mine that has enjoyed a certain popularity. This was the *Letters from John Chinaman* or *Letters of a Chinese Official* as it was called in the American edition, because it was thought that no one would read it there under the other title.

The book was the product of a restless state of mind such as usually, in my case, as in those of greater men, precedes composition. I wanted to make some fundamental criticism of our Western society. But I wanted what I wrote to be read by the general public, and to have some kind of artistic form. I experimented in various ways, trying, to begin with, to utilise one of Swift's myths, in the form of 'Letters from a Houyhnhnm'. These I tried in lodgings at Betchworth, where I was staying to be near Roger Fry, then living at Dorking. The idea was not a good one, and I did not pursue it, but carried my burden about until the reading in Chinese literature to which I have referred suddenly gave me my idea. I was then staying with my family at the Peak at Baslow, and I began there in a meadow with the facility and pleasure that usually follows a long and painful incubation.

The first four letters were printed that autumn in the *Saturday Review* and created some interest, though the readers of that journal, I think, were not deluded as to the authorship; indeed a correspondent wrote pointing out that clearly they were not really by a Chinaman. I never intended any deception, knowing that there was good precedent for that kind of form in English literature, and not supposing anyone would be taken in. The later letters I wrote afterwards, and the little book was published by R. Brimley Johnson, a personal friend of mine, in 1901, with a grotesque picture of a Chinaman on the cover, designed by Gilbert Chesterton. I never liked this, and it disappeared in later editions. I didn't think much more about the book, for I was well accustomed to being ignored. The first copies reached me in America. My brother brought them to my room, when I was in bed in a hotel at Niagara, saying that he had been reading the book, and that it was 'wonderful'. He did not know it was mine, and felt a natural disappointment when I revealed the fact. For who can think as much of the opinions of a friend or relative as they do of those of an unknown author?

They know too much about him! I remember being much excited and pleased at the moment.

But the book would, I suppose, have fallen as dead as my others, if George Trevelyan had not quoted it in an article in the *Nineteenth Century,* which excited some attention. People then began to speculate as to whether it was really by a Chinaman, and a good many copies were sold. It then penetrated to America, and there everybody seems to have accepted naïvely its Chinese origin. It was attributed to the then Chinese ambassador; and Mr Bryan, the famous politician, thought it worth while to write a special reply to it, in which he observed, among other things, that clearly the author had never seen the inside of a Christian home. Before publishing his book, he ascertained that the author was really an Englishman, and he said as much in his preface. But he thought his book none the less worth publication, and it is not for me to dispute that it may have been.

I still think this book well written and its contents true and important; and my condemnation of the treatment of China by the Western Powers has certainly not been modified by later events. The passage cited by Mr Pearsall Smith, in his anthology of prose, is the best in the book. I wrote it in the garden of King's College, with sensations which I still recall. Just as I recall writing there parts of *From King to King,* especially the conversation between Milton and his tutor. That garden indeed is loaded for me with every kind of association; playing tennis there with O.B.; sitting there with Roger and with Ferdinand; some of my sonnets, especially the one:

> I do not bid thee come, although the spring
> Doth in thine absence from herself depart,
> And all her beauty like a painted thing
> Flatters the eye but may not touch the heart

and the one:

> No! not the hand of death! Some other power
> Summon to aid thee in the day of doom!

With its late summer imagery—

> Yet doth the slow-consuming fire of heaven,
> The opiate odour of the glooming rose,
> The languour-laden air of windless even
> Hint at a passion, not a dead repose.

Now, when I go there, inevitably there comes into my mind the figure of one of the youths killed in the war, not a special friend of mine, but one whom I used to see seated in the summer house, and who, for me, will sit there still, till I visit the place no more. He was killed in the first weeks of the war, in Belgium.

CHAPTER FOURTEEN

American Tours and Writing, 1901–1910

In the autumn of 1901 I made my first visit to the United States. This marks, I think, a kind of epoch in my life. I had lived for nearly fifteen years at Cambridge, during the academic year, teaching, studying and writing; though I had also done a good deal of travel in Europe, as well as undergoing my experiences of personal passion. I felt now, in a more acute form, the restlessness which I have always felt in some degree. I was afraid of falling into a rut. And my brother's removal to the States in that year gave an excuse for visiting that country. I arranged accordingly to deliver some lectures, in order to pay my expenses, and made ready to start in the autumn.

During the preceding summer I was staying in lodgings at Betchworth. There was a long garden, ending on the banks of the little river Mole, and there I used to sit and read or write. The Boer war was going on and, in the silence and solitude, a voice used to sing, somewhere out of the green, a then popular song:

> There is not any other
> To take the place of mother.

In this exquisite English summer, in the solitude and the peace, I used to think with a kind of panic of journeying in a few weeks to that vast noise across the Atlantic. And as is so often the case, I seemed first to learn to value what I had when I had decided to give it up. My enterprise looked a gigantic one for a small skinless creature to embark upon. However, once in it, it went easily enough.

I crossed in the Atlantic Transport Line from London, a cargo ship carrying a number of horses, and very large and steady. As I write, I recall standing at night, down on the lower deck, by the bows, and watching the masts sway across the moonlit sky. But I always hated sea voyages, and especially the usually cold and uncomfortable Atlantic; they have been for me mostly a thing to endure and get through as one could. What chiefly strikes me, in memories, perhaps jaundiced, is the bareness of human nature on such occasions, the rapidity with which flirtations develop, the almost complete removal of the restraints observed on land. I don't know why it is so unpleasant to see other people engaged in the sex-rut, while one is free oneself, but I think it is a common experience. And no doubt the violent prejudice of 'normal' men against homosexuality is due to the fact that their own sex is never so stimulated—unless, indeed, one is to agree with a recent writer that the feeling is due to a suppression on their part of impulses they had or might have had. To me, having the homosexual temperament, it always requires a slight effort not to be repelled by the spectacle of sex passion between men and women.

On reaching New York I went out at once to my brother, who was then living in New Jersey, and suffering, with his family, from mosquitoes and other sources of worry and depression. After a day or two there, I went right across to San Francisco. I felt, at first, a throb of excitement at steaming out of the city through country so recently (as it pleased me to think) populated only by Indians. But it is hard to maintain any such sense of romance in America. The train journey of a week or so upset and irritated me almost as much as the sea crossing, and I arrived something of a wreck at Berkeley. There I was entertained by Professor Gayler with the usual American hospitality and kindness.

My lectures went well enough, though I cannot now think they can have been either novel or interesting. I had chosen a subject at which I had been working, the political organisation of the British Empire, and I think that, like too many Englishmen, I probably altogether exaggerated the ignorance of my audience. American audiences, however, are, or were, singularly tolerant, and have an air of being interested which encourages a lecturer, accustomed to the coldness of the English. Thrown thus upon my own resources, I found that I could get on well with people, though I am naturally shy. But I experienced then, what is a common phenomenon with me, the sense that all the time I was acting a part, and that the essential me was looking on, with detachment and some disapproval, at the performing animal. I remember the bright cloudless days in Berkeley and San Francisco, the sea shore with its seals, the Chinese quarter in the city (this of course was before the fire) then a visit to the Yosemite valley, the long drive of two days through primaeval forest, and especially, when I walked ahead of the coach, being quite alone among the huge pines, the black squirrels and the intense silence spread for miles about me.

The Yosemite valley is a deep oval, with huge cliffs and mountains shutting it in. I spent the days walking, mostly alone. Once in the valley I came across two natives devouring raw the decayed carcass of a horse.

Another time, wandering high up in the mountains, my inner life showed itself clearly, and I felt convinced that my business was to discover and illuminate the fundamental notions that should guide modern civilisation. That sounds pretentious enough, and I suppose it was; but not consciously, to me. Only, I did not realise the magnitude of the task nor the pitifully little I could hope to achieve. But the aim was, and is, mine and I cling to it still, for what is left of my life, in a world that seems for the moment to have returned to the purposes of barbarism, backed by all the resources of science. In this place I met two young Germans travelling with their tutor; and it illustrates probably rather my own limitations than the truth about America when I confess that I felt I had come across civilisation again in a land of barbarians. So easily do travellers identify the familiar and congenial with the Good.

Returning from California, I stopped off at Strong City, Kansas, to see my old friend Plump Hughes, then ranching. The 'city' was a single street of wooden houses, with horses tethered all along it, a strip of mud for a road, and a tramway running down it. My friend lived a little outside, with a farmer and his family. All around was nothing but infinite plain. We rode out to round up some cattle and I created some amusement by my inability to compel my horse to adopt the proper form of amble (I forget what they call it, 'lopping' I think). Then back East to Niagara, where my brother brought me my copies of 'John Chinaman'. It must have been in a later visit, not in this one, that I wrote the essay on Niagara published in *Appearances*.[1] Niagara, both the falls and (what impressed me almost more) the rapids, is tremendous, not beautiful. It gives the sense of power detached from purpose more than anything I have seen except Swiss snow mountains. So it served well for my then text. The text, no doubt, is only an 'appearance', but it is one of those that make up America, and one that in all my visits has prominently obsessed me.

On this and later visits I made one or two good friends. One was Miss Norton, sister of T. E. Norton, one of those old ladies America seems to produce, cheerful, intelligent, cultivated and optimistic. She was a lover of Montaigne and has written several volumes on him. I have lost sight of her now. She may be dead. But for many years we used to correspond. I liked her, indeed, better than her brother, who, as I thought, had that air of excessive culture with which that kind of American protects himself against the surrounding barbarism. He had three daughters called by the students at Harvard Paradiso, Purgatorio and Inferno, from their appearance, as I gathered, rather than their characters. I wonder which of them it was that was persuaded to attend the Yale-Harvard football match (the

---

[1] *Appearances*, J. M. Dent & Sons, 1914, a collection of travel articles, mostly reprinted from the *Manchester Guardian*. Ed.

father discouraged football) and, getting there, screamed out at a critical moment, 'Kill him! Kill him'! The story may be apocryphal, but it illustrates well the extraordinarily violent character of American football. The players are armed from head to foot, and there wait in reserve others to take the place of those that are carried out maimed or killed.

Another of my friends made then or at a later visit was G. Dow, then a Professor of Literature at Dartmouth College, New Hampshire, a great ally of Miss Norton and, by nature, what he called 'nonjoiner'. Then, on the crossing back to England, I met Russell Loines, who became one of my best friends. In later visits, I stayed with him in his house on Staten Island, where so many young Englishmen found a welcome, and where, in particular, Rupert Brooke was entertained. I went with him, in my second visit, up to the Adirondacks, where we walked among the hills and rowed upon the lake, while the deer came down to drink in the moonlight. I stayed at his father's house on Lake George, and we paddled in a canoe down the Delaware river. He died suddenly last year (1922), and for me a light has gone out on that continent.

When I said that this visit to the United States marked an epoch in my life, I meant only that it showed me that I could get on well enough with people, and that my natural shyness did not hamper me in intercourse with strangers. Mrs Schiller used to say that my whole manner and appearance was changed for the better. I had certainly more confidence, and perhaps, too, escaped, by that drastic measure, falling into oddity and seclusion, as one easily might, if one is unmarried at Cambridge. On the other hand, it is true, as I have said, that this external social self was a kind of mask, and behind it I felt singularly lonely. Forster once suggested to me that perhaps everyone does, and that we are all posing to one another. But I doubt it. Some men, perhaps most men, seem to find in society the exact expression for themselves. For instance, I am now reading the reminiscences of William Hickey; and it seems clear that he was always his real self, and found that only in company. He was, in fact, what modern inquirers call an 'extravert', and I am certainly an 'introvert'. There always echo about my mind the words I heard long ago in a play of de Musset: 'Quelle solitude qu'une âme humaine.' Nor do I think this is due to the homosexual temperament, for I know at least one homosexual who appears to be an 'extravert' through and through.

During the next years I must have been writing *A Modern Symposium*, which was published in 1905. With the exception of *John Chinaman,* this has been the most popular of my books, and I rather think that, in form, it is the best. I felt still the need, characteristic of me (whether it be a weakness or a quality or both), to write in a form which would allow me to give complete expression to various views, without judging them by my own, which in fact was still only in process of formation. But having experienced the difficulty of the dialogue proper, I tried what I thought would be easier, the form adopted by Plato in the *Symposium*. This form implies less argument and more rhetoric. And the qualities of my book are rhetorical, perhaps, at best, poetic, rather than dialectic. I think it still a good preparation for young men intending politics, and for ordinary citizens, who are able to maintain a more detached outlook. But still it does not solve the problem, which is perhaps insoluble, of making the bridge between speculation and art, and all that side of life, and what is called practical politics. For practical politics involves fighting, and the object of such a book as mine (as it was Plato's object long ago) is to raise the mind above the fighting attitude.

There lies here obscurely the great problem of the relation of ideals to passion and interests, which I do not seem able clearly to formulate to myself, still less to solve. Goethe apparently intended to deal with it in his 'Mahomet', but we have nothing but fragments of that. It seems to be impossible to go into active life of any kind without also being ready to kill, to lie and to cheat. All the men of action we admire did these things, among other things. The only people who did *not* were a few genuine saints. The men of action may reply 'true, but if we did evil, at least we also did good'. I imagine that most of them, if they retain the power of reflecting on their life, would feel that they preferred their own course to that of a fugitive and cloistered virtue. I don't think it clear either that they are right or that they are wrong. What is one really to think of, say, Lenin or Ludendorff, or Poincaré? I say 'think', and suppose a willingness and capacity to discount the mere idle passions of the present. What is one really to *think*? The older I grow the harder I find it to attempt the answer to this question. And the other question—what does one think of Plato (in his political capacity) or (at so great a distance, yet in the same kind) of myself—is but the other side of the same problem. I am conscious, in all I have written and thought, of complete disinterestedness in the pursuit of truth. But it does not seem to follow that the other kind of man need therefore regard me with particular respect. 'What have you done?' he will say, with Kipling. And if I reply 'no particular harm', he will say 'no, and no particular good'. 'Neither have you' I might reply, 'I see nothing but harm.' And somewhere about there the imaginary debate would end. We have not, in fact, either the knowledge or the standards to deal with the subject.

To return: *A Modern Symposium* was published in 1905. I finished it, if I remember right, when we were staying at Baslow in Derbyshire. But I had written it twice over, the first version being unsatisfactory. I suppose it is, in some ways, the best of my books, certainly it is one of the most popular —or perhaps I should say the least unpopular, and it had, at any rate on its appearance, a *succès d'estime*. It brought me for a moment into what is called 'society', or into a chance of it, which I am afraid I did not improve, and I quickly dropped out again. But I found the people I met singularly agreeable, easy and amusing. What was wrong, so far as I was concerned, was that, at bottom, I had nothing in common with them, nor they with me. Probably they found me very dull, and probably I was so, in that atmosphere. As to the book, I take it as a characteristic of me that I felt impelled to state, as far as I could, from inside, what seemed to me the most important of the radically different attitudes about political questions. For I have never been able to rest in an external and merely partisan appreciation of an opponent's view. So far, if I had had the other qualities, I might have been a dramatist. And that reminds me of one of my essays in that capacity.

When I returned from my second American trip in 1909, I was, as usual, restless and discontented, wondering what it would be worth while to tackle, and unable, as I have usually been, to embark on a proper 'academic' book. I had been reading Miss Tarbell's book on the Standard Oil Trust, and it occurred to me to try a drama about it. I accordingly wrote my play *Business* (it must have been in 1909–10) and sent it to the Stage Society, where it was performed on a Sunday and Monday in 1911. I had no experience of writing for the stage, though of course I often went to see plays, and was an admirer of Bernard Shaw. I was not admitted to any rehearsal of my play until the very last moment and then found, too late, that one character had been completely misconceived by the manager, who, however, was otherwise very competent. How successful the play was I cannot tell, as I heard the most opposite opinions, so far as I heard any. It was noticed by the press rather favourably, and I treasured a casual printed remark of Bernard Shaw, referring to me, among others, as a playwright of some promise. I had the personal experience (only too common, I suppose!) of finding my own play very interesting and moving on the stage. But I am pretty sure that was not the general opinion. However, I was satisfied, and thought of writing other plays.

I did in fact, just before the war, finish one, on the subject of Lassalle. I sent it to the Stage Society, and they rejected it. But it was to have been produced by Mr Foss in 1914, at the Little Theatre. He professed admiration for it, and a certainty of success. But the war intervened, and Mr Foss has lost both copies of the play, of which I myself have only two acts of the final version; and I feel now no impulse to try to reconstruct the rest from memory. The subject, I am sure, is a great one for the stage, if anyone should be able to handle it properly. Whether my version had any merits, or what, I cannot now estimate. I am inclined, with the tenderness of authors for their own productions, to think it had.

My next book *Justice and Liberty* was published in 1908. I wrote it with great difficulty, and it sums up my thinking on politics for many years. I am, I suppose, less gifted than most people for what is called practical politics, but the underlying ideas and ideals had always held me, and the actual condition of society had been always a kind of running sore in my mind. What is it not now! I could not write such a book as *Justice and Liberty* now, for I no longer believe as I did for what seems a curiously long time, that men are influenced, or influenceable, by ideas or ideals, except in time of revolution, and then it is the most violent who come to the top. I had, when I wrote the book, the notion which had inspired all my teaching at Cambridge, that political opinions and action might and should be prompted by truth. And I tried to set out important fundamental truths, much as Plato tried for his time, or Ruskin for ours. The book is, I suppose, rather difficult and repelling, in spite of my attempt to recapture the charm of the Platonic form. Anyhow, it has had few readers, though a certain number of copies still sell every year.

Carlyle said that Goethe tried to make men act by light, and when they would not, there came, with the French Revolution, the action of fire. What that fire is we see now in Russia and in some countries in Europe. And I am inclined to think that even I, old as I am, may see it at work in England. If I do not, it will not be any desert of ours that will preserve us. For never, I think, have men so blind and base ruled any country, as those that have ruled in England since 1918 (with the brief exception of the Labour Party in 1924). But it is all too easy to denounce, and in my small way I too am responsible, since I could never so speak and act that men had to attend to me. But in that condemnation much greater men than I are included.

My father died in the December of 1908. He had been failing for some time, and had two slight strokes, but recovered from these without any perceptible loss of faculty. On the whole, till the last weeks, he had kept his health and faculties wonderfully. His last attack—another stroke—lasted, I think, only 30 hours or so. He made one remark I remember: 'What are all these people doing in the room?' apparently seeing relations and old friends. His actual death took some hours and was due to what is called—I forget—somebody's 'Breathing'—a constant rhythm of breath, working up to a climax and failing again, over and over again. The doctor said he was unconscious, and I hope he was. I was suffering from sciatica at the time, in considerable discomfort in the next room, but going in from time to time to his room next door. My sisters knelt at either side of the bed. I think that I did not feel much sense of personal loss, because there had never been intimacy between him and me. My feelings are given in the following letter, written to Mrs Webb, 16 December:

I have never seen anything so beautiful and touching as Janet during that day and night. She somehow typifies for me everything best in women—the things they have and men haven't. She will feel a dreadful void, like a mother losing a child.

That is true. Her feeling for my father had something maternal in it. 'May too,' I add and truly, 'is at her best in a moment of real trouble.' I then go on:

I feel no sense of personal loss. I never had with my father the camaraderie one sometimes sees between fathers and sons. But looking back and seeing him a little in focus, I see what a really remarkable man he was—so many-sided, so human, and, in spite of much worldly success, so fundamentally unworldly. I feel as if I never knew him properly—that is so often the case with near relations. He had a very complete and happy life—gathered the best of all earth had to give —and always kept his horizon open too. To see him dying—it was 30 hours, though I hope he was unconscious—was to me like seeing a machine run down. He wasn't there. Is he anywhere or anything? I somehow think he is; but our thoughts are mere inarticulateness, after all, in face of the fact of death.

In 1909 I went on my second lecture tour to the United States. Some remarks about this have been made above, and some letters dealing with it have been extracted in the chapter on my friendship with Mrs Webb. It was on my return from this visit that I wrote my play *Business* referred to above.

In 1910 I went abroad with my sisters, May and Janet, and Miss Tait, to Sicily. That was a delightful trip, but nothing particular occurs to me to record, except that we took an expedition to see the lava flowing out from Aetna (the remains of the great eruption of that year). I have a vividish impression of a long walk and donkey ride over the ossified lava of the lower slopes, of the slow viscous red stream pouring out of a gash in the mountain side and faintly and ominously crackling, then the very uncomfortable night on straw in a hut, and so back next day to our carriage; a wonderful experience which we all enjoyed—even Miss Tait, who refused to lie down in the hut, and sat upright on a broken chair, remarking occasionally that she was perfectly comfortable. I have come across one letter, to Mrs Webb, from which I will cite. It was written from Girgenti, on 10 April 1910:

The history of Sicily, like all history, is a long series of wars and massacres, and the retrospect depresses my imagination. All these flowers we love—poetry, architecture and sculpture—grow out of a soil of corpses, and are watered with blood. The world looks very sombre to me as I grow older—very great but very terrible, and altogether beyond our intellect and imagination to grasp. I am enjoying myself all right, but in a mild and quiet way. But conversation is out of the question, and I miss a male companion. . . . The past interests me less and less, and the present and the future more and more. 'Let the dead bury their dead' I begin to feel. We can't recover Greece, and we can't recover the Middle Ages. And we ought to devote all our imagination to creating and interpreting our own age, which is great enough, if we were great enough to deal with it. After all, the Greeks were a kind of nest of robbers, crude and irresponsible children in their political and social life.

CHAPTER FIFTEEN

Eastern Travel, 1912–1913

On my return to England from my second lecture tour in the United States I changed my rooms to those I now occupy, and probably shall till I die, in the centre of Gibbs Building over the archway—still a pleasure to me from their dignity and beauty.

I cannot remember anything further definite (except the troubles with Oscar) until my journey to the East in 1912–13. I applied for and obtained what is known as a Kahn Travelling Fellowship. Kahn is a French Jew, of imagination and disinterested genius, who believes that acquaintance with other countries may enlarge mutual appreciation and contribute to peace. He is also a Bergsonian, and when both were poor young men used to expend some portion of his own meagre income for instruction from the philosopher. Later he made a fortune (I believe, in Japanese funds), and is now a millionaire of sorts. I met him for the first time last summer, and thought him one of the most charming, humane, beneficent men I have ever come across. We, the Kahn scholars (so say the British a little ironically), are the extreme forward point of the *élan vital,* and have thus a great responsibility. My report on this tour was published by the Trustees under the title *The Civilisations of India, China and Japan*. I also reprinted articles I had written for the *Manchester Guardian,* adding letters dealing with my American tour of 1909, under the title *Appearances*. Some further facts and impressions I will give here.

I travelled out to Egypt with my old friend J. M. Furness, then the head of a large school in Cairo. I had visited him before, though I think I have not mentioned that. What was then his school had been a palace. It was down in the old city, close to the citadel, and one heard the Muezzin from a neighbouring minaret. There were huge black birds, some kind of crow, in the trees of the garden. Altogether a most romantic spot, I thought and think. The journey from Alexandria to Cairo in the evening, along the Nile, with the little boys riding buffaloes and the long, lean walking figures, lingers still in my mind; and then the arrival in the large cool house, with all doors open, and the Soudanese attendant, silent, young, beautiful as I thought. It was hotter in Cairo that autumn than I remember finding it anywhere in the East, except at Singapore. We lay naked on our beds and took periodic cold baths. In the evening we walked out in the desert, passing through the citadel occupied by British tommies, who in that weather were playing football. The desert, then as before, was the principal impression made on me—like a glacier, that was hot instead of cold and grey, and golden instead of white—the sunset, the moon rising over the fantastic hills of sand, and the air fresh and exhilarating, as in high Switzerland.

After a fortnight or so of this, I joined at Port Said the boat in which my companions had proceeded from England. They were E. M. Forster, the novelist, R. C. Trevelyan, the poet, and G. Luce, also then a young poet, who was going out to Rangoon, where he later married a Burmese lady and became an authority on Burmese history. I remember the voyage, on the whole, with pleasure. The Red Sea was not intolerably hot, and though the company was one not naturally congenial to me, we discovered one interesting figure—a young officer called Searight, of a romantic Byronic temperament, homosexual and perpetually in love with some boy or other, with a passion for literature, and writing an autobiography of which he showed us parts, in a style which also seemed to belong to Byron—not good, I suppose, but curiously moving. We joined him later for a day or two at Peshawar, but I have never seen him since, though he wrote once or twice. So he can linger in my mind with an air of perpetual youth about him. If one actually saw him, I suppose he would be well on into middle age, and probably with nothing to fall back upon, now that the years of romance are past. But he was a charming figure then, and very beautiful. The other passengers, we were informed, used to call our little group the 'salon'. Bob, the most friendly and unselfconscious of men, kept the pot boiling, conversing always on what interested himself, that is literature, to the amused tolerance, sometimes passing into irritation, of his neighbours. 'What is the use,' said one of them once, 'of all these scraps of information?' 'Why, to make amusing conversation as we're doing now.'

India produced on me the kind of impression which runs through my published letters. But, of course, my contacts were of the most superficial. Forster left us rather early, stayed with Indian friends, and got certainly closer to reality than we did; but perhaps (I don't know) few Englishmen can easily get into real contact with it. For the hardworked and conscientious Anglo-Indians I met I felt a sympathy tinged with a kind of despair. For it seemed almost that the more conscientiously they did their work, the farther they were from the native sympathy and mind. But that too may be illusion. I am, however, pretty sure that the irony that brought the English into contact with the Indians is only equalled by that which brought them into contact with the Irish. The barrier, on both sides, of incomprehension

Eastern Travel, 1912–1913

is almost impassable. I feel this incomprehension very strongly myself. Indian art, Indian religion, Indian society is alien and unsympathetic to me. I have no sense of superiority about it, but one of estrangement. What indeed is there or can there be in common between the tradition of Greece and that of India?

After a few days at Bombay Trevelyan and myself went to Ellora, to see the cave temples. In a contemporary letter I find myself writing:

They are 'fearful and wonderful' in the full and proper sense of the words. Even the Buddhist temples have been Hinduised and a great Buddha who should be impressive stares at you with painted ogre eyes and a moustache. There is no fine architectural form, but everything overlaid and overloaded with crude sculpture of Shiva legends, partly grotesque, partly horrible. I feel India very uncanny at present—as if a quite different humanity had grown up in it (which may be pure illusion). Anyhow one seems and is much closer to the terrible forces—disease and drought and famine. Even the sun is terrible. The gait and dress (or nudity) of the people is the great beauty—such reds and greens and blues in the landscape; and primitive goats and cows; and the lovely brown skins. But it is really distressing to feel the gulf—everyone salaaming to the white man, cringing and begging; not allowed to do a thing for oneself; and never knowing what is or is not proper for a sahib.

Next day we went to Ajanta, but I find no contemporary letter about this. I don't think I made anything of the pictures, which are hard to see anyhow in the semi-darkness. But I suppose they may be interesting and even beautiful. The place I remember and the evening sunset while we sat under a tree on the plain. Also the long drive and its picturesqueness. I cannot now and here pursue the various incidents and fatigues of this too rapid tour. We went right north to Peshawar from Bombay to visit Searight. He met us late at night at the station with a military friend, looking superb in his uniform, and we drove back to the camp through moonlit roads. He took us up the Khyber Pass. The officers danced with one another in the evenings and Searight carried Bob pig-a-back in some kind of game. Very faintly, at this distance, I recall the curious excitement due to nothing but Searight's presence.

Returning by Lahore, Delhi, Agra, we landed up at Chattarpur, where, like so many Europeans, we had introductions to the Maharajah. It soon turned out that he was homosexual, in a curious (or not curious) way which combined what would be called perverted sexuality with philosophic and religious curiosity and yearning. He was an ugly little man, who dressed in white drawers, slippers and a very vulgar yellow ulster. He took us drives in his car, the long trains of bullocks leaping wildly into the ditch as he passed, absorbed in questions about Plato or Herbert Spencer.

One philosopher seemed much the same as another to him. I wrote an article on all this, which was published, not with my others in the *Manchester Guardian,* but later in *Basileon,* the King's College annual May week periodical. I cannot, however, lay my hands on it now. Instead, I will quote from a contemporary letter:

I sit on the terrace looking over a wide stretch of trees and hilly ground. A well is just below, where they are always drawing water. And fascinating apes play about, the babies in their mothers' arms, or clinging to their breast.

These apes I remember well. They were sacred and never molested—great yellow creatures.

The Maharajah motored me this afternoon to a ruined palace on the lake—the most beautiful and appealing place I have ever seen. The lake is grown over with lotus leaves; there are water-fowls, and great trees hanging over the water and the usual wonderful sunset light. Sun too hot even at four. The Maharajah offered me the ruined palace (he offered it to Forster before) if I would come and live here. Shall I? I should sit in marble halls and courts and paddle on the lake. And close by is the lovely tomb of the Queen who was a nymph and lived on lotus and was called the daughter of the lotus. This is the Maharajah's account of her. Mosquitoes are getting tiresome and will shortly drive me under my curtains . . . Puṁ Puṁ Puṁ—Tú Tu Tu Tu Tú Tu Tu Tu Tu-Tá, says the drum. It's a queer world. As we emerged from the palace, the car stopped and the Maharajah held a long colloquy with an old woman with a child in her arms. 'It's my cook', he told me, 'She's always running away here to her home, and she says she won't come back this time.' 'Why not?' 'She says her wages are too small. She gets two rupees a month and she wants four.' The ordinary wage for an agricultural labourer is 1d a day. 'Perhaps that is why Krishna does not come.' In explanation of this last I should say that the Maharajah's *sehnsucht*—touching and sympathetic to me—was always for Krishna to come—the ideal friend. As to the cook, he added that the principal reason why he missed her was that, when he couldn't sleep, he sent for her to talk philosophy and religion with him. That, at least, is democratic in a way inconceivable anywhere in the West.

Later I find myself writing from Darjeeling:

It dawns on me dimly, out of a great ignorance, that the Indians once, and perhaps now still, felt nature and her powers more profoundly and audaciously and religiously than any other race—the Greeks were delightful children by comparison. But the Indians never had and have not now a God in history and couldn't have produced Carlyle or Meredith. And I am very deeply unsympathetic to their view of human destiny. Man is a mere episode—rather an illusion—in the eternal life of the Absolute. And the only object is to get re-absorbed into that. Not for me thanks!

Eastern Travel, 1912–1913

This is all commonplace enough. I suppose I still feel it more or less. But my principal feeling is that we know nothing about anything that matters, and that it is unlikely that we humans matter at all in the economy of the universe—not more than fleas matter to us. However, that too is a mere exclamation, and probably quite irrelevant to anything that is true. I go on:

The natives here are a Mongolian type from Thibet and Nepal and Bhopal. They look very attractive to me—so human and so merry. I'm sure I shall love the Chinese. By the bye, the head waiter here comes from Bhotan, three weeks going across the mountains. Eleven years ago his uncles murdered his father, who was a big landlord. So he's never been able to go back. Queer world ain't it?

In a letter from Calcutta at the end of the year I write:

Last night we dined with a lot of Bengalees all graduates of Oxford or Cambridge, very intelligent, very well read, morbidly sensitive, and bitterly conscious of belonging to a conquered race and having no political power. I doubt, du reste, if most of them have any political capacity. But that isn't the point. It's like the suffragettes in England. They feel degraded and slighted. And all this comes out in 'sedition'. They do not hate England, nor the English. They say they owe all they are to her. But they want to be citizens. If Anglo-Indians could understand that, they would understand 'sedition' and perhaps be able to deal with it better. The method of spying on people of every kind, opening their letters, deporting them, etc. and the like, seems to me hopeless. I admit it's difficult to know what to do, for the Indians themselves are as unreasonable and pernickity as all people with a chronic grievance. They thank us for nothing, and abuse us for everything. But if they get hold of Englishmen they think sympathetic they simply load them with kindness and attention; feeling, indeed, as one of them said, that it's like breathing fresh air to talk to an Englishman as they had been used to talk in England. Here, you see, the gulf between the two societies is almost absolute. That's the misery of the situation . . . I dined out with . . . the other night. His conversation was of the kind one could only ignore, unless one decided to insult him. He wanted to pick out a few Bengalees—innocent or guilty he didn't care—and turn the Pathans on them to bayonet them—'play with them' was his phrase—pour encourager les autres. I find *John Chinaman* is a kind of gospel for the 'seditious' here. I didn't know how much. In some queer way I have caught the ideal of the East in that book. Yet really it isn't my ideal. I find myself more and more essentially Western; if the antithesis means anything, which really is what I am trying to discover.

That last sentence interests me. For now, after the Great War and all that has followed, the West begins to seem to me a mere horror, fit for nothing but extermination. Which also, no doubt, is nonsense—a gust of rage, such a one as is always sweeping over one.

The Autobiography of G. Lowes Dickinson

After a visit to South India and Ceylon we went to Singapore and from there to Java, of which I have no contemporary record of interest. Thence returned to Singapore and, having to wait there for a boat East, took a trip to Sumatra. Of that I find the following contemporary account:

It was queer at Sumatra. You land on a mango swamp—it looks like a land unvisited by civilisation. Then a train turns up—the only way through the swamp being the railway. In an hour you arrive at a town and a first-class expensive hotel, with a European menu. The whole town is, on the face of it, Chinese and Japanese. But in every shop they are selling gramophones, bicycles, motor cars, every sort of European goods. You motor a few hours on good roads (so I'm told) and arrive at the Bataks, who were cannibals a few years ago and make the brass work which I have sent home, and which I hope will arrive safe. The interpenetration of East and West is going on at an amazing rate. . . . There are three boy scouts on the pier. (That was at Singapore.)

Thence to China, landing at Hong Kong, where I stayed at the top of the hill, in fog so wet that it soaked one's clothes at night, and descended thence into bright sunshine. Thence to Canton where I stayed with Jamieson, still the Consul there, a batchelor and a character with whom I felt an odd sympathy, which makes me wonder whether he was homosexual. He had to face the Chinese rioters recently, and somehow I feel sure that he did his best to prevent the shooting that ensued. He was certainly, when I knew him, 'pro Chinese'. Canton was amazing, but I have said what I could about it in the little book where my *Manchester Guardian* articles are reprinted.[1] Trevelyan left me there and went home in order to arrive in time for the annual 'Lake hunt', as it was, and is, called—very odd of him, I thought. But I suppose he was restless with long travel. I lost in him a delightful companion, but perhaps saw more of the world than I otherwise should have done, since I was driven to talk to other people. In a letter from Shanghai I find a sentence which expresses what is now, as it was then and long has been, my view:

The older I get the more convinced I become that for us the most important and real thing is the passion to develop a higher, more extensive and more intensive life; and that that passion is just an ultimate fact to be accepted and acted on. It does not help me particularly to say 'God gave us that impulse', but it seems to help many people.

At Shanghai I saw, among other people, Sun Yat Sen, but, being unaccustomed to interviewing people and reluctant to intrude, I didn't get

---

[1] *Appearances, being Notes of Travel,* J. M. Dent & Sons, 1914. Ed.

Eastern Travel, 1912–1913

much out of him. I describe him as 'a quiet rather determined looking man with a tight mouth and looking less than forty, though I believe he is older'. The other day at the Institute of International Affairs the late head of Police at Shanghai described him as the most insignificant and incompetent of the Chinese leaders. But it was admitted that it was he who had inspired Young China and made revolution popular, as much in the North as in the South. What unexpected results had his delivery from the Chinese Embassy in Portland Place (where they had kidnapped him) by the English doctor (whose name I now forget), years and years ago!

From Shanghai, after a rather hectic fortnight or so of visits, etc., I went up the Yangtse by steamboat to Ichang and thence took a house-boat up the rapids. It was wonderful scenery, but I was unfortunate in weather as it rained almost continuously. We did not get up very far, but took ten days over the trip. I was alone with some twenty Chinese and a Chinese servant.

I seem to have written a good many letters on this Yangtse trip—naturally perhaps, as, when confined to the cabin by pouring rain, there was nothing to do but write and play patience. The following may be of interest to reproduce:

I visited two villages and found the people quite friendly and pleasant. In one I visited the school. New please note. This was a tiny spot in the heart of China. On the walls outside were placarded addition sums in our numerals. Inside, drawings of birds and beasts, of the human anatomy, of bacteria! Maps of China and of the world. And the children—very friendly—produced an English reader. What doesn't that imply? It doesn't matter whether there's a republic or no. What matters is *that*.

Again:

The 'joss-houses', as my boy calls them, are commonly deserted and turned into schools. . . . But in one a priest was kneeling in front of a shrine, all by himself, chanting out of a book and hitting a bronze vessel with a little stick. The places seemed to me like disused lumber rooms. The people are always quite friendly and ready to greet one with a flood of Chinese talk.

Returning from the Yangtse, I went up to Pekin. One of the images that persist in my mind is a train covered with Chinese inside and out, roofs, steps, even buffers of the carriages, like a swarm of bees. I spent some weeks in Pekin and the neighbourhood and took one delightful trip into Shantung with my friend Yetts, then a doctor in the British Settlement. On this expedition we ascended the sacred mountain of Taishan, of which I write as follows:

The cuckoos calling to one another across ranges and ranges of hills, bare and grey, green in the sun. And me lying on top of the most sacred mountain in China, where for four thousand years God has been worshipped, according to Chinese legend; where certainly Confucius came, and emperor after emperor, and streams of pilgrims, year after year. A path lined with cypresses and flight after flight of rock-stairs brings you to the top. And there we slept in the temple with images of Taoist gods watching us and saw the full moon over the plain, and the sunrise.

We descended to Tai-an-Fu, arriving late at night, and slept in the great temple there (one carried one's bed and bedding with one as well as two Chinese servants). I write:

The more I see and hear of the Chinese, the more delightful they appear to me. It's not a paradox to say that they are the most civilised of nations. The West perhaps has more possibilities; but in the region of manners, feelings, and art, I think they have a higher achievement. Only, their civilisation is decadent—I don't know when nor why it began to decline and nobody seems to know. Europe, I fear, will swallow it up, not revive it.

I wonder? I am writing now in the May of 1927, in the midst of a 'kind of war' that is not called a war. The British are the most unpopular people in the East, and pretend to wonder why. Anyone who knows the facts could tell them; but for an Englishman unpleasant facts don't exist. However, I must not digress.

On this little expedition we also visited Che-Fu(?) the birthplace of Confucius, where his descendants have reigned, as 'dukes', ever since, and are buried in the huge adjoining cemetery. I write:

We called on the present Duke, who sent a message that he was not up. Yetts considered. It would be 'losing face' to wait. He therefore returned a message that we were sorry to miss him, and proposed to retire. This device immediately produced the duke, fully dressed. We carried on, by an interpreter, a conversation consisting entirely of questions and answers. 'How old was I? Was I married? Why not?' etc. After an interminable time some raspberry vinegar was produced, on which we regaled ourselves. The Duke was rather handsome and looked a rip.

It was here that I slept in a real Chinese inn, of which I speak as follows:

A room opening on the dirty courtyard, with pigs, horses and dogs about; an earth floor; no window, and no apparatus except two chairs and a table. We had, however, of course our own beds and some tinned food to supplement the Chinese. There were no vermin and I was happy enough; though I admit to a

Eastern Travel, 1912–1913

momentary disconcertion on arriving wet-through in pouring rain and seeing the kind of place. A great deal of our time was spent in calling on and being called on by the mandarin, whose attentions and courtesy were rather overwhelming in our humble shed. He conducted us over the temples and the great Confucian cemetery. And we were amused to find afterwards that the doorkeepers had secretly mulcted our boys of two dollars for their fees behind the back of the official—very Chinese.

Yes, and the kind of thing that foreigners are always talking about. But it is a mere reflex of the universal poverty. In July I crossed from Tientsin to Japan, going via Kobe to Kyoto. I thought, and think, Japan one of the loveliest countries I have seen, and it is laid out for walking in a way few countries are. From Kyoto I wrote:

The first impressions of Japan are very delightful. It's so pleasant to find an Eastern civilisation holding its up head and keeping its own. Everything seems capable and efficient and self-respecting. No decay, no squalor, and yet not all Westernised. I suppose Tokyo is like a Western city, but this is not a bit. Japanese costume, Japanese houses and shops, and a great series of temples all 'going' and flourishing, not, as in China, sadly decaying. A Buddhist monastery which I saw this morning is perhaps the most exquisite thing I have seen. A long series of rooms, with the paper walls painted in birds and trees by seventeenth-century artists; colour and design perfect for the purpose; and nothing in the rooms, only the cleanest of matting. In one, two monks were squatting in meditation, and I felt one could meditate to some purpose. You must conceive that the city lies against a line of wonderfully wooded hills; and the temples are on the slope, approached by stairs and backed by gardens. This hotel ('Mikayo') again, the only one I have seen which is not run by cosmopolitan Europeans, is a model of taste, bare walls and floors, all unstained wood and whitewash; galleries for views; charming little Japanese girls to wait; a manager who talks to one about religion and art; and, the centre, of all this, us ugly Westerners, looking by contrast—well! But to think that the Californians treat the Japanese as barbarians! As if there were a single man in the whole continent of America who could hold a candle to the humblest Japanese in the point of breeding or morals. No 'C'en est trop'. And you don't know the kind of Europeans and Americans that come out to exploit the East! It really fills me with horror, sometimes, to look at them. And for such we wage our bloody and unjust wars!

I can't remember now my itinerary in Japan. But I have a few letters from the various places. Here is a bit from Kamakura:

This evening I walked out to a temple on a hill in the woods. It was dusk. No one to be seen. Thatched wooden halls in little terraces among the trees; a great bell in the tower. (Their bells sound like great songs as if the woods had a voice). Noise of cigalas; the little graveyard; images of Buddha in niches of the rocks.

Then I came back and bathed under the full moon rising. Lovely warm sea. Japan is marvellously full of beauty, and somehow it's like England in the way of antiquity and homeliness and peace.

From Kamakura I seem to have gone on my little walking tour with a Japanese friend, during which we ascended Fuji, as described in my book. Then there was Nikko, whence I find some long letters.

I went out in the evening, and fell upon a solitary temple garden full of enormous white lilies. It was all quite still, with that thundery feel that is so exciting. And little shrines all among the lilies. And the hills looking on, very solemn, under a grey sky.

Europeans and Americans seem so gross compared to the Japs. They may have all the virtues (they haven't of course!). But how dreary the virtues are! Why not a little human feeling instead? I think civilisation will die of virtues and vices.

To Trevelyan I write:

The Europeans and Americans really do seem to me a kind of dehumanised, decivilised crowd. The Japs attract me very much. I wish I could talk to them. They are so gay and vital and beautiful (all but their faces). Of course the West is ruining them, as it ruins everything it touches. The horrors of mills and architecture and dress in Tokyo are better not described. And a Western-educated Jap is apt to lose all his manners and all his beauty, like an Americanised Chinese. I really begin to look with horror on our civilisation. I suppose I shall recant and settle down into it again. Anyhow I'm fit for no other.

I can't say that my dislike of Western civilisation has been much modified by time. But I do feel that Cambridge in spring, with its young men, is very lovely. Last night (24 May)[1] I sat out in the College garden with three of them, till 10.30—one of those rare English nights when one can do that. And I was delighted, as so often, by the candour, sensitiveness, and intelligence of these boys—a small minority, no doubt, in the whole mass of athletes and womanisers, but still very charming. It will pass quickly, of course—it's like the bloom on the cheek of youth. But certainly in all my travels I have seen nothing lovelier than Cambridge at this time of year. But Cambridge is a lovely backwater. The main stream is Jix and Churchill and Communists and Fascists and hideous hot alleys in towns, and politics, and that terrible thing called the 'Empire', for which everyone seems to be willing to sacrifice all life, all beauty, all that is worth while; and has it any worth at all? It's a mere power-engine.

[1] 1927. *Ed.*

Eastern Travel, 1912–1913

Having written which—for what is the good of writing reminiscences unless they reflect one's moods?—I read in another letter:

The Japanese Government is suppressing the liberty of speech and thought; all trade unions; all and every outlet of reform movements. The Parliament is useless, the members venal and the parties nothing but personalities without policies. All quite damnable! I am glad I belong to a country still free. That advantage the West has.

But that was written before the war and fascism and communism—in the little oasis of comparatively free and honest government which fills the space between 1832 and 1914. After which? A great note of interrogation!

To return: I write further from Nikko—this time to Mrs Webb:

I'm sitting in a little tea-house on the top of a waterfall. Little Japanese girls in high skirts and sashes and wooden clogs are carrying about tea (green tea, very bad) and cyder (so called). The tea cups, tea trays and tea-pots (quite common) are also quite exquisite. Some boys in divided skirts are stuffing plants they have dug up into tin boxes. And a fat man with several women in attendance has stripped naked, all but his loins, and is quietly eating and drinking. Now this I call civilisation! I just love it. It's just about to pour with rain, but no matter. There are green grassy hills all around, and the noise of the waterfall. Japan is a lovely country! I'm quite alone here, but very happy and very well. . . . The naked man has partially dressed himself now and is preparing for departure with his dear little females. Perhaps I ought to go too, only I don't want to get wet. There's a cuckoo singing with rather a broken voice. And a youth with bare legs and blue spectacles has turned up, and is apparently making himself very entertaining to the ladies of the house. I think I shall go on and chance the rain.

For a few days I went to a little place called Ikao, where there are hot springs, to stay with some American friends.

This is a most enchanting place [I write]. There's no one hardly but Japanese. I'm living in two lovely paper-screen rooms, opening on to a balcony, with a great view of green and blue hills. The village runs up the hill in a steep street, with flights of steps. And the whole place is full of Japanese inns most picturesque. My American friends [I go on to say] made friends of the whole village, by giving some money to a boy suffering from ophthalmia to go to hospital. The whole village turned out with flowers to meet them at the station. As to the boy, he used to embarrass them by prostrating himself with tears every time he met them. . . . Then the extraordinary things they do! A boy of 20, the other day, committed hari kari, so that he might join his teacher who had died. A lot of people killed themselves last year, in hope of saving the Emperor's life. Death and pain seems to be nothing to them. Not because they are insensitive, but because they have this amazing courage, and self-control. Really I don't see where we come in by comparison, either in manners or morals or anything else. But of course they have their dark sides like the selling of their daughters into prostitution. But, from the daughter's point of view, this is a kind of heroism, a sacrifice to the family.

I may as well conclude this account with an extract which shows my consciousness of my own biases:

The only capacity I seem to have is that of interpreting peoples and nations to one another. I shall continue my endeavours in that direction, so long as I can. But I find it hard not to be unjust to the West in my sympathy with the East. It's a bad thing to lose one's temper and I'm always doing it. What a screed about ME!

I returned via the Siberian railway and Moscow to Berlin, Paris, London, very constipated with impressions. London somehow intoxicated me. And my chapter thereon in *Appearances* preserves that mood, and may serve as epilogue and summary for this chapter, if anyone cares to turn to it. It was the autumn of 1913 when I returned. And in less than a year the great catastrophe broke out which has more or less submerged the life of survivors who went through it, but appears to have passed without leaving a trace on the young. What little shallow cups we are, and how few the drops we can hold from the tempests that harry and drown us.

CHAPTER SIXTEEN

The War and After, 1914–1921

I remember well the outbreak of the Great War. I was in Cambridge. Up till the last moment it was impossible to believe that the thing was really going to happen. There had been alarms before, and they had always passed over. Surely this time, we thought, as before, there would be a settlement. Rumours of such indeed occurred up to the very last, even, as I seem to remember, in the evening papers the Saturday night before the fatal Sunday. On that Sunday morning, August 1st 1914, the word 'war' was flaming from the newspaper bills. It was a hot sunny day, and that type of weather continued during the rest of the summer. In the evening I cycled out alone, trying to realise the unrealisable, and I recall the view over the meadows and stream from the railway bridge, on the road between Barton and Haslingfield, a scene associated also, for me, with other deep and tragic, but also healing emotions. Though Germany was at war with France and Russia, it was still uncertain whether England would join. Grey's speech, on the Monday night, made it probable but not certain, and on the Tuesday afternoon I remember sitting for a time in the entrance court of the Union talking possibilities with a young man who still haunts my mind at times, and who a few weeks later was dead. Then came the invasion of Belgium, the end of the old and the beginning of the new. A little later I went down to my friend Bulmer, at Hereford, and we picnicked up the Wye with two of his nephews, one of whom in a short time shot himself, in the Air Force, his nerves broken to pieces.

As we sat by the river, in that marvellous summer, it seemed incredible what was going on over the water in France. Afterwards I spent a few days at Chipping Campden with C. R. Ashbee, and there we read the British White Book. I had written, by request of the Editor of *The Nation*, an article in which I tried to express my feelings, and I received at Campden a few replies from strangers who were grateful to me for saying what they also felt. The perfect weather continued, and the dumb impotent feeling of the gulf between nature, the past, all beautiful true and gracious things and beliefs, and this black horror of inconceivability that nevertheless was true. I had felt nothing like it since my mother's death; but this was infinitely worse. I was fifty-two; there was for me no question of enlisting, though I think I should have enlisted if I had been younger, for I was not a 'conscientious objector', though I had no illusions about the war, nor anything but despair in my heart. I did, in fact, for a time oscillate as to whether I should enter the Friends Ambulance Corps under my friend P. H. Baker, but I decided finally, and probably rightly, that so far as there was anything I could do it must be of a different kind.

I devoted myself, as far as there was any opportunity for such work, to propaganda for a league of nations. Already while I was at Hereford in the first week or two of the war, I had jotted down on a piece of paper two schemes for such a league. As soon as I got to town (still in August), I went round to a few people who might be interested and we got together the committee which Lord Bryce finally joined. We drew up the first plan formulated in England, circulated it to a number of people, received criticisms, amended, and finally published it.[1]

The members of this group, so far as I recollect, were, beside myself, Mr Richard Cross of Scarborough, who had joined the Quakers and whose name is associated with so much good political work behind the scenes. He was a lawyer and a very able as well as good and disinterested man. He acted as secretary for our committee and drafted our scheme. Without him I doubt whether we should ever have come, so to speak, to a point. Lord Bryce attended several meetings during our later period. Another leading and very useful member was my namesake, the Rt Hon. W. H. Dickinson, then a fairly prominent and well-known politician, M.P., and once Chairman of the London County Council. Mr J. A. Hobson was also an active member. Mr Arthur Ponsonby constantly attended, but was opposed, I think, always, to our proposed sanction of force. Mr Graham Wallas also was a member; but he was more concerned to press international co-operation in general than our particular and definite plan for preventing war.

We had, I believe, some real effect, in spite of our small number, and the unpopularity of most of us (so far as we were known at all); for our scheme reached the original members of the American League to Enforce Peace at a critical moment, and encouraged them to proceed, and we used to keep, so far as we could, in touch with them, with some mutual influence on both sides. Our scheme was considered, along with others, at Paris, and one clause of the final Covenant of the League, that defining the disputes generally suitable to arbitration, was taken directly from us. It had been drafted by Cross. But, of course, the League that actually came into being differed

---

[1] *Proposals for the Prevention of Future Wars* by Viscount Bryce and others. (George Allen & Unwin, 1917).

in important respects from the one we advocated; first, by its exclusion, in the first years, of the enemy States,[1] which bids fair to wreck the whole League; secondly, in the important place it assigns on the Council to the Governments of the Allied Powers. Our scheme would have sent every 'nonjusticiable' dispute to a permanent 'Council of Conciliation' independent of Governmental influence. Such a Council was adopted in the Locarno treaties,[2] and it is possible that the idea had filtered through from our draft. As I write, it is impossible to foresee whether the League is going to hold its own against its many enemies on the Right and on the Left. Our scheme, I think, would have reconciled most of the enemies on the Left, but would have been more violently resisted by those curious and powerful people who cannot bear the thought that any order should enter into international relations nor any check be put upon international war.

Our Group, finally fusing with another, formed the first League of Nations Society. That (if I remember right) was in 1915. We gradually built up a very small membership, perhaps two thousand odd. We got several fairly distinguished vice-presidents and finally secured as our president Lord Shaw. Towards the end of the war the idea of a league of nations became more reputable, owing to President Wilson's advocacy of it, an advocacy directly connected with the American League to Enforce Peace and so indirectly with us. Another society was then formed, of different and more 'reputable' people, known, most of them, I think, to have been ardent supporters of the war, and good haters of Germany. This society had money behind it, for the millionaire Major Davies (once an undergraduate at my College) was a member of it. After many to and fro-ings and much discussion, not now worth recalling, the two societies fused under the title of the League of Nations Union. This was in 1918. But some of our stalwarts, notably Mr Hobson and Lord Parmoor, left us when the fusion took place, holding (wrongly, as I think events proved) that we had surrendered some of our points to the enemy. The conditions of union were discussed in a committee whereon Mr L. S. Woolf, Sir W. H. Dickinson and myself represented our Society, and Mr H. G. Wells, Major Davies, and Professor Gilbert Murray the other.

The League of Nations Union is, at the time of my writing, the most influential society pushing the ideal of a league, and under the guidance of Lord Robert Cecil does good work, though its membership even now, and its funds, are very inadequate to its task. I found myself at the beginning a member of the Executive Council; but, thinking the idea was now well launched, and not being able to attend regularly, I resigned and of late

[1] Written before Germany's entrance.
[2] This sentence was a MS addition to the typescript, evidently made later. The Locarno treaties were in 1925. *Ed.*

have been a member only of the literary committee.[1] All work of the organising kind is naturally distasteful to me; and also, no doubt, my unpopularity as a 'pacifist' has tended to keep me in the background in an organisation that intends and indeed is bound to be respectable. I still speak at meetings when I am invited and do what I can to further the idea, though of course circumstances are very much against it. The recent decision about Silesia, for example, has almost killed the belief of many advocates of the League. And the fact that its Council is little better than a replica of the Supreme Council of the Allies, whose main business is to suppress Germany, discredits the League very seriously with good and candid men. I cannot and do not attempt here and now to look forward into the future. But naturally the prospect appears to me very dark. In that darkness two men stand out like angels of light. One is Lord Robert Cecil, the other Nansen.

May 1927. Things change so quickly that it seems worth while to add some words to the above, which was written some years ago. The League is consolidated by the entry of Germany, which is bound to make a great difference. I have visited Geneva several times and observed two things of importance. First, the way in which the permanent members of the Secretariat acquire, almost without knowing or intending it, an international attitude; secondly, how different discussion round a table is, in its results, to the communication by Foreign Offices of telegrams or written despatches. People—and I not least—get impatient and sceptical about machinery. But the fact is that machinery modifies attitudes almost as much as attitudes modify machinery. And by insensible gradation people find themselves feeling and thinking and doing what a little before they would have indignantly repudiated if the suggestion had been made to them. The prevention of the Greco–Bulgarian war shows that the Council, if it wants to, can act quickly and decisively.

On the other hand, the Italian action in Corfu shows the difficulty of dealing with a Great Power, and it seems likely that it was not the League that finally brought Italy to comparative reason, but the despatch of a British warship and Italian fear of alienating this country. Sooner or later a crisis with a Great Power is bound to arise, and then we shall know whether the League will face the music and win. I think the most likely thing is that there will be no declaration from the Council of who is the Aggressor (the British Government, by repudiating the Protocol, has rejected the only complete definition of an aggressor) and that the members of the League will range themselves on opposite sides.

[1] Now abolished, 1927.

The War and After, 1914-1921

To return to myself: I used, from the beginning, to speak in favour of a league, usually to very small and humble audiences, in little schoolrooms. I am not a good speaker for a public meeting either from the physical or any other point of view. But I can put a thing clearly to a small audience that wants to understand, and I may have been of some use in that way. Our meetings were not important, nor public enough even to excite opposition. Perhaps their main use was to bring together the very few men and women in England who were thinking at all about the future, or about anything but winning the war.

I also did all the writing I could. At that time I wrote pretty often for *The Nation* and used to attend their weekly lunches where the very few who were (comparatively) 'pacifists' were to be met. I also wrote for *War & Peace*, which became later the 'International Review'. I wrote, when I could, for the *Manchester Guardian*, especially four long letters, to which the Editor gave great prominence, on the League of Nations solution of the problems of the war. Besides this journalistic work, I wrote my two books on the war, the first entitled *The European Anarchy* (1916) and the second *The Choice Before Us* (1917). I made also two expeditions abroad. The first was in the early spring of 1915 to the Hague (it was before foreign travel, even to neutral countries, was cut off). There met there a small international gathering which included representatives from Austria and Germany; among them were Professor Schucking and an Austrian sociologist whose name I forget. Dr Lange, the very able secretary of the inter-parliamentary organisation, was also present, and I was drawn to him by a certain fundamental agreement in our notions of what ought to be done and how. I was the only Englishman present except Mr Baker (father of Phil), the M.P., who turned up at the end, but took no part. He died later during the war, and his son P. H. Baker, a member of my College, who was then running the Friends' Ambulance, later became a leading figure, behind the scenes, of the League at Geneva, and a great ally of Lord Robert Cecil.

At this meeting at the Hague there was formed the Society for a Durable Peace, among whose resolutions was one in favour of a League of Nations, drafted, if I remember rightly, by myself. This organisation continued to function, though no more international meetings were possible. It published a large number of papers, which were collected in three large volumes and some of which were interesting and important. On my return I was confronted by a statement in the press that Mr Baker and myself had gone to the Hague with the approval and under the commission of Sir Edward Grey. This, of course, was quite untrue. But on my return I had an interview with Sir Edward, explained what we had had done, and showed him our resolutions. He expressed no objection to these, but of course I foresaw that the kind of peace we wanted would become impossible by the mere fact that there had been a war. For that matter, I myself always knew that I was engaged on a forlorn hope, but saw nothing else on which I could engage with conviction.

My other journey abroad was to America in the spring of 1916. This trip was undertaken in order to lecture on the idea of a League of Nations. I lectured at a number of universities and other institutions both in the East and in the Middle West. It was of course before America came into the war. What may be called, I suppose, or would be called in England, the 'upper' classes were very sympathetic to England and anxious to enter the war on our side. Their's was a not uncommon attitude in the East. In the Middle West there seemed to be a complete indifference to the war, no idea of taking part in it, and a general sense that it was another of the fool enterprises of Europe, which of course it really was. The comparative sanity of America at that time, the mere contact with people who were not war-mad, was a refreshment to me. But how superficial and transitory that state of feeling was, was shown a year later, when America came into the war, and, according to all accounts, precisely the Middle West was the most intolerant and savage part of the country. The intolerance and cruelty of England was bad enough during the war. But anything that happened here pales into insignificance before what happened there. A modern democracy is a mere cloud of dust, and blows any way the wind blows.

As to my general attitude towards the war, it is sufficiently shown in my books and articles on the subject. I did not think, and I do not think now, that, after the invasion of Belgium, England could have kept out of it. I stated this clearly in the preface to my *Choice Before Us*. But neither was I ever under any illusion as to the real causes of the war. I knew it was impossible and absurd to suppose that this war (after all the wars of history, this particular one!) was due to the sole crime of one nation, deliberately forcing it upon an innocent world. Although I had made, at that time, no special study of international relations, I knew enough to know that Europe had long been a powder magazine, and I saw that nothing would cure that, no victory, no defeat, except a complete and radical change of policy, not in this or that State, but in all States. This led me at once to the idea of a League of Nations. It led me also, on the other hand, to a study of the circumstances and events that really led up to the war. I stated my first results briefly and clearly, in my *European Anarchy*. And, so far as I know, that book contains a true and well-balanced account of the real causes of the catastrophe. Everything there said has only been confirmed by the mass of material that has since been published.

It was clear to me that, unless the public here and elsewhere could be induced to see that causation in the true light, there was little chance that they would adopt the only remedy. But that they should see the causation

The War and After, 1914-1921

proved, of course, to be impossible. My friend, Mr Morel, the organiser of the Union of Democratic Control, clings to the view that, so long as it was thought that Germany alone was to blame, so long all hope of a good peace was ruled out. I did my best at the time to dissuade him from making an attack on allied policy the centre of his propaganda. But substantially he was right; though also he was wrong, in the sense that nothing would have induced the public to look at the truth.

With almost incredible rapidity the whole temper of England changed. This was, no doubt, assisted by the deliberate propaganda of press and government. But perhaps it hardly needed that propaganda. For it is a law of war (if the phrase may be allowed) that the combatant nation must believe itself to be wholly right and the enemy to be wholly wrong. This of course, is true of every country, on both sides, and governments merely used the means of publicity at their disposal to exploit a sentiment only wanting to be exploited. As it was then, so it will be again. Before a war people are too indifferent to study the truth about international politics. When the war has broken out, they are too passionate. And on those two facts is based, and apparently securely based, the power of a comparatively few men and interests to maintain war and destroy mankind.

To me, the worst kind of disillusionment was that connected with universities and historians. Hardly a voice was raised from those places and persons to maintain the light of truth. Like the rest, moved by passion, by fear, by the need to be in the swim, those who should have been the leaders of truth followed the crowd down the steep place. In a moment, as it were, I found myself isolated among my own people. When I say isolated, I do not mean in any sense persecuted. I suffered nothing in Cambridge except a complete want of sympathy. But I learned, once for all, that students, those whose business it would seem to be to keep the light of truth burning in a storm, are like other men, blindly patriotic, savagely violent, cowardly or false, when public opinion once begins to run strongly. The younger dons, and even the older ones, disappeared into war work. All discussion, all pursuit of truth ceased, as in a moment. To win the war, or to hide safely among the winners, became the only preoccupation. Abroad was heard only the sound of guns. At home only the ceaseless patter of a propaganda utterly indifferent to truth. A few people only, far more unpopular than myself, were my companions and sympathisers. I worked with them, or alone at my own table.

In some sense my cause came to have, at the end, a sort of formal triumph. But the character of the peace, the old kind of peace, with the old vices exaggerated to lunacy, has more than counteracted any advantage which might have been hoped for from the League of Nations. Europe, as I write, is being torn to pieces under our eyes, and this solely on account of the policy of the victorious Nations. As I write these words, those Governments have just condemned twenty millions of Russians to perish of famine, because they desire to get the Russian Tsarist debt acknowledged. I do not think history shows anywhere an example of Shylock policy on such a scale. But the men who govern Europe have as little humanity as they have sense. They are so used to the daily perishing of millions, that they would hardly be happy without it.

While my main interest and occupation, during the war, was as I have described it, I was still carrying on my work at Cambridge lecturing twice a week in term. But my class was naturally composed almost entirely of women. Cambridge had become a hospital and a camp. In my College there was almost nobody left but a few dons and the nurses who were quartered in the building by the river. My sense of alienation from common opinion, my melancholy, and my clear sense of fact (for so I must call it) caused me to retire altogether from such life as there was in the place. I lived and ate alone, when I was in Cambridge, and saw almost nobody. The long winter evenings still linger with me. Shut into my room, I seemed for a time to have shut out the world. My dim reading lamp, the rich red wall-paper, the flickering fire, were my background. It was there I used to think about Oscar, and write to him. It was such a mixture of love, of fear, of hope, of all conflicting emotions, as must have been common to so many who loved. I never really believed that he could return alive; and indeed it is something of a miracle that he did, for, in 1917, the whole of the officers of his battalion were killed, he alone being kept back for some purpose in the rear. Whether he is the happier to have been preserved it is not easy to say. To me, it makes, even in this terrible world, all the difference.

30 October 1921

The preceding chapters were drafted during a very few days in the summer and early autumn of 1921. Today is 30 October, and I feel inclined to set down something about my present state.

I resigned my lectureship at King's in 1920, retaining a life Fellowship, and being granted a pension of £100. This should leave me quite enough to live on, if ordered society, or rather the present order or disorder, persists at all. When I resigned my lectureship, I thought, first, that I had taught long enough; secondly, that I had lost belief in my teaching, or (perhaps it would be truer to say) that the development of political and social facts had outgrown my powers, as a now ageing man, to deal adequately with it; thirdly, that I did not want to have so much of my time tied to work which began to seem to me less important. I did not doubt that I should find stimulus and interest and power enough to continue to study and write. This may turn out to be true. But I find my present state rather unpromising.

Returning to College late this term, I find myself lonely, out of touch, and disinclined for such society as is easily open to me. My thoughts are sad and hopeless. I see little reason why I should go on living, and little hope that I can add anything of any importance to such work as I have done. The state of Europe and of the world is desperate. Such religion as there is is impotent and absurd. Reason and humanity hardly begin to make themselves felt. Violence and greed and low ambition seem more dominant than even before the war. I am myself without any influence on events. And I am out of touch with young men, who have always been my principal interest. Looking back or forward, my life appears, and indeed is, an insignificant and meaningless thing.

I have been rereading Wordsworth's *Prelude* and I am clear that his flight from life to the Lakes and his plunge into English conservatism, though it made him in some sense happy, was a mere evasion of the problem. 'Nature' teaches nothing about moral evil and good. She made Wordsworth happy and gave him some mystic feelings, which may have been worth having. But life went on as before, to Chartism, to the Crimea, to 1870, to 1914. Poverty went on as before; disintegration went on as before; so did the murder and practical enslavement of negroes, and all the lying cant and horror of the world. One might forget all this in 'Nature'; one could never alter or cure it. Nor, if there existed the world behind which he thought he divined, does the existence of that world alter in the least the facts of this one. Though, therefore, I can still get something from reading Wordsworth, I get from him no truth or illumination about life. He had feelings about nature. He did not comprehend life. Nor has anyone, sage or poet or religious leader, comprehended it.

Through all this chaotic horror I find one thread running which seems to me true and beautiful; that is, the activity of the Quakers. Wherever in Europe is trouble—and where is there not?—these few men and women are to be found, talking little, doing much, bringing relief to Germany, Austria, now to Russia, while the big guns talk and do nothing. That is one way of life which is clearly good. But it is not my way. I set myself at the beginning to discover all the truth I could and to state it. The result is meagre enough: perhaps it is less than nothing. But I have no other path. I do not know whether this frame of mind will persist to the end, which may be yet several years, or whether it will lighten and clarify. Meantime, since I can do nothing else, I have settled down once more to the pre-war diplomacy, with the idea that perhaps I might yet write something that would be of use.

For the last few days I have spent most of my time reading despatches.

It is dreary work enough, but there is a kind of dramatic interest in it, to see this catastrophe approaching, to see everyone afraid of it, yet everyone hoping to profit by it, to see how inevitable it is while the European system prevails, and how necessary a complete change of system is, if mankind is not to move quickly to its final destruction. That final and quick destruction I would far rather see accomplished than the continuance of the hideous life which we are still leading. But I can, of course, see no way into the future.

Everyone around me, all my best friends even, seem to have settled down to live as before, pleasantly, cynically, or whatever may be their attitude. I, almost alone, rise and go to bed with the constant obsession, is there to be a continuance of the old, to the new war, or a radical transformation? The pain becomes almost unendurable, and I can only stave it off by plunging into some kind of work, which yet must bear upon it. I have never felt so utterly lonely and so utterly impotent. True it matters little, from a universal point of view, what I feel or am. But unfortunately one is not only universal, and cannot escape from one's particular body and all that it involves, includes and excludes. So much for that.

2 June 1927.

I leave the preceding passages as they were written, for they are a record closer to the events and my feelings about them than I could now compose. Some things have happened since which give a rather different complexion to a world still reeling and staggering and uncertain whether it can recover its feet. The League is strengthened by Germany's belated admission. Some kind of attempt is at last being made to deal with that question of armaments which is in fact the whole of the question of war, though men are reluctant to admit it. England has drifted into a kind of stolid opposition to any development of the power of the League, while France has really begun to rely upon it, or at least to try to get other States to make it possible for her to rely upon it. We are in a state of quasi-war in China, and we have very stupidly (to say the least) broken off relations with Russia. But all this may be a temporary set-back, such as always occurs when a Conservative Government yields to its diehards—that curious brood which is always to be found in England, and which has done so much harm to our policy and our reputation. I think it would be true to say that, outside Italy (standing, for the present, for all the causes the war professed to have been fought to defeat), there is no Power regarded so generally as the centre of reaction as Great Britain.

I have published (last November) my big book on the origins of the war, *The International Anarchy*. I know that this is a good book—I believe it to be possibly the best book on the subject; because it is the only one I know which stresses the only important fact, that it is not this or that nation nor its policy, but the anarchy, that causes wars. The book was considerably and favourably enough reviewed, but it has not sold as much as a thousand copies. Another testimony to the general truth that truth is the last thing people care about.

Meantime I have been occupying myself largely with the translation of *Faust* which Miss Stawell and myself have been working at, and which is now complete. It has been, and is, an infinite relief to me to deal with a mind so sane and so great as Goethe's. But we have not yet found a publisher for our book, and I anticipate the usual fate for it. I don't seem to care much now. I am getting very old and have little left to do but to keep myself innocently occupied so long as I can, or must. I still enjoy myself much and often. This term in particular Cambridge has been so lovely in the almost perpetual sunshine that it has been enough to be alive and look at it. And still the young men exercise their perennial fascination, the few I know, who are certainly also fit.[1]

---

[1] This strange concluding sentence calls for a word of explanation. It is a reminiscence of the concluding sentences of *The International Anarchy*, which must have been fresh in Lowes Dickinson's mind when he wrote it:

> A book of this kind . . . cannot hope to be read by very many. It is of necessity complicated, like the facts, and it can hardly help being tedious to any but trained minds. But the facts it deals with may nevertheless be mastered by young students, and through them filter down to larger audiences. It is for such young men that I have written. They may be few, but if they are also fit their influence may reach far.
>
> *Editor.*

The Wandering Jew

The Wandering Jew

It was in the early spring of 1919, at the end of February or the beginning of March, that I first saw him. I had turned into the Luxembourg garden, as I was in the habit of doing when I could escape for an hour or two from my labours at the Conference. The sun was shining, though it was still cold, and I was tempted to sit down for a few minutes and watch the crowd of passers by. There were the nurses and children as usual, the students, the old men and women, moving among the trees just coming into bud. And presently, among them, I saw coming towards me a figure that arrested my attention. The first thing of which it reminded me was a figure I had seen, some years before, in a picture representing John the Baptist. It must have been the face, and the way the hair and beard were worn, unusually long. But the hair in the picture is red, and this was grey. And the clothes, of course, were different. In the picture, I remember, St John wears a green robe and leather undergarments. This man was dressed in modern costume, but with the peculiarity that he had a long blue cloak, that made me think of Teufelsdröckh. He was tall and had a curious air of dignity, so that, though some children were following him and evidently making comments, they did not dare actually to accost him.

He passed before me and, as he passed, turned and looked at me. His eyes were extraordinary, and had on me an extraordinary effect. I thought I had seen him before, and in a different scene. The garden, the budding trees, the gay crowd became unreal. I had a feeling of great heat, of olives and vines and bare hills. Different people in eastern dress seemed to gather about me. The present reality drifted away. I felt confused and lost. And, clinging to my seat, I kept saying to myself, as though it were a charm that would hold me: 'Paris 1919. The Hotel Majestic.' How long this went on I cannot tell. It seemed to me an infinity. But I was startled from it by a blinding flash, followed by a tremendous clap of thunder. I jumped to my feet. The rain began to pour in torrents. Everybody was running for shelter. I did the same and, as I did so, heard a passing voice cry: 'It must be the Wandering Jew.' I got back somehow to the hotel, following my feet rather than my mind. I was shivering all over and went to bed, and remained there some days with a severe chill.

When I got about again, arrears of work claimed me. There were the usual dances and entertainments in the evening at the hotel, and life resumed its busy gay complexion. But I could not forget the old man and his eyes; and as soon as an opportunity presented I went back to the Luxembourg, half in the hope, half in the fear of seeing him. Neither hope nor fear was cheated, for there he sat, in the place where I had seen him sitting before. As I met his eyes, the same curious feeling began to come over me, but this time I was determined to meet and crush it. I went straight up to him, sat down beside him and made some remark about the weather. Thereupon something snapped. I saw him as an old Jew, dignified indeed and handsome, but no longer uncanny, and I was half sorry I had spoken to him. But I had, and he replied; and then what struck me was his voice. It was the most beautiful I had ever heard; but, more than that, it had overtones in it—I don't know how otherwise to put it—which made everything he said seem more important than it was.

What he did say struck me as curious but not remarkable: 'It is a long time since we met.' His French was perfect, and removed the impression I had had that he was a foreigner. I know French myself as well as English, for my mother was a Frenchwoman, and it was partly for that reason that I was seeing so much of the leading personages at the Conference. 'Not so long,' I replied; 'perhaps a fortnight. But I am surprised that you remember it.' His next remark startled me: 'I was not thinking of that. I was thinking of long ago.' Now I have a good memory for faces. Even if a man grows a beard, I seldom fail to recognise him. If I had seen this man before, I was sure I should not have forgotten him. True, I had had that strange feeling when we first met, but that, I now knew, was merely the effect of illness. So I said: 'I think you must be mistaken. I should not have forgotten you.'

'Nor,' he said, 'have I forgotten you.'

A shiver came over me, and, remembering how I had been chilled before, I got up and proposed that we should walk.

It was a Sunday, and the garden was full of people. I watched with delight their gaiety and their solidity, for there was something ghostly about my companion. And, feeling I must say something and following my thoughts, I exclaimed: 'I like the French.'

'They are like everyone,' he replied, 'I see no difference.'

That remark too struck me as odd, especially from a Frenchman, and, to draw him out, I continued: 'They seem to me very different from the English, the only other people I know well.'

'I see no difference,' he replied; 'the French, the English, the Italians,

The Wandering Jew

the Germans, the Chinese, the Japanese, even the Indians, all are the same. Nothing that matters alters.'

'It is what alters that matters,' I replied. 'Human nature is nothing. The whole interest lies in its varieties.'

'Until you have learnt,' he replied, 'that there is no interest. But that takes time.'

'Longer, I hope, than my lifetime,' I said laughing.

'Longer than yours or than anyone's, except mine.'

I looked at him. After all, he could not be more than 60 or 65 at the most, to judge from his appearance. So I said lightly: 'Come, I hope you do not intend to kill me off before I am your age.'

'What age do you suppose me to be?' he asked; and I hazarded, 'Sixty?'

He smiled. 'You will live as long as that,' he said, 'and you will have learned very little when you die.'

I confess I was rather nettled by that remark, because I have an observant nature, and it seemed to me that by sixty I ought to know a good deal.

'Why do you say that?' I asked.

'Because sixty years, or seventy years, or eighty years, is too short. That is why no one learns anything.'

'Except yourself?' I asked maliciously.

And he replied gravely: 'Except myself.'

'And how do you learn?'

'By observation and experience.'

I remembered then that he had referred, as though he knew them, to various nations east and west, and I observed: 'You have been a great traveller?'

He answered 'Yes' rather wearily and did not seem inclined to pursue the subject. So I continued: 'And from which people have you learnt most?'

I was, I confess, half jesting, but he took me up with that curious simplicity and seriousness which I have learnt to belong to his character. He seemed to reflect, and then said slowly: 'I learnt most at the beginning, for then I was most ignorant. But perhaps my teachers at that time were not the best. I might have learnt quicker and better from the Chinese and the Indians. But it was not till later that I met them, and my first teachers, after the Jews, were the Romans.'

I realised then what I had to do with. 'You have studied Roman history?'

He ignored the question, and went on: 'The Romans taught me the essence of all empire. A little people fighting, as all peoples fight, has the luck to conquer its neighbours and the wisdom not to destroy or enslave them. They become its allies without becoming its equals, and fight at its side to conquer others. Every enlargement means new contacts, new dangers, new victories. Like the threads of a spider's web, administration and law bind together what war has first united. These externalities flourish, and the inner life decays. A huge case hangs in the air, covering up from sight millions of atrophied insects, decaying walls, crumbling cells, the ruins of what once lived. A crowd of lawyers and soldiers keeps the peace among dead men. Till something pricks the crust from outside and all falls in dust.'

His views about the Roman Empire were obviously old-fashioned. I knew that, for I had recently read Mr Belloc on the subject, and I realised that that great political structure had continued into modern Europe with the single exception of the Germans, who had never been properly assimilated, leaving it to the Great War to perform that necessary task. However, I was not inclined to argue the point, and the less so that for the first time the old man seemed to be inclined to talk. A curious far-away look came into his eyes.

'Yes,' he said; 'I saw Rome conquer the Jews. It was well for the Jews to go. They have been better since than they were when they had a kingdom. But Rome was Empire and did as all Empires do.'

'You saw?' I enquired. But he took no notice of my question. He seemed to plunge into a kind of dream, and I think he ceased to know that I was there.

'There had been sieges before, they say. Josephus reminded us of them. Sennacherib lost before our walls two hundred thousand men. The king of Babylon took Zedekiah and destroyed the Temple. We built it again. Antiochus came and took and sacked. Pompey came, and Antigonus and Sosius. So they said, and so I believe, for that is the course of all who pursue power. So it was from the beginning, and so it will be to the end. Sooner or later—what matter whether it be years, or decades, or centuries—conquerors are conquered, but always by conquerors, who fall themselves in turn to new conquests. They say so, and I believe it, for, in all the centuries since, I have seen nothing else. But I was not there. I was there when Titus came.'

It was when he said this that I realised fully, for the first time, that he was mad. The reader must take that fact along with him in all that follows. But if he does not think this madness worth recording, the fault will be mine, not the Jew's. For he had built up out of his visions a world of consistency which stands for me always up against the real world, challenging it as night challenges day, or death life. I have wondered which is the truth. Do I know even now? A kind of terror came over me, which was not the terror of the insane. I could not speak, and he did not expect me to. He continued, as though lost in his vision:

'Titus was like all representatives of Empire. He said he would spare the city if it surrendered. But those who would have surrendered it were with him, and those in power were robbers and fanatics. Among them one cried "A voice from the East, a voice from the West, a voice against Jerusalem and the holy house, a voice against the bridegroom and the bride, and a voice against this whole people. Woe, woe to Jerusalem." They took him in vain, they beat him in vain, he went on crying, till a stone from the engines killed him as he added "Woe woe to myself". I was there, but the stone would not smite me. I lived and I live. The city was full of rumours. They spoke of comets, of battles in the clouds, of the temple gates opening of themselves and refusing to be closed, of voices heard in the sanctuary, crying "It is time for us to go". The terror grew as the hunger grew, but in those that had power it was the terror of despair. Within, they killed every man who spoke of surrender; without, they attacked, they burned and destroyed; and the Romans of many campaigns fell back astonished before these madmen. They separated their souls from their bodies and used both as though they themselves had no property in them.

'The Roman who had come to conquer grew angry as these grew mad. He did as men always do, outdoing cruelty by cruelty, under pretence that the sum of cruelty would be less. He cut off the hands of his prisoners and sent them back to their friends, saying: "Thus do I treat my enemies. But be my friend and I will be yours." One day I saw from the wall a man crucified. He writhed on the cross like Jesus, and I looked at him, as once I had looked at Jesus. And presently, in every vacant place, the crosses rose, to north, to south, to east, to west, the Jews hanging in torture and the Roman soldiers laughing. They crucified till there was no wood left for crosses. For miles and miles what had been gardens and crops and woods was a trampled wilderness, and the trees that were not crosses were towers and rams and roads to the walls. And still, while they could, those within would escape to those without, hoping against hope for more mercy from their enemies than from their countrymen. But the Romans opened their bellies to see whether they had swallowed money. They paddled their hands in the bowels of their foes by thousands and thousands. I saw it and I could not die.

'That was at first. Then Titus enclosed the whole city in his wall, and no one could go out. The famine began to rage. The bodies of dying and dead filled every room. The young men and the children wandered about the streets and fell down where they must. For lack of food they swelled up in a dropsy. There was no one to bury the dead. The smell of corpses filled the air, and those who went to fight waded over the bodies of the fallen. I saw a woman in a house eating her own baby. Half she had consumed, and the rest those hungrier snatched from her. I saw, I lived, and I live, to see always the same things. For an infinity of time that went on;

for time is measured by suffering. But the end came. The city fell. The temple was burned. I had seen it shining afar like a mountain covered with snow. I saw it now flame scarlet. I saw the Romans, mixed with Jews, crowding and perishing together. I saw, about the altar, dead bodies heaped, falling down into steps for those who still pressed on, till assailants and defenders perished in the flames—all but myself, who could not die. From top to bottom, from end to end, the city was razed to the ground. The old and infirm were killed, the beautiful and young selected for the triumph, others picked out to perish in the spectacles, the rest sent in chains to Egyptian mines. I too went to Rome. I saw the triumph. I saw the sacrifices and the feasts. And through them all I saw the crosses before the walls of Jerusalem, and behind those the cross of the lord Jesus. As it was, so it has been, and so it will be, until or unless he comes again.'

He paused, looked strangely about him, and wiped some foam from his lips. He had been talking, I think, to himself, not to me. But now he seemed to remember me. 'I was saying,' he said, 'that that is empire.'

And, feeling that I must say something, I said, what was obvious: 'It was an episode in the Roman Empire.'

'A type,' he replied, 'and it recurs for ever. I saw Jerusalem taken by the Romans. I saw Rome taken by the Goths. I saw Hangchow taken by the Tartars. I saw Jerusalem taken by the Crusaders. I saw Delhi taken by the English. I saw Moscow taken by the French. I have seen fire and famine lay waste the fairest cities of the world. But I had to wait till the twentieth century to see whole nations starved in the name of righteousness and law.'

'What do you mean?' I said rather hotly. 'Do you dispute, what is obvious to the world, that the allied nations, and your own countrymen at the head of them, were fighting a war of defence against aggression?'

A kind of weariness came over his face. 'Everyone,' he said, 'always is. I have watched history for centuries and never known a case where any combatant admitted he was an aggressor. The war from which we have just emerged is like every other in that. Both sides claim to be fighting defensively, and no doubt both sides believe it. What difference does it make? It is like all wars. It began as they began, it has ended as they ended. One side is down, the other up. Millions of the poor, the credulous, the weak have been slain. The rest are reduced to helpless poverty. The few have got advantage. Empire has shifted its base. And all is in train once more for the new war for the old causes. The rest is talk, and known to be. And Jesus does not come.' I was so angry, so perturbed, and so perplexed that I got up and left him without a word. And it was some days before we met again.

The Wandering Jew

HOW THE CURSE FELL ON THE JEW

'The relation of what you ask for is of all that I suffer the bitterest to bear. But that too from time to time I must bear as part of my punishment.

'At that time in Jerusalem I was different from what I am now. It was the beginning of my life; and I knew and understood less even than many of those who had lived no longer than I. I was a Jew then in experience and feeling, as I am now only by the accidental fact of my birth, which centuries ago has lost all meaning. I was also an ignorant and fanatical Jew, as most of us were, and I was poor. My trade was a shoemaker, and my name Cartophilus. Ignorant though I was and vain, I was not altogether stupid; yet without right feeling. Two ideas possessed my mind, one that of the Jewish race, the other that of the poor. But I cared for either only because I was myself a Jew and poor. The Jews were to me, as still even now they are to so many of that nation, the chosen race. In my ignorance of all history except theirs, and even of theirs, since I knew it only by the books the priests had doctored, I thought them destined one day—and why not in my time?—to rule the whole world.

'For of that world even at that brief moment of time I knew nothing outside Palestine, and of all literature not a word but the scriptures of my race. But those Jews who were to rule I thought would be the poor Jews like myself. For the priests, the doctors, the Pharisees, all that was in authority and power, I had the hatred and contempt of the oppressed. I was sharp-witted, bitter in my way, even sceptical, in the small region where I could see at all. The injustices, frauds and cruelties of our society were clear to me, for I myself suffered from them. But my notion of the remedy was that I and my like should come into power and do to others as they did to me. That has been the motive hitherto of every revolution; and that is why no revolution has ever cured anything. Those in power see that, and infer a right to continue in power. Those out of power suppose that their zeal is for righteousness when really it is for domination in their turn. So it was with me, though I did not know it, and about that little sore point of error, suffering and pride gathered the abscess which I called knowledge.

'So I lived vainly enough, as all men live, and happy in my vanity, taking pleasure in my sharp speech and in my visions, in my satire on the present, and my dreaming of a new future, till middle life. Then I heard of Jesus. He was preaching in Galilee and drawing after him great crowds. What I knew, or thought I knew, was only by word of mouth, for he did not come to Jerusalem until he came to his death; and of what I heard I chose out, for emphasis and memory, what suited my way of thinking and feeling. Two things in particular dwelt in my mind: one, that he attacked, as I did, the ruling classes of my nation, who were the Pharisees and Sadducees; the other, that he said he was the Christ of prophecy, that he would deliver my people from their oppressors and make them, that is, us, the poor and despised, the rulers over the world. This I believed, as all men believe, because I desired to believe it; and what did not harmonise with it I put aside as error.

'When, therefore, Jesus came up for the Passover, I was more than ready to welcome him. I thought that the end of my poor and humble life was at hand. I thought that he was coming to overthrow both Herod and the Pharisees and the Romans, to put me and my friends into power, and to fill us for ever with all the things I then thought good—with eating and drinking, fine houses and rich couches, women servants, authority. For all this I thought I had warrant in the books I had read and re-read, which I supposed to contain the wisdom I myself contributed out of my own ignorance resting on my own passions. Jesus entered Jerusalem riding on an ass. Crowds surrounded him, spreading before him palm branches and garments. But my eyes were fixed on himself. There has never been a face so beautiful nor yet so sad. I saw that. But it filled me with rage and disappointment. For I saw also that there was nothing there of the king and conqueror. Being myself full of hate, I looked for hate in him, and I found only, under love, despair. Being full of sensuality, I looked for that in him. And I found only intellect and spirit. Being full of the love of power, I looked for that in him. And I found only insight and persuasion. The man in me loved these things. But the Jew hated them. What was *to be* in me rose in rebellion against what *was*. For the first time I knew what doubt was. Under the heat in the shouting crowd and the narrow streets, amid the smell of sweating men and the noise and cries, this struggle within me took away my consciousness. I fell down in the doorway where I was standing; and when I came to myself, the crowd had passed. It was silent and lonely, and the sun shone down out of the cloudless sky.

'For those next days I followed Jesus about in the city, yet never approaching him to speak. I was half in doubt, half in hope, now angry, now despondent, waiting for the fulfilment of my old desires, yet also aware that they themselves, with the chance of their fulfilment, were giving way within me. He behaved in those last days like a man of authority, but not like a prince. He drove the money changers out of the temple, and the sellers of doves. He healed the sick, or so they said. He attacked without scruple or reserve the Pharisees and Sadducees. Yet this did not satisfy me. For about the coming of his kingdom he was vague. He seemed to accept the Roman authority. He foretold, for those who followed him, persecution, not triumph. He spoke of a long future of evil and sorrow. And though he seemed to think a time would come when he would be recognised as lord, he could not, and did not, say when it would be. This disconcerted me. But most of all, behind all that, was the struggle going on within me between the hopes I had held before and those which seemed to be his.

'Then came the betrayal. He was taken, tried, condemned to the cross. What that meant, the shame of it, the despair, the rage, you Christians can hardly know; for you have made of the cross an image of glory and triumph, reserving for the men like Christ whom you have killed, what is disgraceful to you, the gallows or the sword. At that time there was not one of the followers of Jesus who stood by him. All had expected him to assert himself against his enemies, to escape, to triumph, to appear as the visible king. But he made no resistance, and everyone deserted him. On me a kind of rage broke out. The test had come. He had failed. He had deceived us all. He was about to perish by a death as shameful to Jews as it was to Romans. I waited for him on the day of execution. He had to pass my house carrying his cross. He was weaker than the two thieves who were to suffer with him, and he stumbled before my door, and tried to pause and rest. Then there broke out in me all that had been struggling through those days. I struck him and mocked at him: "Go, go, Jesus king of the Jews. Go quicker to your kingdom." Then he looked at me. And that other new self in me came up and looked back at him. Everything I had believed in, hoped for, dreamt of, fell away. I knew nothing except that I had followed vanity and folly, and that I must now follow some new thing written in those eyes. Not in anger, but in pity, justice, and wisdom, like one announcing a doom he cannot help yet did not choose, he said: "I go; but you will remain till I come again."

'With the words I lost consciousness; and when I came to myself, I was alone in the street under the blazing sun. Instantly, without thought or doubt, I got up and followed to Golgotha. I stood and watched, His mother was not there, nor John, nor any who had known or followed him. He died alone, while the soldiers set as a guard played dice, and the Jews who were his enemies mocked him. There was one cry and one only that came from his lips, an inarticulate cry of death. I heard it and knew the end had come. I left on my wanderings, and I have wandered ever since.'

It was only once, and somewhat in these words, condensed, short, thrown out with a kind of passion, as though each word were a stab, that the Jew told me the history of Jesus. What he said, of course, left everything in doubt. Did Jesus think he was the Messiah? If so, in what sense? Did the Jew think so in any sense? Did he rise again? Was he to come, or did he think so, to judge the world? If so, when? On these questions hung the whole truth of the Christian religion. What I myself thought about that I knew. But I wanted to know what the Jew thought. At the time I did not like to question him further, so great plainly was his trouble. But afterwards from time to time, directly or indirectly, I was able to ascertain his view, though not altogether to understand it.

As I have already said, what he called the coming of Christ was always in the Jew's mouth. He spoke of it both as the redemption of the world and as his own deliverance. I asked him therefore once how he thought the coming would be, and whether in the form of orthodox Christian belief. He shook his head.

'The first disciples,' he said, 'were like me. They expected a triumph and they witnessed a death. But the transformation that came upon me did not come upon them. I was to grow into a man, with all the pains of manhood. They were to remain children in their hopes and fears, their achievement and their failure. After the death of Christ came the story of his resurrection. It came much as it is related in your gospels, full of confusions, incompatibilities, improbabilities. He had appeared, he had been seen by several; then he had ascended into heaven. This kind of thing it was easy then to believe in Judaea, and indeed, as history was to show, it was to be easy to believe in the world. The story of the Messiah was now changed for those who were to believe in Jesus. A death and a burial were to be the preliminaries of his coming. But, after that, he was to come before men then alive died. That was the belief of the earliest Christians. That gave them their enthusiasm and their faith. That, above all, inspired Paul, the great founder of the religion.

'The belief failed. There was no second coming in those early years, and it became necessary to transfer the belief to some later indefinite time. Again and again, as you know, in times of horror and despair men have supposed it to be near. Always it has failed them; but the first hope gave to the first Christians such strength that their church was able to survive its disappointment. It grew in the way you know, drawing its strength from the world it conquered, as a seed does from earth and soil, and moving always further from Jesus as it moved nearer to man. Christians ceased to be heretics and became supporters of the State and the world. And at that time and ever since, had Jesus appeared again, he would have been put to death by whatever agency of shame was then the one recognised among men. His life came like the lightning. It passed in a flash, and after its passing all was as it had been before.'

'Yet you believe in him?' I could not help saying.

'I looked into his eyes,' he replied, 'I and I alone.'

'And you believe in his coming?'

'He must come.'

'On the clouds?'

'In the hearts of men.'

'It is long,' I could not help saying.

'For me, yes. For you who can die, some three score years and ten, and then at least you can escape. I must wait. And, as you say, it is long.'

I did not press the point further, so evident was his pain. But, trying to take his point of view and to imagine how it would feel to think one had lived two thousand years, I wondered whether he saw, or thought he saw, any process of history making for the consummation in which he believed. I did not raise this point at the time, but on a later occasion found opportunity to ask him what he thought of the doctrine of progress. I was struck, as so often, by the candour of his answer, and the thought and knowledge that he showed.

LLOYD GEORGE

The personality of the Jew began, after a time, to take such hold of me that I found it natural to speak of him. Especially, I had spoken of him to one of my chiefs, whose name I will not mention (I should be sorry to add to the indiscretions of some of my colleagues) but who had honoured me with an unusual measure of intimacy. He had an omnivorous curiosity and an energy for acquiring impressions which not even the arduous labours of the Conference could exhaust. He was interested as soon as I spoke of the Jew. He asked me all about the curious mediaeval wanderer with whom my friend chose to identify himself. From time to time he would question me about his opinions; and, growing more curious, at last he suggested that I should ask him to lunch. It was the first invitation of the kind I was commissioned to bring to the Jew, though it was not, as we shall see, to be the last. I rather expected that he would refuse. But he assented at once, without appearing either flattered or surprised, as though such things had happened before and would happen again, and had for him no more interest when he was their subject than when it was another event.

When the day came, he made no change in his dress. That, fortunately, with my chief did not matter. He appeared, as usual till his interest was aroused, dignified and remote. But what I was not prepared for was the reaction of his appearance on his host. The latter looked to me—I hardly like to write it—vulgar. His gestures seemed exaggerated, his features bloated and coarse, his expression cunning; and even his manners, so justly famous for their ease and familiarity, struck me, for the first time, as elusive and false. That, at least, was the immediate impression he made, as he came into the room, a little late, and bursting, as usual, with vigour and health.

'Sorry to keep you. This your friend? How do you do, Mr . . . delighted to meet you. Let's get to lunch at once. My time is short. We're slaves, Mr . . . slaves.' And so he ran on, turning his eyes on and off the face of his visitor, who bowed deeply and said the least he could. What he did say was in English, and that so perfect that I began to revise my original impression, which I had never questioned, that he was French. What was he then? I began to wonder, while that curious feeling of unreality came over me again and prevented my attending properly to the conversation, or rather the monologue, that was going on. What startled me into attention was a remark of the Minister's, very characteristic for its frankness and unconventionality: 'I expect you think us a precious lot of scoundrels, Mr . . .'

Most people, I suppose, would have passed the matter off with a laugh. But the Jew, with his usual gravity, replied simply: 'You are what you can be.'

The Minister appeared delighted. 'Precisely, precisely. What we can be. And everyone talks as if we were what we want to be, with a free hand to do what we like. The fire-eaters want us to get out of Germany the whole cost of the war, and at the same time to destroy the whole German people. The pacifists want the kingdom of heaven on earth. And we meantime, who are up against the real facts, are considering one minute how to keep Austria alive for a fortnight, the next what to do with the Turks, the next whether we can save the Armenians, the next how to keep the Poles quiet, the next how to deal with Soviet Russia, and all the time how to get reparations out of Germany without allowing her to compete with our trade. No joke, Mr . . . I assure you.'

'Those who start wrong,' replied the Jew, 'go more wrong with every step they take.'

'We started wrong, you think?'

'Yes.'

'What ought we to have done?'

'Prayed, all together, for forgiveness, and then set to work together to restore the world you have destroyed.'

'Forgiveness! It's they who need that, not we. We fought for the Right against aggression. We won, and we have to punish as well as to restore. There must be justice done as well as mercy.'

I had heard these words often enough before; I knew that they contained the simple truth and that my chief believed them; and yet I was impressed by the comprehensive gesture, as of one in despair before palpable lies, with which the Jew appeared to sweep them away. He did not, however, argue, he never did, he simply said, as though he spoke with authority: 'Vengeance is mine, I will repay, saith the Lord. There is no man who can impute guilt to another, still less is there a people. Guilt is everywhere, and therefore, so far as human punishment is concerned, nowhere.'

I never quite know how my chief will take any remark. He is so quick to see its bearings, so clever at taking new ground when an unexpected diversion threatens that on which he stands. 'As a private man,' he said, 'I might agree with that. But, worse luck, I'm a statesman. I live and work in a fire of passions. And you yourself, who know history, will admit that your principle has never been applied.'

There came into the Jew's eyes that strange far-away look that they bore when he reverted to the past. 'Never,' he assented. 'I have been at most peace conferences since such things have existed, and never have I seen, in any of them, any humanity or any religion. But those, all of them, were councils of kings and princes, seeking only each his own power. There could be, as there was, nothing but changes of territory and changes of trade. Now France took provinces, now Austria, now Prussia, now Russia, and always England. The conveyance of slaves from Africa to Asia and America was fought for and won by men; and that too England in the end acquired, and English merchants, and pious ones, grew rich upon it. The history of wars and of peaces is the history of men, that is, of evil. But one thing you have invented in the twentieth century was unknown to earlier ages. You have said that you fight for right, and you have conscripted soldiers on that plea; you have fought for five years and murdered more men than ever before were killed in that time, by means more terrible. And in the end a handful of you are making the peace on the old lines of dividing the spoils.'

'Not at all,' interposed the Minister, justly, as I thought, annoyed. 'For the first time we are applying principles. No territory is passing except in accordance with the wishes of the people. That is what was ignored in every previous treaty. That is our new contribution to history.'

The Jew looked at him, and, for the first time since I had known him, something like irony transpired through his expression.

'Alsace-Lorraine,' he said, tentatively.

'Certainly, and that is the principal case. It was brutally taken in 1870. It is now righteously restored.'

'What language do the people speak?'

'Largely German, I believe; and in German they would have announced their determination to be French.'

'Perhaps they would. They were not asked. But I remember them German, and glad to be so, not three hundred years ago.'

The Minister looked askance at me with delight, and winked. But he continued gravely:

'Three hundred years! What have we to do with that? In three hundred years everything alters. We don't profess to go back to the beginning.'

'Why then are you restoring to Palestine the Jews, who have had no home there for two thousand years?'

The Minister made one of his characteristic thrusts: 'You ought not to complain of that anyhow,' he said. 'For your countrymen profit by it.'

'I have no country,' the Jew replied, 'and I wish for none. Let us pass on. Are the peoples of Turkey being freed?'

'Are they fit for freedom? They will have good guidance instead of bad.'

'Guidance that even now is killing them by thousands in Mesopotamia, in Syria, in Cilicia, because they do not wish to have it.'

'You will see all that will settle down.'

'As it would have settled down had the Germans won, only under them instead of you. I see no difference.'

'No difference between us and the Germans?'

'None, except that you are less competent. You all seek power and trade, and none of you seek anything else.'

I thought the Minister would be angry, but he had determined to take the matter humorously. He saw, of course, that the man was mad.

'Well, at least,' he said good-humouredly, 'we do it less efficiently than the Germans, and that is always something.'

The Jew took no notice. The intense light was in his eyes, and he was pursuing his idea.

'What are you doing about India?' he asked. 'Are they to have liberty?'

'They are to have a new measure of self-government, and a very generous one.'

'Why then have you massacred them by thousands at Amritsar?'

'That was no massacre. It is the first duty of a government to keep order.'

'So thought the Germans in Poland. Why have you turned them out?'

'The Germans were beaten.'

'Precisely. And perhaps, had they won, they would have turned you out of Ireland on the same principle.'

'Ireland is a very different case. There is a minority and a majority.'

'As there is in Silesia. As there is in the new Poland you are making. As there is everywhere where there are people at all.'

A kind of bulldog look came over the Minister. He felt strongly, as I knew, on the Irish question. 'So long as I am in power,' he said, 'there shall never be a republic in Ireland. The security of England depends upon that.'

'And is Prussia secure with her bitterest enemies within seventy miles of her capital and no sea between?'

'Prussia was beaten,' the Minister replied shortly. The Jew threw out his hands as though his case had been proved and rose to go.

'You see,' he said. '1919 is like 1648, 1713, 1756, 1783, 1815. Nothing changes but the words and phrases of men. But we must not keep you from your labours.'

The Wandering Jew

The asperity had departed from his voice, and his bearing showed now only his usual courtesy under what I recognised by now as his usual despair.

But the Minister is a curious man. I never know how he will take things. He was, I knew, pressed for time. The Jew had certainly been provoking. There was every reason, I thought, for letting him go, and I should have been glad for him to go without a scene. But suddenly my chief smiled his irresistible smile, signed to the Jew to resume his seat, and, getting up himself, began rapidly pacing the room while he talked.

'You're candid, Mr . . . I will be candid too. It is not often one has the opportunity. What you say is true, much truer than it ought to be. I see that you blame me. But you are wrong. If I were a free agent, we should have a very different peace. But I am not. Who, in fact, makes the peace? Representatives of five nations, of which four are mad, and one impracticable. Japan wants China and some islands, and leaves us alone only if we give her that. Italy wants the Adriatic coast and the German Tyrol. France wants everything—all the money she can get, and also the ruin of the Germans, out of whom she means to get it, together with the left bank of the Rhine, which she assured to herself by a secret treaty with Russia of which we knew nothing. We want all we can take everywhere outside Europe, and also an indemnity. America wants nothing, except the one thing she can't have, a good peace. In all this, I have to play the best game I can. It's not a good one, I admit; but then think what it might have been. Really, Mr . . . when I think of what is demanded by the wild men behind us, I stand, like Clive, astonished at my own moderation.'

'Who gave the wild men power?'

'The war.'

'And the election? Who controlled that?'

'The wild men.'

'And yourself. That was your moment. The paths of good and evil stood open before you, one one way, one the other. You hesitated a moment, then you plunged for evil; and from that moment Evil has been your master.'

It was really extraordinary what this Jew could say. He seemed to dominate the situation. I had seen my chief in many situations and never known him to fail in courage and resource. Yet now he was on the defensive. He was apologetic, and, as it seemed, anxious to excuse himself.

'You are wrong,' he said. 'I was assured by those who ought to know that only by taking the line I took could I secure my majority. That majority was necessary. The country must present a firm front, if we were to take the place we deserved in the councils of Europe. And I don't mind saying it was necessary that I should be the leader. There was not, there is not, anyone else.'

'And so, if you could not lead the right way, you would lead the wrong.'

'Right? Wrong? Are those words relevant at all? The older I grow in affairs, the more it seems to me that there are forces in the world and nothing else. By chance, by luck, by ability, by I don't know what, I was at the head of those forces. The same thing that brought me there kept me there. What was it? Did I choose it? I was its instrument. I seemed to lead. I pretended to lead, but really I followed. If Evil is triumphing, I am not responsible. So far as I can, I do good. You see the Evil that is. You do not see the Evil that might have been.'

The Jew looked at him with an expression that seemed to mean at once comprehension and condemnation. 'I see the faces of the ignorant and the poor, and I hear their cries. They are millions, you and your friends are tens. If the war has been won, it is they who won it, they who paid in their bodies and in their substance, they who perished, they who survive mutilated, broken, without work, without pay, with no better prospect than to resume where they were a hundred years ago, and climb again, if they can, from out of starvation to subsistence. These millions, these hundreds of millions, in all countries, in those you call enemies as well as those you call friends, have had no voice in the making of your peace. No one of them has been considered at any moment or at any point. You have thought of the rich, you have thought of the titled, but you, the Minister of democracy, have never thought of the mass of the people who raised you to power and kept you there. What they wanted was not indemnities—it is not they who will profit by them; not territory—it is not they who will exploit it; not revenge—it is not they who will enjoy it. All you have done and are doing is for the powerful and the rich. And not twelve months will pass after your treaty is concluded before, in every country of Europe, and most of all in your own, millions will be starving because you have pursued the profit of the few. Then you will struggle in vain against the issue of your own policies. You will plunge deeper and deeper in the mire. I cannot tell what the issue will be; it may be that all Europe will perish; it may be that only a few millions will die, and slowly what remains will begin to build itself up again, towards the new catastrophe and the new war. Either way, for the mass of the people, for the children of Jesus, there is no hope and no escape. You chose revenge instead of justice, the rich instead of the poor, falsehood instead of truth. You will not pay for it. You will die in the odour of sanctity, thinking yourself a great man. Those who will suffer and pay are the innocent you have betrayed in the war, betrayed in the peace. This war has been like all wars, this peace like all peaces. And you have served only to hold the veil, painted with a picture of democracy, before the eyes of the people, while behind its screen you pursued the policies that all rulers have pursued since the foundation of states.'

As I have said, it was extraordinary what this man would say, and what the chief would take from him. He listened as if he were fascinated, and and for a few moments there was silence in the room. Then he seemed to pull himself together. But he spoke without his usual confidence, and as if he had met, for the first time, a man who had the right to judge him, and was anxious to make a good defence.

'I don't deny what you say,' he said, 'from a certain point of view; from the point of view, if you like, of the Absolute. You are a student and a spectator, and you see the most of the game. But you don't feel it, nor the forces nor the facts, as we do, who are in the midst of them. And you judge us as hypocrites, who are only caught in events. When I went into this war, I believed that we had no alternative. I hate war, and I had shown it in the past, at the risk of my own popularity. I was a democrat. I did believe in the people, and I wanted to make their lot better. That too I had shown by what I did. But, once in the war, there was only one thing to do, to win it. And we were in danger of losing it. No one in England, I believe, could have won it but myself. But to do so I had to use every means.

'To make the rich work, I had to let them pay themselves well. They are like that, and I was bound to recognise it. The poor were easier. They have simple feelings. Some of them believed in the cause and gave their lives for that. Some, many, loved adventure and change and gave their lives for that. Some were cowardly and lazy. Them I compelled. Some had conscientious scruples. Them too I punished. Once plunged into that torrent, do you suppose I ever had time to think of anything but reaching the other side? I set my mind on that, and refused to think of anything else. I needed at my side the adventurous, and they are not the scrupulous. I chose the one, and thrust the other aside. I made Parliament a passive instrument of my will. I filled it with placemen, to make and keep it subservient. I overthrew the whole structure of the constitution that centuries had built up; for I knew that constitutions exist for the State, not the State for them. I signed personally, or I endorsed, every treaty required to keep our allies at our side. But I saw to it too that those treaties comprised clauses that would increase the power of my own country. I thought of nothing but success. In the end success came. And then, looking round, I found that everything for which I wanted success was already thrown away in order to secure it. I could disarm the enemy, I could not disarm our allies. And I would not, I admit, disarm my own country. I could take provinces from the defeated, I could not prevent their being added to the victors. I could see democracy established where had ruled the autocracy we fought to destroy. I could not prevent that autocracy from having established itself among ourselves. Worse, I saw and I see that democracy passing into anarchy, and nothing to counter that but the very forces we fought to destroy, plutocracy and the army. I find myself siding with those forces because the alternative seems even worse. I find myself—the champion, and, believe it or not, the genuine champion, at first, of liberty, peace and democracy—supporting everywhere tyranny, war and wealth. It is true. But is it my fault? I swear it is not. It is the force of events that have carried me, while I thought to control them. And you yourself, had you been a man of action instead of contemplation, would have been as I am and done as I have.'

It is a curious thing but long and, as I thought, well as I had known my chief, I had never heard him speak like this. And even while I was held by the interest of the conversation, I observed that his ordinary manner, compared to that which he had now assumed, was insincere, and that while he seemed to be admitting the worst that the Jew had accused him of, he gained in dignity, as perhaps a sinner does in confession. The Jew seemed to feel this too, for when he replied, he had abandoned the tone of a judge and recurred to the curious and remote melancholy with which I principally associate him.

'What you say,' he began, 'has been said to me in how many languages by how many men of action! I have had it from Tiberius, from Titus, even from Marcus Aurelius. I have had it from Genghis and from Kubla Khan. I have had it from Mahomet the Second, who took Constantinople. I have had it from Frederic the Second of Sicily, from Henri IV of France, from Cromwell of England, from Frederick of Prussia. It is the constant cry of all who have had the impulse to act and the honesty to measure what they have done. And it is eternally true. Not by power, not by force, is the fate of man bettered. Those are but waves succeeding one another on a sea that is always the same.'

'By what then?' asked the Minister quickly with something of his accustomed confidence.

The Jew thought. Then he said: 'By some of those men whom you killed in prison as conscientious objectors?'

My chief countered with increasing confidence. 'Fanatics, and many of them not even honest. Try something better.'

But the Jew went on: 'My master was surrounded by fanatics, and many of them not even honest. It is always so, and I, like you, once misjudged the wheat to be tares. The tares are many, and we know by whom they were sown. So even the corn. It is sown, some on waste places, some among thorns, some on good ground. It is that which is sown on good ground that alone can deliver mankind.'

'The world has waited long for that,' was the reply, and it rather surprised me, for the Minister is a good practising Christian.

'It will wait,' replied the Jew strangely, 'until Jesus comes again.'

Once more my chief winked at me in his odd way. Then, rising quickly, he said, 'Well, Mr . . . your conversation has been so interesting that it has made me forget my engagements. I shall get into trouble. Good-bye, and I hope we shall meet again.'

I showed my friend out, and when I returned, the Minister was walking up and down the room. He seemed to have shaken some weight off his mind, and was quite himself again.

'Queer old boy,' he exclaimed. 'I'm glad to have met him. Mad as a March hare, of course; but he sees some things. But I must go.' And he whirled down the stairs to his car, which had long been waiting, and (as I happen to know) achieved that very afternoon one of his most notable diplomatic triumphs. Certainly he is a very remarkable man. But I could never get the Jew to admit it. He says merely: 'He is like the rest.'

CLEMENCEAU

It was the English Minister who brought about the interview of my friend with the great Frenchman. The latter does not love Jews, nor anyone who is not French. But he has curiosity, malice and intelligence, and my chief, reporting to him with the humorous and vivid exaggeration of which he is a master, had aroused his interest and perhaps his apprehension. The old man received us with his accustomed vivacity—one would never have supposed him to be over seventy—and then, when he heard the Jew speak, expressed surprise and pleasure that his French was so excellent.

'I had supposed,' he said, 'that you were English.'

And I put in: 'If you heard him speak English, you would think so still more.'

The old man said, a little maliciously: 'Cosmopolitan, like so many of your race.'

But the Jew replied with his usual simplicity: 'Too many of them are nationalistic.'

'When they are that,' said the Minister, 'they are more extreme than the rest. But it is a good fault, if it be one. Let me confess, I hate a cosmopolitan.'

Knowing my friend's opinions, I thought this a bad beginning. The Minister perhaps intended it to be so, for, as I have said, he was malicious. But I endeavoured to postpone a direct clash of sentiment by a digression.

'The Jews,' I said, 'are as patriotic as the institutions of a country allow them to be. In East Europe, where they have been deprived of all political rights, they have been either money lenders or, as now, leaders of revolution. In England they have been, for a century, pillars of the State. One, at this moment, is Governor of India, and another Secretary. There are no better Englishmen than they.'

'Annas and Caiaphas,' said the Jew, 'are always good nationalists, whether in Judaea or elsewhere. Wherever there is a Jesus to be crucified, they are there to do it'.

The Frenchman laughed sardonically. 'You must not outrage our friend's feelings,' he remarked. 'England, we know, is the land of liberty and tolerance.'

I was annoyed, I confess. My diversion had resulted in an unjust combination against what is, after all, the best and freest country in the world. And the comparison of Lord Reading and Mr Montagu with Annas and Caiaphas was merely grotesque. So I said rather stiffly to the Jew, 'You obviously don't know much about modern England.'

'Perhaps,' the Minister riposted, 'he reads the *Morning Post*.'

'I read no newspapers,' the Jew interposed.

'Or he may have heard of the telegram I remember years ago from India: "A new god has appeared on the frontier. The police are on his track." The English, I admit, are not represented by Caiaphas. But I am sure Pilate was an Englishman.'

'Who tried to save Jesus?' I interposed.

'And ended by washing his hands. And so do your countrymen always. You are all consideration, reasonableness and fairness, so long as people submit to your rule. But let them refuse, let them ask to govern themselves in their own way, even though they do it badly, and no people are harder and more ruthless.

'I often laugh at your great Minister, for whom (I need not say) I have the profoundest respect. He has taken for the English most of Africa and most of Asia Minor—all, of course, in the name of good government. When the people resist, he shoots, in six months, more of them than their oppressors have killed in centuries. He gives the rest of us good advice, and preaches resignation and moderation. And meantime just across the St George's Channel lies an island that has been struggling for centuries to be free; and he tells them all plainly that he will shoot them all down in a war of extermination rather than concede their request. For my part, understand that I admire him. It was at that cost that the British Empire was built up, extended and retained. But I sometimes think, I have indeed sometimes said, that perhaps he might be a little more tolerant of the actions of other nations conducted on the same principle and for the same end. We have had unfortunately to kill people in Syria, as you have in Mesopotamia, though naturally not nearly so many. But you have not shown much sympathy with us. And I think that, if you had the Germans next door to you instead of across the seas, it would not have been long, principle or no principle, before your frontiers would have been carried to the Rhine. You are not quite like Pilate after all. You wash one hand and crucify with the other. But the hand you wash is extended towards the world outside. The one with which you crucify spreads over your own Empire. You are surprised and even outraged when we comment on that hand. But do you really suppose it is not seen?'

I began to think, what indeed I afterwards discovered to have been the case, that there had been some difference of opinion on the Supreme Council that morning. But it is not my business to discuss such questions, and I endeavoured to steer away.

'At any rate,' I said, 'the English do want the end of war. There are no such supporters of a league of nations.'

The Minister laughed again. 'Oh yes,' he said, 'I grant that. When one has eaten up a quarter of the world, one wants time to digest it. Perhaps, too, you have eaten too much; perhaps you are not quite sure what might be the result of another conflict. At any rate, the League, to which, of course, I take off my hat, suits your book, for the present time, and in the present circumstances. It's the Germans that it is not likely to suit, nor perhaps the Turks, nor perhaps, who knows? the Russians. And meantime we perhaps may be forgiven if we hanker after other means of security. What do you think,' he added, turning to the Jew, 'of the League of Nations?'

The Jew answered in his quiet way: 'Nothing. For it is nothing.'

The Minister laughed his malicious and yet good-humoured laugh.

'You see,' he said, 'what an impartial person thinks. You are a realist, sir, like myself? You believe in self-protection?'

'I believe in peace.'

'Naturally. The trouble always is that the others do not.'

'The trouble is that you do not and that your colleagues do not. The world would be glad enough of peace. The statesmen, the soldiers and the adventurers will not give it them.'

'Ah, my friend, if you knew how powerless we statesmen are!'

'All men are powerless who have no faith, or whose faith is a faith in evil. You believe, but you believe in France. The others believe, but they believe in England or in Italy or in Germany. Those who believe in Man and in Jesus, the prophet of Man, are few and weak now, as they have always been. And the mass of men, believing in nothing, are the victims of those who believe in lies.'

The Minister dropped his irony, as I have seen so many men drop their masks before this grave and passionate sincerity of the Jew. There was one thing in which he did believe, and he said so:

'Not lies, but truth, and the only truth. That truth is the nation; for an Englishman England, for an Italian Italy, but for a Frenchman France. Could I, do you think, at my age have fought through these years, and won, if I had not believed? I believe in France! In the vineyards of the East and South, the Seine and the Rhone and the Loire, the white Mediterranean sun, the far-gleaming snow of the Alps. I believe in the people, in the little Celtic Breton, the grave placid men of Normandy, the Southerner, passionate and quick, the peasant clinging to his land, the Parisian, all intelligence; the warmth, the life, the movement, the soul and the body of France. I believe in her history, from Caesar to Clovis, from Clovis to Louis XVI, from the Revolution to now and beyond now; in her patience and her madness, her littleness and her grandeur, her nobles and kings and those who cut off the heads of her nobles and kings; her soldiers, royal or republican; her scepticism and her faith, her ideas and her materialism, her sombreness, her brilliancy, her castles, her cathedrals lighted through visions, her ships of the sea and the air, her science, her art, her rhetoric, her poems, histories and tales. I believe in the soul that is incarnate in a million million bodies, and in twice a thousand years. I believe in France; and outside France, I believe in nothing. Let her live, and the rest may die. Gare aux autres! Let them look to themselves: I look only to France.'

The Jew listened without any sign of impatience, but with that curious air of having heard and known it all before; of expecting to hear it all again, which made one doubt whether his manner was more of patience or of despair. He sat silent for a moment when the Minister paused, as though wondering whether it were worth while to speak; and then, as if obeying reluctantly an inward need, replied:

'You look to France, but you do not look to the French; and the French are real, but France is unreal. To save France you have killed two million Frenchmen. And what is it you have saved? You do not know yourself. Your kings and nobles, your cathedrals and castles, are dead, or live as vampires. Your wars are dead as those who died in them. What lives lives with other thoughts, other hopes, other fears, and these not more of France than of her enemies or her allies. That they should be enemies or allies is but a transitory fact. For centuries I have watched this little Europe, this threshing floor of human life, that gathers up the chaff and wastes the grain. There is no one country that has not fought with or against another, and that will not, if war goes on and men survive. Against whom have you not fought? Against the English, the Russians, the Spanish, the Italians—to say nothing of Austrians and Germans and Turks. With whom have you not fought? With English, with Russians, with Italians, with Turks. There is no more sense in your combinations than in the clashing of motes in the beam.'

The Wandering Jew

'There is the sense that the combinations have sought the advantage of France.'

'And achieved only her ruin, so far as they have achieved anything. Your great and glorious king Louis XIV fought for sixty years to give you the frontier of the Rhine. He left France exhausted of men, of treasure, of everything but his own glory. Your Napoleon did really try, as you say the Germans did, to subjugate the whole world. For twenty years he killed your young men and wasted your substance, to leave you at the end where you were, save for the men he had tortured and slain. In 1870 you challenged Germany, as much as she challenged you. What was the result? In 1914 she challenged you. What is the result? You are acting so that she will be bound to challenge you again. What will be the result? It isn't even worth while to ask, so certain is it that it will be the ruin of both nations.'

'Were we responsible for the war just ended?'

'History will say, or try to say. You yourselves, who have thought all your life of nothing but revenge, would have been responsible if you could. But no nation is ever solely responsible for a war. The ideas, the passions and the ambitions of them all are responsible. And while they continue war will continue.'

'There will not be another war between France and Germany,' the Minister replied grimly.

The Jew looked at him and understood him.

'Will there not?' he replied. 'Even if you could succeed in your intention to kill by starvation twenty or thirty million Germans, there will remain forty millions—as many as you have in France.'

'Disarmed, poor, without colonies. And we have a million black troops.'

'As Rome had her barbarians. What became of her, and of them?'

'That is for the future. I am eighty. I have done my work.'

'And there have perished thousands of youths of twenty who would have done, if they could, a different work from yours.'

'They died for France.'

'They died for mankind.'

'It is the same thing.'

'They did not think so, and they were right.'

'What do you know of them? You are not French.'

'I am human—not English, not Italian, nor German. I have become through suffering and through the years, human. I can tell you what you do not know. Among the generals of this war, far behind the lines, were men like you. They thought of their country, and they meant by their country themselves, their honour and glory, their power and wealth. The moment of their life had come. Were they likely to shorten it? The German general, the French general, the English general, all were alike. They must prolong their authority and secure their fame. You at home, all old men at home, supported them. But the others, who were perishing daily in their thousands, they felt otherwise. Most were as sheep driven to the slaughter, dumb, hopeless, blind. They did not hate, at least, not the enemy. Perhaps, not knowing it, they hated you. But among them were some who knew that they were dying for a vain thing, that every moment of their suffering was making the world not better but worse, that it was for you and your like, not for their country, nor for man, that they were killing and dying, and that, when all was over, all would be irredeemably worse. It is so, and in your heart you know it to be so.'

'Did I make the war?'

'Not alone, but with all men like you. All your life you have thought of nothing, believed in nothing, but war. And even now you look forward to war again, and war worse.'

'Did I make the world?'

'You helped to, and helped to make it wrong. You had power, as few men have had it. What have you done with it? Just because you had led the war, and led it to victory, you could not make any peace save one that must lead to a new war. Because you loved France, you hated mankind, and because you would make her strong, you have handed her over to destruction.'

'You talk like an Englishman, like an Italian, like a German, like anything but a Frenchman. This war was fought to re-establish Right. The rest may follow: that must come first. In 1870 the Germans made war on us. They took Alsace-Lorraine. They laid upon us an indemnity. Till that Wrong was undone, there could be no Right. All my life I have waited and worked to set that right; all France has waited and worked with me. We did not make the opportunity. They made it. But when it was made, we used it to the full. You talk and think of the future. I think first of the past, and so does every Frenchman. In the very place where Germans humiliated us we have humiliated them. What they took from us we have taken back from them with interest. Justice has been done. And if to that justice all the future had indeed been sacrificed, France is ready for the sacrifice. Light-minded Teutons may forget. We never forget. They may condone the past in the name of the future. We will not. Fiat justitia: ruat coelum. That is the Latin maxim. Let France perish, let the whole world perish with her, rather than one jot or tittle of her Right be abandoned by her.'

'Two thousand years ago my master was crucified in Jerusalem. Forty years later Jerusalem was captured and destroyed by the Romans. Christians said it was punishment for crime. But who was punished? Not those who crucified Christ, but their little children. And so it is always, and always will be, where nations remember and act. A set of ideas and sentiments cuts into living flesh and blood. The sins of the fathers, if sins they be, are visited on the children. You now are killing by hunger and disease, and mean to kill, men and women and children who were not alive when you suffered what you complain of, who had no part in it, no power over it, no knowledge of it. A nation is nothing but a name for the chronic rancours of men. The only reality is real men and women. But to your phantom you sacrifice these by millions, not only in countries called enemy, but even in your own. If you had taken no revenge and no compensation, your own people, as well as the others, would now have been richer, happier and more prosperous. But for the sake of revenge you have sacrificed well-being, calling your revenge justice, and your well-being materialism. You are yourself an old man, well-to-do and what is called glorious. You will die contented and prosperous. But it is the others, the millions of your own country and of all countries, who suffer that you may feel happy.'

'Justice will have been done.'

'Justice is never done. Had justice been sought or attained, where would now be France, France who through her whole career has sought nothing but conquest; who has never cared for the right or the claims of others; whose Louis XIV, whose Napoleon, were Wrong incarnate, of the same kind that you attribute to the Germans, only on a scale infinitely bigger? Where would you have been in 1815 if justice had been done, such justice as you now claim and enforce? France would never have lifted her head again. You appeal to the past. Be then judged by the past! By that judge the sins of France are scarlet, and those of Germany white as snow.'

'You speak like a German.'

'No, I have no nation and I speak for none. All nations are and have been and will be unjust. For no nation has ever thought of anything but its own power. If indeed you want the reign of justice, you must get rid of the nation.'

The Minister laughed with a kind of fierceness. 'If that were so, perish justice and long live the nation! But it is not. The nation and justice is the same thing when that nation is France. When one dies, the other dies. And that is why I have chosen justice and not security. And I know I have France with me.'

'Not a hundred years will pass and there will be no France, not a thousand years and there will be no England. History will report of you and of them to schoolboys yawning over their books as it reports of Babylon or of Rome.'

Poems

Contents

	Page
Dedication	233
To the Heavenly Love	236
To the Heavenly Love II	239
'It is enough! Prolong not now'	241
'If, in this house of music, where I spend'	244

SONNETS:

	Page
Dedication	249
I	250
II	250
III (A)	251
III (B)	251
III (C)	252
IV	252
V	253
VI	253
VII	254
VIII	254
IX	255
X	255
XI	256
XII	256
XIII	257
XIV	257
XV	258
XVI	258
XVII	259
XVIII	259
XIX	260
XX	260
XXI	261
XXII	261
XXIII	262

XXIV	262
XXV	263
Epilogue	263
From Theognis	264
'My love, I saw the roses glow'	265
'How wide the sweep of happy fields'	265
'A month ago! At length the breeze'	266
'By star-white meadows daisy-sown'	266
'Oh, thou didst make the summer sweet'	266
'Under the western skies'	267
'Deep in a wood the foxglove grows'	267
Sunrise	268
'We live and die, and every task'	269

DEDICATION

O Athens! Athens! brain and soul,
Wisdom and love divinely blent,
Who bendest o'er a mystic scroll
Thy head of roses redolent,
Then all unwearied risest up
To drain with boys the purple cup.

Athens, although the feet are still
That thronged the streets of Pericles,
And fallen on thy sacred hill
The music of the marble frieze,
And lone along Cephisus' vale
Mourns the neglected nightingale.

Though Socrates no more enchains
His eager boys with honeyed pleas,
Nor out of lips rebellious rains
The music of Euripides,
Nor to a theatre mad with joy
Is thundered out the tale of Troy.

Though when the midnight moon is low
No music clangs in woods of pine,
Nor sudden torches light a glow
On ruddy lips and flashing wine,
Nor dizzy hills give back the shout
Where Bacchus leads his drunken rout.

Yet Athens! Athens! we have heard
'Neath paler skies and sadder trees
The song impassioned of the bird

That sang of old to Sophocles,
Have listened for the cymbal-kiss,
And heard the horn of Artemis.

For us the spring is mad with Pan
As once upon Colonus' hill,
For us his blood divine that ran
In Attic vines is ruddy still,
And still his breath is on the breeze
That stirred of old his olive trees.

We too, though late, have dared to stand
Before a pagan altar's fire,
Have felt the gods on either hand,
The breath of Mars, Apollo's lyre,
Have caught at Aphrodite's hair,
And quailed before Athene's stare.

For who but we have idly paced
The walk beneath the chestnut trees,
And started, half in jest, and chased
The thought we yet were loth to seize,
Then sunk to silence while the night
Circled and sung for our delight.

And who but we have held discourse
Of peace and tumult, weal and woe,
Nor even so have made divorce
'Twixt tears and laughter, fire and snow,
But looking sorrow full in face
Have turned to jest for heart of grace.

And who but we with eager eyes
Have gazed upon the world of chance,
And felt our equal spirits rise
To mingle hands and join the dance,
Till heaven was cleft, and lo! the dove,
The tongues of fire, the breath of love!

O Cambridge! Cambridge! small the need
Of plighted faith to honour thee;
Thine is the hand that sowed the seed,
The gathered fruit thy guerdon be;
'Twere wasted breath to bid thee take
The creature thou thyself didst make.

What need of vows to bind the will?
Enough that thou hast given us birth,
Hast led us on, and leadest still,
To health or sickness, grief or mirth,
We need not seek to make or mar;
What thou hast made us, that we are.

  1887.

TO THE HEAVENLY LOVE

Lord, who art Lord of all, of those who know
And those who know Thee not or know in part,
In things that live not like a life dost show,
And in the living like a life apart,
Who ever art the more than all that is,
The Perfecter that waits on Perfectness.

Thou, who art Lord of beauty! when the sense
Anticipates the promise of the soul,
And in a moment of divine suspense
Feels in a part the secret of the whole,
'Tis Thou dost bid conception live in act,
And reconcile the symbol and the fact.

Lord, who art Lord of consolation! Thou
Who weighest out the loss against the gain,
And wilt not have Thy meanest servant bow
Where fraud or folly consecrates the fane,
Nor when the last accounts are gathered in
Wilt reckon up a failure as a sin.

Who from the many noughts Thy wilful One
Not for his proof or promise dost select,
Nor for achievement wrought or merit won
Dost honour, nor for lack of these reject,
But to the Would-it-were that was not his
Preferrest still his unrepentant Is.

Healer of limit, who with more than more
Dost recompense the willing choice of less,
And to the spirit self-impaired restore

What very self-perfection bade repress,
One with Another blending to supply
What to the Self its self-ness doth deny.

Thou, who art Lord of liberty! the tie
That binds by law, by passion to divide,
Fashioned by man in weakness to supply
Ease to his fear or solace to his pride,
Thou for Thy chosen servants dost remit,
Heedful of them who heedless are of it.

They in their freedom comfortless and lone,
Yet to their genius true where'er he shine,
Though bare of all possessing still their own,
Though by the world rejected marked for Thine,
Not for an aimless pain are set apart,
Or trivial end, to travail and to smart.

But rather, in division taught to grow
By difference endeared more subtly one,
Gather in grief the lore which not to know
Is knowledge little worth and wisdom none,
How, in their self-dependence incomplete,
Soul into soul may echo and repeat.

Lord, who art Lord of purity! the flesh,
Never by Thee, as some have erred, rejected,
Feeds and sustains, but may not mar nor mesh
The souls Thou hast in eminence selected,
And with such hunger edged their amorous mood
As covets more than perishable food.

To Thee not only roses and the dance
Are consecrate, and sleep by summer seas,
Not only strange concurrences of chance,
Sudden delight and sorrowless release,
With such ambiguous kisses as betray
Even their inglorious promise of a day.

But more supremely Thine, and whollier bent
On Thy behest, the finer fellowship
Of soul and flesh so mystically blent
That the strong hand and half-reluctant lip
Not for a passing pleasure meet and part,
The solace of a transitory smart;

But rather, acquiescent in a pain
That hints at satisfaction not its own,
Even of the body's passion make a gain,
Not for itself, but for that Power alone
Whose fire, consuming that whereon it feeds,
Transmutes the flesh to serve the spirit's needs.

Till, by transcendence of the barren bliss
That flies upon the running rope of time,
Raised from the level ruck of Now and This,
And in the Everlasting made sublime,
Fixed as the stars the splendid moments ride
Over the shifting waste of time and tide.

Lord, who art Lord of promise, hear! and take,
From hearts too full for supplication, praise;
Praise for the past's eternal-present sake,
And for its implicated future, praise!
Praise for Thy world, and, of all selves the Self,
Praise, O Thou Lord of lovers, for Thyself!

1893.

TO THE HEAVENLY LOVE

II

Once more, Thou Lord of sorrow, not for praise,
But supplication ere the day of doom,
Looking across the wilderness of ways
To where they meet and vanish in the tomb,
Here at the turning-point of age and youth
I turn to Thee for solace and for truth.

Not that I quail before the law of life,
Whose strength I own, whose justice I arraign;
Not that I seek remission of the strife
That quickens while it tears the rebel brain;
Or ask for one erasure in the scroll
That seals the sombre secret of my soul.

What He, the master not the mate of man,
Less than the life He quenches as He gave,
Lord of the mazes of a loveless plan
None but the despot honours and the slave,
What He, the God of strength, hath bade us bear
The breath were base to deprecate in prayer.

But Thou, but Thou, the Lord of spirits, Thou
Who soughtest me when least I thought to find,
To whom in that obeisance I bow
That binds at once the passion and the mind,
Breather of hope and caster-out of fear,
Light of the world and Saviour, hear, oh, hear!

Under the stress of His remorseless years,
Temper in His despite the stubborn soul;

Turn to her health the poison of her tears,
Her pain to power, her passion to control,
And with the fuel of her dead desires
Foster her inextinguishable fires.

Whate'er He bid her suffer, let it so
Work in the stuff and substance of her life
That by a shaping virtue in the blow,
Though by the bludgeon dealt her and the knife,
She by His very malice may but be
Fashioned the closer to her type in Thee.

Or if He set her, in His high disdain,
Far from the road His happier victims wend,
Unvisited of pleasure or of pain,
Sapless and sad to sicken to her end,
There let her learn to ripen not to rust,
Root on the rock and blossom in the dust.

And when He makes the last and worst essay,
When one is taken and the other left,
And stripped of every shrine the stony way,
Even of Thy passing presence is bereft,
Then, even then, past hope, past comfort, still
Steel to Thy task the unconquerable will.

That so, when all is finished, one by one,
We, with the sweat of labour on our brow,
The work achieved, whate'er be lost or won,
Not He, not He hath laid on us, but Thou,
May claim at last, made by endurance free,
Thy crowning gift of immortality.

  1895.

Poems

It is enough! Prolong not now
The season of the bended brow,
Of withered heart and bitter lips
Bodeful of no apocalypse.
This is the mood with passion fraught
Forecasting all the gains of thought,
This the brief hour of respite given,
And this the path that leads to heaven.
Stay not to question, though the cloud
Is spread beneath us like a shroud,
And what it hides, for weal or woe,
We know not yet and may not know,
Mooting in vain the secret sense
Of hieroglyphic evidence;
Whether for ends divinely fair
The spirit stirs and quickens there,
Or, as the sadder sceptic deems,
All is the wilful woe it seems,
Where pashing hoof and hornèd head
Mangle the living with the dead.
Upward and on! for lest we stay,
Behold, to guide us on our way,
Comes the late moon in mourning mood
For loss of that bright plenitude
Whose shadow doth her crescent fill;
Her, as she hastens o'er the hill,
Lifting above its dusky brim
Her silver chariot's violet rim,
With streaming hair and burning eyes
Orion follows through the skies.
And while we linger all too near
For us who long have housed with fear
The labyrinth of the sullen stream,
Trackless to this elusive gleam,

Troubles the sense with noises. Hark,
How from the caverns of his dark
Unfathomable abyss he howls
Oracles to the hooting owls!
Pause not for him! the smoother lawns
Are all above us, and the dawn's
Unutterable promise. Here
The pines are sweeter, and more clear
The lucent space of sky; and lo!
'Twixt yonder peaks, not yet aglow,
Troubling the solemn eyes of night
A miracle of crystal light
Brightens apace; the moon grows dim,
And the pale constellations swim
Under a violet sea. And now
Our feet are on the very brow,
And to the dim horizon's bound
Above, beneath, and all around,
Like petals of the mystic rose
Peak upon peak of splendour grows
Up to the central wheel of fire,
Whose shafts of radiance high and higher—
Oh! from what presence half-divined,
What power of what imperial mind,
What heart, what soul, what more than these,
That tongue can speak or spirit seize,
Dart the quick throb which—turn and see—
Wakes the whole west to sympathy.
For that ethereal spirit of green
That passed across it like a dream
Is fled, and all the world of snows,
Cleft into tongues of burning rose,
Rises like altar-fire to greet
Him who—behold, beneath his feet
What once was earth transfigured lies,
Lifts to him answering lips and eyes,
Breathes to his breath, to his embrace
Reaches the mirror of a face,

That gives him back nor he nor she,
But undivided Me and Thee.

The hour is fled, the vision fades,
And still across the lower glades,
Muffled in mists that vainly shroud
What to the listening ear is loud,
Rise, from the nameless pit below,
Hurrying alarms and cries of woe,
With one mechanic undertone
In the dread pauses heard alone.
The vision fades, the hour is fled,
The splendours of the pageant shed,
And shorn of plumage thou dost wait
At the sad city's open gate.
But though the mark is on thy brow,
No bondman of the flesh art thou,
And though thou enter, thou dost bear
This in thy heart for comfort there:—
Only the morning reads aright
The sombre secret of the night;
Only the free divine the laws,
The causeless only know the cause.

1893.

IF, in this house of music, where I spend
The bitter pause before the piteous end,
Over the wailing flood of lyric woe
That floats the fate of Tristan, come and go,
Like breezes on the water, memories
Of solitary rocks and silent skies
Far in the heart of mountains; if the thought
Of that remoter nature, yet untaught
What only man can teach her, presses in
To mar the tale of love's immortal sin;
'Tis but because it pleased the One Divine
Even in the wilderness to build a shrine,
And from the heaven descending like a dove
Light in the wild his holy lamp of love.
Therefore it is, before the eyes be dim
And dumb the lips that fain would honour Him,
Not for themselves I labour to record,
No, but for Him, the mem'ries I have stored,
To fashion thence, so He but lend me grace,
A shrine of song for His immortal face.

So, while the curtain lifts, I close my eyes.
The Breton castle where the lover lies
Fades into mist, with all the tale of dree
Blown from the horn across the dolorous sea;
'Tis night, and I alone. Beside the stream
I labour upward, stirred as in a dream
By subterranean thunders that enact
The terrors of the hidden cataract;
Pause on the pass, and in the sudden light,
Hung like a jewel in the naked night,
See like a magic exhalation grow
Up to the cloudless moon the world of snow.
The stars are bright; but even as I gaze

The change begins; hands that I see not raise
Far in the east the sluices of the dawn;
The lesser lights are one by one withdrawn;
And swiftly rolls against the waning moon
A silent sea of lustre, all too soon
To brighten into shafts of gold, and smite
By that divine apocalypse of light
From every dome of ice and rocky spire
The quivering image of a world of fire.

Higher I climb, by cataracts of ice
Chasm and cliff and emerald precipice
Flung in a frozen foam that never falls,
And is for ever falling; over walls
Of moving rock, and on the upper snow,
Hour after hour, with weary feet and slow,
O'er the abyss suspended, till at last,
The summit gained, what was the Power that passed
Before my troubled sense? For where I stood
The straining earth, as to a central node,
Drew to a point, then broke and fell away,
Peak upon peak, to that diviner day
Where, as it seemed, the valley waters found,
Far-gleaming to the dim horizon's bound,
Among the cloudy islands of the Blest
In that most ancient river Ocean, rest.

Fair was the vision, fair as heaven! but oh!
The Power that works beneath for weal or woe,
Indifferent which, and rounding life with death,
Blasphemes Himself His own creative breath;
Who if He light the rainbow-arc of bliss
Hangs it above the bottomless abyss,
And if He build the mountain bids it blanch
Before the thunder of the avalanche;
Who is not beauty, no, 'tis we who smite
With that allure the nakedness of night;
Who is not wisdom, no, 'tis we who draw

From that perplexèd skein the thread of law;
Who is not love—ah, let me turn and go!
The God I worship I have left below,
Where on the golden alps the cattle ring
Their chime of bells beside the bubbling spring,
Where the great woods descending softly shield
From these impending horrors flock and field,
Where in the sleeping valley far below,
Brightly by mead and mill the freshets flow,
And happy peasants draw contented breath
Under the shadow of the hills of death.

And where—O figure flitting like a dream
Here where I follow up the phantom stream
O eyes that haunt the valley like a song,
O soul of sorrow pitiful and strong!
Spite of the world so absolute to part
Flesh from the flesh when heart is knit to heart;
Spite of the flesh so cunning to conceal
The very soul it labours to reveal;
Spite of the soul so subtly set to spin
A mesh of moods to hide her essence in;
Yea, spite of all, from thee to me the fire
Of that eternal Spirit of desire
That is the Self within the self and lies
Behind the last illusion of disguise,
Flashes the truth of the redemptive plan
Incarnate in the bleeding heart of man.

That was the God we sought! And though we be
Sundered by more than that remorseless sea;
Though we be set in so diverse a way,
To labour thou, and I to watch and pray;
Though with the years that ripen thou shalt gain
Strength to the hand and cunning to the brain,
Even in thine own despite with that endowed
That conquers while it charms the warring crowd,
And, though thy soul be set apart, akin

To those that wager and to those that win;
While I, by that which dwells within me driven
To prove before the time the promised heaven,
The proffered good too careless to pursue,
The good denied too eager to eschew,
Deeper with every lustre am withdrawn
Into the silent kingdom of the dawn,
A shadowy captive in an alien host
And in the world of living men a ghost;
Yet I believe, when spirits once have met,
Though in a wilderness of error set,
With so imperfect vision to divine
Under a veil so thick the mystic sign;
When at the touch of some diviner day
The curtain of the flesh has rolled away,
And at the secret heart of Being shown
The Spirit each embraces as his own;
When with an alien element at war
Once they have heard across the battle's roar
The diapason of the myriad soul
That is the master-motive of the whole;
O then, O then not all the sundering years
With their obliterating rain of tears,
Not all the thin disguises woven in vain
By our illusive labour of the brain,
Nor that obliquity beyond control
That is the very habit of the soul,
Shall hide from us the truth which—words are vain!
But hear, O hear, in that imperious strain
That from the heart of all creation cries,
And from Isolde's passion ere she dies,
Cooling the fire of those tormented strings
With droppings from the harp's ambrosial wings,
What from the flesh in anguish doth suspire,
The woe and wonder of the world's desire,
Upward through all the range of arduous art,
Toil of the brain and tumult of the heart,
To countless crosses nailed of priceless pain,

In countless resurrections risen again,
To find at last, on what eternal breast,
In what impassioned consummation, rest!

1895.

Sonnets 1893–1894

DEDICATION

Here where the dews of sorrow
Drop from a sky of lead,
I set myself to fashion
A garland for thy head.

Perhaps on that to-morrow
When we are counted dead,
By some diviner passion
It will be perfected.

I

DEAR, in these days of over-precious art,
What shall I say to justify my song?
Shall I declare it crieth from the heart,
And to that judge refer it, right or wrong?
Only because I may not take your hand,
Nor look upon your face, nor hear your voice,
And there is nothing in this empty land
To wake my very soul and say, rejoice!
Because the laughter rings, but not for me,
And not for me the happy voices call,
And friendless are the faces that I see,
For lack of one that is the friend of all,
   Only for that I sing—how happier far
   To rest in silence where my wishes are!

II

I NEVER asked for more than thou hast given,
The benediction of a brother's love;
Fairer to me than all the stars of heaven
That argent planet beacons from above;
And in thy spirit's ample firmament,
Where'er the orient sun may rise and shine,
Think not that I shall murmur or repent,
Craving a fuller light that is not mine.
Let but thy star of consolation lighten
Over the twilight meadows of my soul,
Larger across the gathering darkness brighten,
Surelier fix and fire the heavenly goal;
   Then though the dawn delay or fail me quite
   I am content to wait and watch the night.

Sonnets 1893–1894

III (A)

Not for thy presence only, though thine eyes
Unseal the frozen fountains of my soul,
And in her woods of winter bid arise
Music that mocks at her austere control;
Though like a god from heaven thou dost reach
To this poor fleshly clod the fire of life,
Stir the dumb lips to pentecostal speech,
Kindle the heart to love, the hand to strife;
Not for thy presence only, but because
Present or absent—oh, that woeful Or!—
Thou over such an Ought as never was,
And such a Was as will be never more,
   Yea, over all the past and future thou
   Triúmphest in the holy name of Now.

III (B)

Therefore I love thee; yet let Therefore end
Ere it begin so poor a task and lame,
Seeing I love thee first, and after spend
Mere idle breath in reasons for the same.
Is it thy hand, thy hair, thy face, and all
That more luxurious lovers use to praise?
Oh, no, not these, nor any sweets that pall,
Or flowers that wither in the wintry days.
Is it thy soul then? Yet that soul of thine,
What is it but the spirit of thy flesh?
Are they not lips that make it known to mine,
Are they not arms that fold and eyes that mesh?
   Then is it undivided flesh and soul,
   Thy very self, the perfect and the whole?

III (c)

But no, saith one, for still the Spirit hath
Over the flesh her high pre-eminence,
And every Form in his appointed path
Moveth to her celestial influence.
She through a thousand tenements may pass
And still, in every new creation, be
The fine elixir in the glitt'ring glass,
The soul and elemental part of thee.
And though she chafe against her crystal cage,
And with her silver fretting wear it thin,
Yet doth she still renew from age to age
A fairer prison-house to harbour in.
   So be it, love; yet still must I demur!
   Without the house, what were the sojourner?

IV

My soul is knocking, hark! and all in vain.
Where is the gate that she may entrance win?
Thine eyes are guarded with a crystal pane,
Too straitened are thy lips to let her in.
Disherited of her corporeal stuff
Round and about she wanders like a ghost,
Closer she strains yet never close enough,
When most she thinks to win defeated most.
Oh, many a year must pass and many a pain,
And many a sorrow run its purging course,
Ere she may hope by patience to attain
What never yet was yielded up to force,
   And unimpeded clasp the sister-soul
   That rounds her broken crescent to a whole.

Sonnets 1893–1894

V

SINCE thou didst cross the threshold and didst pass
Here where I linger up the vacant stair,
And to the length of yonder dusky glass
Lend the dear image of thy face and hair;
Since from this attic window thou didst glance
Over the muffled city blurred in rain,
And from the shuddering coil of circumstance
Turn for thy comfort back to love again;
Shall not a shape, now thou art far away,
Sometimes across the empty chamber shine,
Shall not a phantom hand that may not stay
Reach through the gathering gloom to close in mine,
   Oh, and the grey eyes stoop, the faithful heart
   Beat against mine a moment ere we part!

VI

WILT thou not come, my love? behold, I cry!
What are a thousand leagues of ocean brine,
What the tumultuous winds and angry sky,
What heaven or earth to that true heart of thine?
The fire is burning, see, the kettle sings,
The music waits that thou dost love to hear;
Hath not thy spirit swift immortal wings
To ride the bluster of this wintry year?
But no! thou dost not hear, thou wilt not heed,
I shall not lay my head upon thy knees,
Nor feel thy loving fingers pass indeed
Here where I fondly feign them for my ease,
   Nor open happy eyes to read in thine
   All that without thy telling I divine.

VII

If you are sad, I may not bring you solace,
If you are sick, I may not help or heal;
In pleasure there is no communion for us,
In labour no alliance or appeal.
Day after day our destinies are thwarted,
Weary of work, by leisure unrelieved,
Solitude void, companions ill assorted,
Ambition dead and purpose unachieved.
Hath it been ever thus, and will be ever?
Or was there once a star-enchanted lake,
A mountain-path for us to climb together,
A night to vanish and a dawn to break?
    Oh, feeble heart, take courage in thy pain!
    What hath been, is, what was, shall be again.

VIII

The thing that hath been, is. Those heavenly lights
That made a marriage of the hills and sky,
Those azure-shining days and shadowy nights
With all their golden candles set on high,
Even in this wintry fit of rain and snow
Fade not nor fail because the summer's dead,
But all unblemished in the mem'ry grow,
By sorrow's secret affluence fondly fed;
Nor is there any word that thou hast spoken,
Nor any touch of thy most loving hand,
Nor any message sent me for a token
From those dear eyes at whose behest I stand,
    But liveth yet though thou art far away,
    And serveth at thine altar night and day.

Sonnets 1893-1894

IX

Dear, though the way be long, the country bare,
Open to every wind to pinch or parch,
Yet is it will, not fate, that set me there,
Yet is it love that heartens me to march;
And at some station of the dusty road,
Some plot of grass edging a quiet stream,
Halting to ease my heavier-urging load
Or warm my agues at the fitful gleam,
Haply across the blank and vacant light
I shall behold a sudden shadow fall,
Or in the silent horror of the night
Hear the sweet voice of consolation call,
    And in a moment meet the bending bliss
    That cancels years of sorrow with a kiss.

X

As I have seen the mimic flowers of frost
Blossom and bud on every barren bough,
And for the loveliness of summer lost
With comfort cold the wintry woods endow;
So in the dull December of my days
Fain would I counterfeit a summer zest,
Filling my hungry soul with empty praise
Of her diurnal round of toil and rest.
Only at night I set her free to roam
The forest of her mem'ries ever green,
Then from her flowery wanderings call her home
To tell the wonders she has heard and seen;
    Whereat she bids me look, and lo! I trace
    Deep in her eyes the image of thy face.

XI

This is the birth of Christ; and if he be
All that they boast who groan beneath his grace
I know not, nor if he be aught to me,
Who have not heard his voice nor seen his face.
But one I know whom in a field apart
I heard the angels herald from the skies,
Whose birth was in the manger of my heart,
Whose hand of healing on my lips and eyes;
And if he suffered on the cross in pain
That rent the woven veil of present bliss,
Oh, yet he is not dead but risen again,
And folded in his heaven of faithfulness,
    Where like a shepherd he his wandering sheep
    In pastures ever green doth guard and keep.

XII

Now do the birds, though yet their woods are sere,
Waken the viewless voices of the sky,
Till from their hearts of fire I seem to hear
The ancient motherhood of nature cry.
Hers are the bleatings of the sheep, and hers
The trumpet-note of pompous chanticleer;
Her spirit is the wind among the firs,
And the whole motion of the hurrying year.
And thou, for whom no dim and shadowy dawns
Break the fierce ardours of the intemperate east,
Who seest not on dew-bespangled lawns
The day beginning ere the night has ceased,
    Hear in the song thou promptest me to sing
    An echo of the music of the spring.

Sonnets 1893–1894

XIII

This is the hour of Pan. The happy birds
Bid their loud song of salutation cease,
And in the quiet fields the flocks and herds
Gather in silence round the god of peace.
The primrose and the violet overblown
Open their eyes to feed upon his face,
And where the white anemones are strown
The dreaming earth is locked in his embrace.
And I without the help of ears and eyes
Feel with a still and spiritual motion
While He without a murmur or surprise
Comes floating in upon me like an ocean,
   Till with a start I wake and—was it He
   Or, absent-present, thee and ever thee?

XIV

How do the waves along the level shore
Follow and fly in hurrying sheets of foam,
For ever doing what they did before,
For ever climbing what is never clomb.
Is there an end to their perpetual haste,
Their iterated round of low and high,
Or is it one monotony of waste
Under the vision of the vacant sky?
And thou, who on the ocean of thy days
Dost like a swimmer patiently contend,
And though thou steerest with a shoreward gaze
Misdoubtest of a harbour or an end,
   What would the threat or what the promise be
   Could I but read the riddle of the sea!

XV

WEARY and wet in this belated June
That came not up with summer or with spring
I listen to the lamentable tune
Of birds that have not any cause to sing.
Wide is the wood where onward I do drive,
Hung with the foliage of the quick and dead,
Where that which lives is only half alive,
And that which dies is never wholly dead.
Wide is the wood and dark, and worse than foes
The muffled apparitions of the night,
As one by one in silence comes and goes,
Waves me a sign and then is out of sight.
   Yet in this wood I know there is a tree,
   And one without a mask who waits for me.

XVI

SINCE it is so, my love, and since I bear
Deep in myself the causes of my woe,
And must, as though it were my native air,
Let the long breaths of sorrow come and go;
Since it was never aught of time or place
That clipped my spirit's wings when she would soar,
But of herself, albeit of heavenly race,
She centres ever earthward more and more;
Since it is so, and since my only hope
Is rest no more, but courage to endure,
Fixing an ever-thwarted aim and scope,
Even in a world where that alone is sure,
   Since it is so, oh! in that cruel stress
   Be with me, love, to comfort and to bless.

Sonnets 1893–1894

XVII

I DO not bid thee come! although the spring
Doth in thy absence from herself depart,
And all her beauty like a painted thing
Flatters the eye but may not touch the heart;
Though her voluptuous lilacs all in vain
Summon the mem'ry to a joy that's dead,
And the perpetual doves perturb the brain
With burdens of a tale for ever fled;
I do not bid thee come! let absence try
The quality and temper of our love,
Let years of drought and famine drain it dry,
And doubt and disappointment probe and prove,
 And then, oh! then, when these have done their worst,
 Then let us meet and ease this cruel thirst!

XVIII

I DO not bid thee come, I said. But now,
When I am tired of questioning earth and sky,
Waiting in vain the lyric answer 'Thou'
To this eternal declamation 'I';
Now that I weary of the feignèd foe
Who bids me stand and wrestle in the night,
Whose challenge I must answer though I know
'Tis but myself that summons me to fight;
Now for a moment come, oh! come, and be
The simple sense of this perplexèd seeming,
Open the ears to hear, the eyes to see,
That are perturbed and blind with hideous dreaming;
 Yea, angel foe, tear off the mask, and be
 Thy very self and therefore very me!

XIX

ONCE more, my love, a week of happy days
We rowed the river from his reedy source,
By ancient meadows where the cattle graze
And homes and hamlets of his upland course,
To where the volume of his silver flood
Comes with a mightier motion sweeping by,
And solemn heights with all their weight of wood
Hang in the void of his inverted sky;
Once more we climbed the hill, and far away
Over the rolling hollows of the plain,
Behind the borders of the dying day,
Sought for the dim Beyond, not all in vain;
   Once more, once more! but, thou away and he,
   That happy week how happiless to me!

XX

ALAS, my love! to think the very sun
Who now declines upon the silver Thames,
Where by his isles of emerald he doth run
Liquid enamel diapered with gems;
He who, though now behind the purple hills
Sunk in a golden glory out of sight,
Yet with a crystal after-lustre fills
To northward all the watches of the night;
Even he returning to his eastern lair
Not as he fell in mercy doth arise,
But with a blast of pestilential air
Fans to a furnace heat the smouldering skies,
   Where thou from dreams of fever heavily
   Awakest to the fever of the day.

Sonnets 1893–1894

XXI

This is the sabbath day; the clangorous air
Beats to the bells that shake a hundred spires,
Loud in the loft the solemn trumpets blare,
And pealing organs lead the choral quires.
But while the joyous worshippers ascend,
I, like a pagan in an alien land,
Close up my doors, as fearful to offend,
And sadly at my secret altar stand.
Poor are the rites and unadorned the cell,
Faded the flowers, and the taper dim,
Feeble and few the verses I can spell,
Unworthy me, then how unworthy him!
   Yet is my god a god of love indeed,
    And looking to the will forgives the deed.

XXII

Let us not grieve, my love. The eastern rose
May languish for her lover of the west,
And unregarded die before she knows
The consolation of a hope possessed;
The snowy pine upon his northern height
May sicken for the champak and the balm,
Where in the splendour of a southern night
Blossoms in vain a solitary palm;
But thou and I, spite of the sundering seas,
Once having won possess the thing we sought,
Careless though one may burn, the other freeze,
And one in action grow and one in thought;
   For so do all our currents subtly cross
    That each makes good with gain the other's loss.

XXIII

Now when the passion wanes that made my days
Under thy bright dominion ebb and flow,
Possessing thee, a morning song of praise,
And, in thy loss, a wailing and a woe;
Now when the current more serenely runs
To music no tumultuous motion mars,
From more immediate mast'ry, moon's or sun's,
Delivered to the keeping of the stars;
Yet is it thou from that celestial sphere
Who with thy soul dost call and kindle mine,
Thine is the tone, whate'er the song she hear,
Whate'er the form she see, the beauty thine,
   Nor may she any grace or virtue know
   That doth not ever from thy fountain flow.

XXIV

No, not the hand of death! some other power
Summon to aid thee in the day of doom;
Earth shall reveal in one immortal hour
More than was ever garnered in the tomb.
Prophet or seer hath never rightly taught
What may be learnt by living, late or soon,
The sense of that unutterable thought
Hid in the dusk of an autumnal moon.
Yet doth the slow-consuming fire of heaven,
The opiate odour of the glooming rose,
The languor-laden air of windless even
Hint at a passion, not a dead repose;
   And more than ever thou didst dare to dream
   Wakens, perhaps, and works behind the screen.

Sonnets 1893-1894

XXV

THOU knowest, love, of love's immortal tree
Strength is the root and tenderness the flower,
And more luxuriant sweet the bloom will be
The deeper drawn from elemental power.
Therefore the fate was kind that set the seas
Inexorable against a low desire;
We were not born to load a bed of ease,
No, but to climb the rock and cleave the fire.
Hark, what a note the loud heroic horn
Peals from the height of that enchanted hill!
What low delights must he have learnt to scorn
Who to that trump attunes a tempered will!
    Yea, for the road is rough that leads above,
    And they must labour well who well would love.

EPILOGUE

CRUCIFIED, dead, and buried! be it so.
What falls to earth has of the earthly need;
The flower must wither that the fruit may grow,
The fruit decay to shed abroad the seed.
Crucified, dead, and buried! but the soul
That hath betrayed the petals of the spring,
Yet in her core and centre doth control
Rudiments of a rarer blossoming.
Crucified, dead, and buried! but that death
Hath from that burial resurrection strange;
The passion that has perished on the breath
Lives in the heart and works immortal change.
    Then though the lips be dumb, the music still,
    Take in their stead the re-created will.

FROM THEOGNIS

Lo! I have given thee wings, wherewith to fly
    Over the boundless ocean and the earth;
Yea, on the lips of many shalt thou lie,
    The comrade of their banquet and their mirth.
Youths in their loveliness shall bid thee sound
    Upon the silver flute's melodious breath;
And when thou goest darkling underground,
    Down to the lamentable house of death,
Oh! yet not then from honour shalt thou cease,
    But wander, an imperishable name,
Kurnus, about the seas and shores of Greece,
    Crossing from isle to isle the barren main.
Horses thou shalt not need, but lightly ride
    Sped by the Muses of the violet crown;
And men to come, while earth and sun abide,
    Who cherish song, shall cherish thy renown.
Yea, I have given thee wings! and in return
Thou givest me the scorn with which I burn.

My love, I saw the roses glow,
   The sweet wild roses, newly blown,
I wondered how they bear to grow
   So far from thee, so lone.

My love, I heard the plovers cry,
   The dreary plovers on the moor,
I pitied them to live and die
   So far from thee, so poor.

My love, I saw the great moon rise,
   The tawny moon across the lea,
I wept for her, because the skies
   Keep her so far from thee.

How wide the sweep of happy fields,
   How fresh the broad and moving air,
How sweet the scent the garden yields,
   And that one wandering star how fair!

And yet, and yet, all these above,
   I miss my only best delight,
To call thee by the name I love,
   And press thy hand, and say 'Good-night!'

A MONTH ago! At length the breeze
Awoke, and pent among the trees
Panted impatient for release.

The labouring clouds were all astrain
To void the burden of the rain
And let it through to drench the plain.

But while the night her tumult spent
A calm and blessed element
Retained me at thy side content.

BY star-white meadows daisy-sown,
   Where weedy pools obscurely shine,
Through copses thick with bracken strown
   Where breezes waft the scent of pine,

When summer eves are cool and grey
   I walk alone, intent to find
In what new language I may say
   How sweetly thou art in my mind.

OH, thou didst make the summer sweet
   As never summer wont to be,
While every evening I might meet
   Beneath the stars and speak with thee.

And now that thou art far away
   I will not think thee out of sight,
But always at the close of day
   Will turn to thee and say 'Good-night!'

UNDER the western skies
A windless water lies,
Red with the heavenly fire
That blazes ever higher,
Blazes away and dies
Until, in ashen skies,
The stars arise and pass
Over the sea of glass,
The windless sea that lies
Under the western skies.

DEEP in a wood the foxglove grows;
The valley set with burning rows
From dawn to dusk in silence glows.
But when the peering day is done
The clusters wake, and one by one
Ring their sweet bells in tune
Under the pausing moon.
The trees bend down their branches high,
The brook forgets to bubble by,
The climbing rose and elder pale
No longer hear the nightingale,
And those holy spirits that walk
Twilight woods in solemn talk
Forget almost their ancient pain,
And dream the world is young again.

SUNRISE

Apollo! Apollo! arise,
For the stars are awake in the skies,
And silently look to the east, to the east and to thee,
　　Till the light of their longing is pale,
　　And they dyingly dwindle and fail
At thy coming, eclipsed in the shine of a silvery sea.

Apollo! Apollo! arise,
For thy palace is decked for thine eyes,
Its chambers of vapour compounded and eddying fire;
　　Thy curtains of cloud are ablaze,
　　And redly resplendent the ways
That are spread for thy chariot, Lord of the quiver and lyre.

Set thy foot on yon easternmost hill,
Then spring to the heaven, and fill
With the light of thy shining the shadowy spaces of earth;
　　Let the streams be aglow in thy praise,
　　Let the forests be shaken and raise
To the Master of music a hymn of Beginning and Birth.

Apollo! Apollo! awake,
For the land is astir for thy sake,
And Darkness has shaken her wings and is sped to the west;
　　Awake and arise and pursue,
　　Let thy feet be as fire on the dew,
And as fire in the heaven the wavering gold of thy crest.

Apollo! Apollo! awake,
From the poise of thy pinions shake,
For the land's renovation, a quickening rain of delight;
　　That the earth may break forth into song,
　　That her youth may be lusty and strong,
And forgotten her desolate days as a dream of the night.

Oh! god of the quiver and bow,
   Young golden-haired god, who art foe
To the night and the shapes of the night, be at hand to
      release;
   On thine enemies empty thine ire,
      Then sweep on the strings of thy lyre
That thy sons may be ware that the times of their tarrying
      cease.

We live and die, and every task,
Prosper or no, is duly wrought;
Our task is not the thing we thought,
Our guerdon not the good we ask.

We live and die, and dying rise,
For, O thou world that movest still,
Thy work is ours and ours thy will,
And while thou livest nothing dies.

Body and Soul

Body and Soul
A Dialogue

Soul: What is it that you want? Come, spit it out!
     What's this eternal worrying about?
Body: As if you didn't know!
S   No matter! Say!
     Or are you ashamed?
B   I? At this time of day?
     With me at least it's always been the same
     Since we were born. It's you who've crabbed the game.
S   Go on!
B   I want a youth.
S   Well, so do I!
B   But there begins and ends our harmony!
     Mine must be dressed with most consummate taste,
     Broad at the shoulders, narrowing at the waist,
     An exquisite distinction in his ties,
     His shoes as bright and shining as his eyes.
     You wince?
S   Oh no! A youth may have his pride!
     I've no objection if he's dandified.
B   You hypocrite!
S   Continue!
B   We're alone,
     I and the youth I dream of as my own.
     He sits and at his feet I take my place,
     He plants them firmly on my neck and face,
     Both pleasing me and pleased himself at heart,
     Because he loves the dominating part.
     I snuff the scent of leather at my nose
     And squirm and wriggle as the pressure grows,
     While he, more masterful the more I gulp,

Cries 'Quiet! Or I'll tread you into pulp!'
So, half in earnest, we contend, till he,
Kindling towards the final ecstasy,
Falls down upon me, with his lips on mine,
And fused in one we taste . . .

S   The life divine?
B   Satanic, if you like! What does it matter?
     D'you think I care for all that idle chatter?
S   I know you don't. The question is, do I?
     For we are bound together, that is why
     What raises you, you see, may lower me,
     And I've a stake in what your boy may be!
B   Take your part then. Let the lad be kind,
     Add to his body a spirit and a mind,
     Let him be tender, delicate, and true
     And have a deep fidelity to you.
     So will his soul be yours, his body mine,
     And life satanic blend with life divine.
S   Say rather, if so fair a dream can be,
     The two combine to make humanity.
B   Why not?
S   Ah why! Go back with me and trace
     What we have known since we began our race.
B   To the beginning then—our glad accord
     When you were hardly born and I was lord,
     And led you where I would and made you lie
     Under the foot of any passer by.
S   Yes I remember, though that earliest fate
     Lies back of any years that I can date.
     With none to know or warn me, I was driven
     O'er a dark sea under a starless heaven,
     Before I knew I had a sex at all,
     Predestinate to stumble and to fall.
B   But you grew older, and timidity
     Half tore you from your servitude to me.
     Your dreams I still possessed, but nothing more,
     Nor even those when, one fine day, you swore
     To cut me off from even the stolen delights
     With which I soothed your miserable nights.

Body and Soul

S I swore and did it, and at last outgrew
　　The life in death I used to lead with you.
　　My chrysaloid integument I cast,
　　And the bright psyche spread her wings at last.
　　What vast expatiations then I knew,
　　What flights towards the Fair, the Good, the True!
　　What troops of bright companions came and went
　　Floating upon that heavenly element!
　　You were forgotten!
B 　　　　　　　Yes, but I was there!
　　For those companions—well, you found them fair!
　　And one warm night, beside a glimmering bed,
　　You stroked and kissed a dear and tangled head!
S Yes! Then, then first, I loved!
B 　　　　　　　　　You, only you?
　　Did I not have my pleasure in it too?
S Hardly, I think. For you were drowned in me
　　So deep that you could neither hear nor see.
B Yet from that sleep how quickly I emerged
　　And with what fierce persistence wrought and urged!
　　Those nightly kisses! Have you then forgot
　　In what strange mood you sought your lonely cot?
　　How, while you heard Platonic music chime,
　　I, taut and tense, was torturing all the time?
S Well, what of that? I rather choose to dwell
　　On the release from that long winter's spell,
　　When on the western shore we walked together,
　　You, I, and he, through the bright summer weather,
　　Or by the dusky river took our ease,
　　And saw the peacocks roosting on the trees.
　　Naked we lay upon the warm sea shore,
　　Your hand in his—what could you wish for more?
　　Then ate and drank while the late sun went down
　　On golden waves behind the shining town.
　　The night came on. Together in one bed
　　We rested, foot to foot, and head to head,
　　We kissed good night . . .
B 　　　　　　　　And he—oh deep damnation—
　　He offered, you refused, the consummation.

S I did not want it.
B   Oh, be honest do!
    Was it not ignorance? And cowardice too?
S I did not want it. More I cannot say.
    We wakened to another happy day.
B I was in hell!
S   Indeed! I did not know it!
    You seemed to me to have become a poet
    While, like the seven planets, you and I
    With summer, sea, and sand and air and sky
    Revolved in one harmonious ecstasy
    About the golden centre that was he!
B Romantic nonsense! I was far too stout
    To travel in that crazy roundabout.
    I watched my chance, till, when we went to town,
    Your waxen wings began to flutter down.
    Your boy was there, but hid behind a screen;
    This, that, the other always came between;
    Until one sultry night they asked you down
    To their high-gardened house above the town.
    What hopes were yours! Yet you were doomed to miss
    Even your one, your miserable kiss,
    And take instead, at parting in the hall,
    A pressure on the arm—and that was all!
    Your lips were parched with drought, you stumbled blind,
    Went on, stood still, turned round, and looked behind,
    Your knees gave way, you sank upon the ground,
    The lights of heaven and earth went round and round,
    And I took charge! The seven lean years were passed.
S It's true. You had your victory at last.
B Victory, d'you call that brief intoxication,
    Cheating desire with mere imagination?
S Oh, call it what you will! At least you had it,
    Though world and flesh and devil all forbad it.
    It slaked your thirst and left me sadly free
    To follow my austerer destiny.
B Austerer! Did you not pursue for years
    That body of his, with sighs and groans and tears?
S No, that was you! He gave you what he could,

Body and Soul

    A meagre and an insufficient food,
    But I the while, expatiating free,
    Was turning passion into poetry.
    For neither women, absence, nor pursuit,
    Mine of the ghostly, his of the sensuous fruit,
    Could wear away that first supreme emotion,
    Nor staunch the fountain of my deep devotion.
    Clearer it flows, not feebler, as I age,
    Till now, confronting the penultimate stage,
    To the long years, to him, and even to you
    I give my thanks—and add my pity too!
B You're very kind! But, if I might inquire,
    Was not the purity of your heavenly fire
    A trifle mixed? No doubt they all were brothers.
    But still, as I remember, there were others.
S Yes, as there are a myriad stars above,
    And each the brighter for the other's love.
    Come, let's recall them! Saddest, darkest face,
    Return to me across the fields of space,
    Shining once more, in fashion as you were,
    When there was nothing in the world so fair!
    Come to me in that chamber in the tower
    Where once I waited vainly, hour by hour,
    Symbolically tasting, once for all,
    The long lean years predestined to befall.
B Yes, twenty and more. And you, through all that time,
    Glued to a memory like a bird to lime.
S His letters were the nutriment of love,
    Sped to me weekly like the obsequious dove.
    The rest was work and silence, as I grew
    Daily and yearly more remote from you.
B There were returns.
S   Not one, but three or four,
    And each revealed him dearer than before.
    An apparition and a sudden light,
    He broke upon the borders of my night,
    Melted the ice of my austere control
    And woke a choir of singers in my soul.
    High in the mountains, through the leagues of pine,

Air like a nectar, water like a wine,
Clinging to rocks, suspended on the snow,
Or through the valley arm in arm we go,
In the full day of spirit and of mind,
The dawn before us and the night behind.

B   And did no Body hunger for your friend,
No 'softer love that hath a fleshlier end'?
My memory is of one who tossing lay
Through wakeful night to unrefreshing day
Because a certain person had not been
To kiss good night. Do you recall the scene?

S   Yes, very well. That was the chaff of pain,
Flung from the stones in grinding out the grain.

B   The chaff was most abundant! It was me!

S   But grain alone, and richest grain, was he.

B   Well, he came home at last, and came for good!
How was it then with that aetherial food?

S   He was the same.

B   Perhaps! But, as it seemed,
Not quite the kind of paragon you had dreamed!
Was there not pain and suffering?

S   I agree!
The fault was yours!

B   Oh put it all on me!

S   But when you dropped him, then I held him fast!
He was my own eternally at last!

B   Much good may he do you! Don't you find it pale,
This spiritual love, and just a trifle stale?
You don't reply! No matter! Who came next?
Let's take the blue-eyed darling for our text.
What, are you blushing?

S   I was wrong to add
New trouble to that trouble-burdened lad.
But oh, how dear he was! He's in my eye,
Even now, on horse-back, staring at the sky!

B   I don't complain of him! I had my pleasures
Freer with him than with your other treasures.

S   You more, I less—yet still I can't forget
How first he kissed me. I can feel it yet.

Body and Soul

B Nor I the pressure of his little feet
    Just where I loved them—that's what I'd repeat!
S You did, too often, till he shied away!
    A rupture was the price I had to pay.
B But that was mended.
S   If such mend can be!
    Yet he it was reconciled you and me!
    The war time came, the boy was sent to France,
    Whether he lived or died was all a chance;
    And then, cut off from any hope for you,
    More poignant and more clear my passion grew.
    That lad, enveloped in the cloud of war,
    I loved as I had never loved before!
B But he returned.
S   He did, to go again.
    Oh what was then my rapture and my pain!
    We met—he took my arm—
B   And nothing more?
S I'm coming to it—you lay upon the floor
    And kissed his dear bare feet upon your face
B While you?
S   Confessed that was their proper place.
B And then?
S   All fragrant from the bath he came,
    Back to my bed, lit by the leaping flame,
    Crept to my arms, and, tenderly inspired,
    Gave to us both what each of us desired.
    'Tis the one reconcilement I recall
    In our long duel.
B   It passed. And that was all.
S You cynic! Will you never learn to see
    In time the symbol of eternity?
B I only know that we began again
    The round of disillusionment and pain.
    He never loved you, but was bored at best,
    Outraged at worst till—well, you know the rest:
S He's married, and my friend! Again I win!
B Oh yes, no doubt! But where do I come in?
S You were at once the challenge and the goad

      That drives me on. It's I that choose the road.
      Now for our next adventure.
B   I admit
      Of all your crew he only had the wit
      To treat with lightness what in fact is light
      And took some joy in giving me delight.
S   But you forget! Only the other day
      He asked to be exempted from that play.
B   And you consented, as you always do!
S   Of course, because I love him more than you.
B   He was the last; the *next* remains untold.
S   Why should there be one? You are growing old.
B   Oh don't deceive yourself! I shall not tire!
      After the frost will always come the fire.
S   And after that, for me, the still small voice.
B   Why not have both, my pleasure and your choice?
      You've lost your scruples now. You would approve
      The finest ecstasies of masculine love
      So that they were not merely sensual lust,
      So that you chose, not fell because you must,
      So that he gladly gave his body too
      In recompense for what he had from you.
S   It never can be, and I'll tell you why,
      Since we are bent on candour, you and I.
      The trouble is, in honesty and truth,
      You never had a charm for any youth.
B   I! Not?
S   No, never! No one ever drew
      Nearer to me because he cared for you.
      I was the magnet, and in your despite,
      For sake of me, they gave you your delight.
      How could you, so supremely misendowed,
      Hope to attract the sensitive and proud?
B   You're candid with a vengeance, but your bow
      Has shot a little further than you know.
      I've heard you quote, unless I much mistake,
      That 'soul is form and doth the body make'.
      If so, the vileness you impute to me
      Implies, it seems, your own obliquity!

Body and Soul

S   But I have heard, when souls come up to choose
     The body they will welcome or refuse,
     That chance or folly, ignorance or fate,
     May yoke them to an inappropriate mate.
B   Romantic metaphysics! You and I
     Began together and together die!
     One did not choose the other! Something grew
     Into this quarrel that is me and you.
S   Whatever be our origin, we grow
     More and more dissonant as the seasons flow.
     Glued to the earth you settle more and more,
     Greedy and covetous, sorry, sick and sore;
     While I, more aery soaring and more vast,
     View from above the present and the past.
     Disinterested from my own desire,
     Secreting joy from grief and light from fire,
     With a detached and independent mind
     I view the changing fortunes of mankind,
     Trace the first totterings of their infancy,
     Their boyish fights, their idle reverie,
     The lunacies of their romantic youth,
     Their blind and bloody quest of truthless truth,
     Till at their manhood's verge I see them stand.
     With the bright torch of science in their hand.
B   It sounds sublime! Yet, privileged to peep
     Behind the scenes, I've heard my poet weep,
     'The more he knows, this ill-conditioned boy,
     The more he uses knowledge to destroy,
     Till, in the end, his stately pilgrimage
     In fire and sulphur fumes departs the stage.'
S   And so it may! But Mind, although she grew
     In such a brief anatomy as you,
     Can yet outgrow not only your low place
     But the whole continent of the human race,
     See it without a shudder disappear,
     Engulphed and swallowed in the aeonic year,
     And even against her very self take sides
     With what above eternally abides.
B   Flamboyant rhetorician! Well you know

You are securely anchored here below!
I give a little tug and down you tumble
To tooth-ache or . . . Remember, and be humble!
S I don't forget. But every new escape
Restores me nearer my primaeval shape;
Till, in the end, the cord is snapped and I
Am free at last to join infinity,
In that same hour in which, deprived of me,
Yourself revert to your plurality.
B For me, agreed! But you? Is that so clear?
What would you be without my eye and ear?
Without a something else, which, though abused,
Has kept you curious, active, and amused?
S Detached from you, I shall be free to climb
Beyond the furthest bound of space and time.
B The gesture's noble! But I think I heard
The muttering fear behind that shining word.
Wait till the last, the fiercest struggle, wait
Till I invade in force your every gate,
Flow over every passage, every cell
Of the proud fort you engineered so well,
Till you become a passive registry
Of the triumphant agony that is I.
S I know it, I have had it, have endured
The very thing you threaten, and been cured;
And, if you snap the tie that then was strained,
By my endurance I shall have attained.
B What if I choose, abandoning assault,
To undermine that dome's imposing vault,
Starve to submission eye and ear and brain,
Make you an idiot or a child again,
Till strangers mutter curses on your head,
And even your friends can only wish you dead?
S All that you can and may, I don't deny it,
You have the power and if you will can try it,
But this I know, up to the bitter end,
I to my purpose all my force will bend,
Believing that the passion of the soul
Is rooted in the nature of the whole.

Body and Soul

B So, last as first, you miss the best of life,
    Waging with me this vain and desperate strife.
S That was imposed upon us by our fate.
    But listen! Though I fight, I do not hate.
    For you, my enemy, have been my friend,
    Driving me desperate to my proper end.
    We enter now the last most tragic scene
    That sums in symbolism all that's been.
    Do you your worst, as I shall do my best.
    What lies behind us both must do the rest.

Index

After the War 3n
After Two Thousand Years 26, 28
All Souls Place 41, 57, 92, 115
America *see* under 'Travel'
Apostles, Society of 18, 29, 68–9, 90, 92, 142, 161
Appearances 169, 177, 182, 188
Aristophanes 21, 56, 162
art, artist 19, 74, 76, 92, 132–3
Ashbee, C. R. 27, 65–6, 67–8, 70, 73–4, 77, 85, 189
autobiography 6–8, 9, 12, 23, 43

Baker, the Rt Hon. P. H. 190, 193
Belloc, Hilaire 206
Bloomsbury Group, the 4, 31
Body and Soul 20, 271–83
boots *see* fetishism
Boyd, Mr 51–2
Bridges, Robert 157–8
broadcasting 26–7
Browning, Oscar 63–5, 151, 157, 166
Bryce Group, the 3, 190
Bryce, Lord 159, 190
Buddhism, Esoteric 67–8
Bulmer, Fred 189
Business 21, 172, 174

Calcutta 98, 101–2
Cambridge 6, 24, 59–69, 125, 145, 150–1, 157, 170, 186, 195–6, 199, 235
Cannan, Gilbert 120
Carpenter, Edward 104–5, 156–7
Cecil, Lord Robert 191–2, 193
Charterhouse 8, 52–7
childhood 35–44
China *see* under 'Travel'
Choice Before Us, The 3n, 193, 194
Christianity 61, 133, 134, 156, 211–12
Clemenceau 21–2, 221–7
Coleridge, Christabel 39, 50–2; the Rev.

Derwent 39; Edith 39; Ernest 49–50, 56
conscientious objectors 23, 190, 219, 220
Contribution of Ancient Greece to Modern Life, The 26
Cox, Harold 69, 72
Cross, Richard 190

Daniel, Sir A. M. 161–2
Dante 94, 126
Davies, Major 191
death 28–9, 60, 134, 149, 173–4
Dennis, Admiral 39
Development of Parliament During the Nineteenth Century, The 2n, 84, 144
Dickinson, the Rt Hon. W. H. 190, 191
Dow, G. 170

Eckhard, Mrs 14, 16; Oscar 8–9, 12–17, 123–6, 134–5, 196
Economic War After the War 3n
Edwardes, Mrs and Miss 40
Egypt *see* under 'Travel'
Emma (nurse) 36
Ertz, Susan 121
European Anarchy, The 3n, 193, 194

Fabian Society, the 144
Fellowship 78–9, 137, 140, 144, 147, 150, 196
fetishism 8, 10, 43–4, 50, 53, 90, 125
Forster, E. M. 1, 6, 7–8, 9, 21, 27, 170, 178, 180
friendship(s) 12, 62–3, 89, 116, 121, 127
From King to King 2n, 84, 142–3, 166
Fry, Roger 4, 8–9, 12, 31, 68, 78, 84–6, 90–3, 116–17, 123, 140, 143, 144, 150, 157, 161, 164, 166
Fuller, Reginald 1–2, 30
Furness, J. M. 177

Index

George, Henry 62, 63, 69
Germany *see* under 'Travel'
Gersau 93, 106, 112–13
Goethe 20, 27–8, 44, 73–4, 78, 126, 133, 138, 163, 164, 171, 173, 199
Goethe and Faust: An Interpretation 27
Graham, George 60, 63, 140
Grant, A. J. 63, 139
Greece *see* under 'Travel'
Greek civilisation 22, 25, 148, 160, 163, 175, 180, 233–4
Greek View of Life, The 25, 110, 148, 161
Grey, Sir Edward (Lord Grey of Fallodon) 193

Haffenden, the Misses 40
Hanwell, childhood's home at 35–41
Headlam, J. W. (Sir J. W. Headlam-Morley) 77
Hegel 5, 99, 141–2
history 2, 93, 142–4, 159, 195
Hobson, J. A. 190, 191
Holland *see* under 'Travel'
homosexuality 7, 9–12, 18, 31, 62, 89, 104–5, 111–12, 126–7, 146, 157, 168, 170
Hughes, Pip 45, 75; Plump 45, 169; Tom 45, 75

immortality 5, 134
India *see* under 'Travel'
Inge, Dean 79, 137
International Anarchy, 1904–1914, The 3, 22, 23–4, 151, 198–9
Italy 198 (*see also* under 'Travel')

Jacob's Ladder 83, 157
Japan *see* under 'Travel'
Jesus 22, 61, 207–12, 221, 222, 223, 226
Justice and Liberty 3n, 4, 172–3

Kahn, Albert 177
Kahn Travelling Fellowship 177
Keynes, Maynard 1, 6, 22, 24, 65
King's College, Cambridge 1, 25, 30, 59, 62, 123, 137, 166, 177
Kipling, Rudyard 29, 116, 171

Lakes, the 139
Lassalle, play on 20, 172
Laurie, A. P. 63

League of Nations, The 3, 190–5, 198, 223
lecturing 69, 73–4, 75, 76, 140, 146–7, 149, 168, 193–4, 196
Letters from John Chinaman 3n, 5, 165–6, 169, 181
literature 118, 119
Lloyd George 21–2, 213–21
Loines, Russell 170
love 3, 90, 106–8, 111–12, 115–16, 118, 126, 141, 154–5, 196
Lowes Dickinson, Sir Arthur (brother) 42, 59, 165, 168, 169; Cato (father) 35, 41–2, 76–7, 89, 123, 173–4; Janet (sister) 173–4; May (sister) 29, 42, 57, 174; Mrs (mother) 35, 57, 60
Luce, G. 178

Macnaghten, Sir Malcolm 119–20
Magic Flute, The 22
Maharajah of Chattarpur, the 179–80
masturbation 8, 10, 50, 53, 54
McTaggart, J. E. 68, 83, 92–3, 99–100, 117, 119, 120, 141–2, 144, 161, 164
Mayor, Robin 161
Meaning of Good, The 3n, 4, 119, 162, 164
medicine, training for 19, 76–7, 79, 89, 139
Middleton, Professor 138–9
Mirabeau 20–21, 140
Modern Symposium, A 2, 3n, 4, 18, 159, 170–2
Moore, G. E. 4, 24, 164
Moorsom, Raisley 163
Morel, E. D. 195
Munro, W. A. R. 53
Murray, Gilbert 128, 148, 191

Nansen 192
Norton, Miss 169–70
nurse *see* 'Emma'

Ord (father of Bernhard) 66–7
Overcote 31, 117

pacifism 24, 192, 193
Page, T. E. 56
Paris 20–1, 84, 140, 150
Parmoor, Lord 191
passions 6–7, 8–9, 12ff, 89–135

286

Index

Plato 4, 5, 18, 20, 26, 67–8, 90, 93, 111, 120, 126–7, 150, 155, 160, 164, 171, 173
Plato and his Dialogues 26
plays 20–1
Plotinus 69, 74–5, 78–9, 137–8
Poems, 1896 19–20, 229–69
poetry 18–20, 61–2, 81–7, 93–6, 107–9, 158, 166
Points of View: a Series of Broadcast Addresses 26n
politics 3, 23, 62, 119, 144–5, 173, 195–6, 198
Ponsonby, Arthur (Lord Ponsonby) 190

Quakers, the 75, 190, 197

religion 61, 132, 197
Religion: A Criticism and a Forecast 3n, 5
Religion and Immortality 3n, 5
research 3, 23, 24, 151
Revolution and Reaction in Modern France 2n, 18, 84, 143–4

Salt, Henry and Mrs 71–2
Samoens 128–32
Savary, Peter 8, 12, 127–34
Schiller, Canning 93, 99–100, 108, 120; Ferdinand 8–9, 10, 12, 18, 19, 84, 92–6, 97–113, 115–16, 120–1, 123, 154–5, 166; Max 93, 95, 100, 112; Mrs 93, 95, 100, 106, 108, 112–13, 170
school, boarding 49–57; day 45–7
science 4, 76–8, 89, 120, 132–3
Searight, Kenneth 178, 179
sexual experiences 8, 10, 20, 43–4, 50, 53, 54, 90, 124–5, 127–9, 140, 273–83
Shakespeare 42, 108–9, 111, 142
Sharpe, Mr, Mrs and Miss 39–40
Shaw, Bernard 72, 126, 144–5, 158–9
Shaw, Lord 191
Shelley 20, 61, 76, 85–6, 107, 157

Sicily *see* under 'Travel'
Socrates 22, 61, 150, 151
Spearman, Sir Alexander 38; Miss 38
Stawell, Melian 27, 199
Stephen, J. K. 157, 159
Strachey, Lytton 4, 164
Stubbs, Dr 75
Sun Yat Sen 182–3

teaching 3, 146–7, 150–1, 161, 196
Tilford, farm at 69–72
travel in America 21, 123, 152–4, 165, 167–70, 174, 194; in China 182–5; in the East 124, 177–88; in Egypt 177–8; in Germany and Holland 66–7, 193; in Greece 161–3; in India 178–81; in Italy and Sicily 138, 174; in Japan 185–8
Trevelyan, R. C. 165, 178, 179, 182

Wallas, Graham 190
Wandering Jew, The 21–3, 201–27
War, the Great 3, 23–4, 124–5, 189–90, 193–6, 215, 218–20, 224–6
War and Peace 21
War and the Way Out, The 3n
Webb, Mrs 75, 124, 149, 154, 156
Webb, Sidney (Lord Passfield) 144
Wedd, N. 68, 119, 144, 161
Welldon, the Rt Rev J. E. C. 63
Wells, H. G. 191
Westcott, Dr 156
Whitman, Walt 92
Wilde, Oscar 104
Woodman, the Misses 45–7
Woolf, L. S. 191
Wordsworth 116, 118, 139, 197
writing 3, 119, 143, 145–6, 147–8, 159–60, 164, 193, 196–7

youth 3, 150, 186, 197, 199